UNTIL
HE IS DEAD

CAPITAL PUNISHMENT IN WESTERN NORTH CAROLINA HISTORY

James Thomas Rusher

2003

Parkway Publishers, Inc.
Boone, North Carolina

Available from:

Parkway Publishers, Inc.
P. O. Box 3678
Boone, North Carolina 28607
Telephone/Facsimile: (828) 265-3993
www.parkwaypublishers.com

Library of Congress Cataloging in Publication Data

Rusher, James Thomas.
Until he is dead : capital punishment in western North Carolina
history / James Thomas Rusher.
  p. cm.
Includes bibliographical references and index.
ISBN 1-887905-73-1
1. Capital punishment—North Carolina—History—Case studies. 2.
Murder—North Carolina—History—Case studies. 3. Trials
(Murder)—North Carolina—History—Case studies. I. Title.
HV8699 .U5 R87 2003
364.66'09756—dc21
2003001792

Editing, Layout and Book Design: Julie Shissler
Cover and Graphic Design: Aaron Burleson

Introduction

Few activities are more effective in the desirable process of civilizing persons than the reading of trial transcripts or other reliable accounts concerning persons who have been placed on trial for a capital offense. Thereby, one quickly becomes aware of the pitiable fallibility both of humans (victims, the accused, jurors, and justices) and of judicial procedures. Furthermore, both alarm and sadness may be evoked by realization of the severity of criminal codes, both past and present. None of this, however, mitigates the need for justice that is just and equitable and that likely is a goal of the present massive publication.

Until the present volume, no one has gathered and analyzed the raw data provided by the courts of a large section of Western North Carolina. Thomas Rusher is familiar with such records from his service as District Attorney for the Twenty-Fourth Prosecutorial District, the counties of Avery, Madison, Mitchell, Watauga, and Yancey.

As a historian of much of the same geographical district, I had formerly thought of myself as (at least) modestly informed with most of its "goings on." Nonetheless, I was immediately surprised and pleased to have available much that I did not know and concerning which I would not always have immediately known where to find. The breadth and depth of Rusher's research is quickly evident by a quick glance at his bibliography, all of it obviously consulted and digested: criminal court dockets and transcripts by the dozen, state criminal codes and court reports, an amazing spectrum of newspaper accounts (both regional and national), Governor's Papers, and published volumes.

Students of law will find much of interest here as changes in the criminal code are frequently mentioned, along with the sentiments, public and judicial, that helped to bring them about (usually softening their harshness). Consider, as a minor example that revealed my own deficient knowledge, the case of teen-aged mother Frances Stewart, hanged (likely unjustly) in Burke County in 1833 for the killing of her husband, Charles Silver. Widely known regionally is the long poem that this unfortunate illiterate girl reportedly recited from the gallows. It contains the line that she has been sentenced to death "For murder in the first degree." Rusher immediately realized, as I did not, what this implied for the final date of composition of the poem: North Carolina statutes did not distinguish various degrees of murder until 1893.

Successively, Rusher traces the attempts to render execution less brutal: from hanging, to electrocution, to lethal inhalation, to lethal injection. The sensitive reader will applaud these changes, while experiencing revulsion as eyewitness descriptions of the application of the first two methods are recited. It might have been mentioned that one of these methods of execution, lethal inhalation, was initiated by a bill that was introduced in the North Carolina Legislature by a native of the area under discussion: Dr. Charles Peterson of Mitchell County.

Nearly forgotten episodes of local history are recovered, knowledge of the advancement of a more humane penology is chronicled, and the reader peers into the heart of a District Attorney who has been deeply affected by what he has experienced. However, he is not a strident polemicist for his conclusions. May his tribe increase!

Lloyd Bailey
Barrow Distinguished Professor of Religion
Mount Olive College
Adjunct Professor of Religion
Methodist College
Retired Professor of Hebrew Bible
Duke Divinity School

Foreword

For criminal defendants in North Carolina, the last words they never hope to hear from their trial judge are "until he is dead." As methods of execution have changed, so have the judges' words. Early on the judges used the words "to be hanged by the neck until he is dead." Later, they used the words "to cause a current of electricity to pass through his body until he is dead." More recently, the judges said, "to cause the condemned to inhale lethal gas of sufficient quantity to cause death, and the administration of such lethal gas must be continued until he is dead."

The current preferred method of executions requires the use of the words "to administer to the defendant a lethal quantity of an ultra short-acting barbiturate in combination with a chemical paralytic agent until he is dead." The changes in methods of execution represent an historic uneasiness with the administration of the death sentence. It is important that the condemned person not suffer, but it is also important that the witnesses to the execution not be compelled to observe an agonizing death.

As a prosecutor, I tried numerous death cases. I have observed a number of presiding judges pronounce the sentence of death. Sometimes the judge labors over the pronouncement. Veteran Judge James Davis of Cabarrus County, North Carolina, noticeably gasped and had difficulty forming words when he falteringly sentenced Phillip Lee Young to death in Watauga County. Judge Charles Lamm's voice rose to a high falsetto when he read the jury verdict recommending death in the sentencing hearing of Daniel Brian Lee in Avery County. I saw jurors cry as they stood and recommended a sentence of death, or not done so, often by one dissenting vote. Death litigation is profound, and judges, both at the trial level and the appellate level, have professed difficulty in dealing with the issue. The death sentence threw communities into turmoil, jurors were known to reverse their opinions, and popular opinion has vacillated over the necessity of capital punishment. Legislators often changed the laws, and an historic trend is clearly discernible which continues to exempt certain types of persons and cases from death sentences. At one time, laws required a physician to be present at the execution. The physicians protested, citing the ethical dictates of the Hippocratic Oath, which asserts that physicians have a duty to save lives, not participate in the taking of lives.

The North Carolina Superior Court trial judge first sets a date for the execution. There was an era when the condemned person was not obligated to appeal. Current law makes the appeal automatic. When there was an appeal and the appellate court affirmed the death sentence, the matter was returned to the Superior Court to set a new date. At one time, the law required the governor to issue a death warrant. Governors did not seem to like this responsibility and soon the practice of setting the date of execution reverted to the Superior Court. During one era, the law stipulated a formula to determine the date of execution after a judgment was affirmed. Later, the procedure provided that any stay of execution granted by any court or judge required a new period of waiting time before the sentence could be carried out. For a short period, probably due to an unanticipated consequence by a rewrite of the law, a person could not plead guilty to a capital offense. Now, any person who faces the death penalty is entitled to two attorneys.

Perhaps the first instance where the law sought to treat men and women equally occurred when the North Carolina Conference of Judges (the precursor to the Supreme Court) ruled that women were entitled to "Benefit of Clergy." Previously, Benefit of Clergy was a legislative pardon granted only to literate men who were charged with a capital offense for the first time.

The 1868 North Carolina Constitution limited the types of cases where the death penalty could be applied. In 1893 murder was divided into two degrees, and only first degree murder was punishable by death. To stem the number of death sentences, two procedures were developed. First, whenever a person pleaded guilty to a capital crime with the consent of the judge and the district attorney/solicitor, that person would be sentenced to life imprisonment. Second, juries were given unbridled discretion to recommend mercy, meaning life imprisonment.

Eventually, rape was divided into two degrees, and thereafter, only those guilty of first degree rape were subject to the death penalty. Rape was later eliminated as a capital crime. There came a time when the North Carolina General Assembly prohibited the death penalty for persons under seventeen years old at the time of the offense. Later, the state prohibited the execution of the mentally retarded.

The purpose of this book is to describe four cases of historic significance in western North Carolina. I chose to discuss four particular cases and events, together with lore and legend, where the death penalty was applied or was an issue. These cases focus on events that happened in the counties of the district where I was a prosecutor.

The Race Riot of 1923 in Spruce Pine is unique in that it involved a forcible eviction of all black members of the community, and yet no serious work ever chronicled its history. A person now reading the official documents of the time might well think that "colored" was a part of John Goss's name because wherever the name appeared it was followed by the word "colored."

The execution of 63 year-old Peter Smith for the forcible rape of a teenager brought about a sea change of attitude on hangings, and led the Governor of North Carolina to declare that hangings were barbarous.

The crass outlawry of a small group of men in a small remote area of Watauga County and the antics of those men should be of compelling interest to serious historians.

The trial and eventual parole of Reid Coffey in Avery County shows the indifference of our law toward victims or their survivors. Mrs. Lilly Coffey stood alone against an organized effort to obtain parole. However, men who avoided the death penalty by escaping or by obtaining parole sometimes became productive citizens.

Finally, this book chronicles several death sentences handed down in Yancey County where several jail escapes prevented the sentences from being carried out.

In these pages, both supporters and opponents of the death penalty will find material that buttresses their positions. My purpose is neither to support nor to refute, but rather to accurately report events of historic significance in western North Carolina that have been largely ignored until now.

This book also addresses the larger scope of crime and its devastating effects on the victims. I seek not only to describe criminal trials, but to bring forth community events which occurred at the time, some of which were more remarkable than the trial itself.

There are several limitations in writing about historic trials. Transcripts of trials were made only when there were appeals. In the Goss trial, for example, contemporary newspaper accounts became the better sources. The judge's notes in the Goss case are illegible and provide scant information.

In instances where there was an appeal, North Carolina's appellate rules required that the lawyers narrate the evidence. For example, the lawyer may have asked the witness several questions such as: "What is your name? Where do you live? What is your occupation?" In composing the transcript the lawyer was required to eliminate the question and answer format. Therefore, the lawyer would prepare transcripts as: "I am John Wilson and I live at Newdale and I work for Claude Higgins." Transcripts were editorialized and to a degree propagandistic. Yet that is the state in which a researcher finds them.

I have, over the years, talked with many people who have an interest in history and I am grateful to those people who helped my research. In this book I give credit to those individuals who made observations or provided information on the cases I report.

I visited the North Carolina Archives and the State Library dozens of times. I researched public documents, Governors' loose files, Supreme Court original records, various indexes showing clemency, death warrants, rewards, public laws, and Central Prison records.

During my research I have worked in the following libraries: Rowan County Public Library; Appalachian State University Library in Boone, North Carolina; East Tennessee State University Library in Johnson City, Tennessee; Isothermal Community College Library in Spindale, North Carolina; the University of North Carolina Library at Asheville; Mars Hill University Library in Mars Hill, North Carolina; the public libraries in Burke, McDowell, Caldwell, Watauga , Mitchell, Madison, Avery, Yancey, Iredell, and Ashe Counties in North Carolina; the Boston Public Library in Boston, Massachusetts; Pack Square Library in Asheville, North Carolina; the Patrick Beaver Memorial Library in Hickory, North Carolina, the Spruce Pine, North Carolina Public Library; and Spartanburg County Public Library in Spartanburg, South Carolina. In addition, I studied loose files, case files and court minutes in the clerks of court offices in Watauga County, Avery County, Mitchell County, Yancey County, and Madison County, North Carolina; and Commissioners' minutes in the Watauga County, Avery County, and Mitchell County, North Carolina register of deeds offices. I researched old documents and records at the Spruce Pine Town Hall. I communicated with and received material from the Wyoming Department of Archives. Through the staff at Appalachian State University, I ordered materials from Cincinnati, Ohio.

I was helped by Professor Lloyd Bailey at Duke University, Durham, North Carolina, whose knowledge about genealogy and history of the three counties of the Toe River Valley is extensive. Ben Blackburn was most helpful. His collateral ancestor, Spencer Blackburn, was the only person from Watauga County ever to serve in the United States Congress. Ben's great interest in Watauga County history proved to be a boon to my own research. Not only did he help with research, but he also had a family connection to the Howell family. He had a photograph of Amos Wellington Howell, but never knew the subject until Mrs. Fairchild identified him. Working with Ben Blackburn, I was able to find Wellie Howell's gravesite.

E. Y. Ponder introduced me to people who knew where Peter Smith's grave was located. Ponder served as sheriff of Madison County from 1952 until 1966 and from 1970 until 1986. His knowledge of Madison County, North Carolina, was vast. Joe Snyder from Cane Creek near Bakersville, North Carolina provided information. Harold Bailey, who worked in my office, introduced me to several sources and helped me discover information.

For the most part, I sought to stay out of the stories, but having been an attorney in North Carolina since 1967 and a prosecuting attorney since 1971, my experience and insights may be helpful at times. To that extent, I found myself occasionally adding an interpretation or an opinion.

I began my prosecutorial career as an assistant solicitor, and ended it as a district attorney. The Office of Solicitor was crafted from the North Carolina State Constitution. As such it is often called a constitutional office. The usage of the term "district attorney" is more modern. Legislators wanted to change the name of the office, but to do so required a constitutional amendment. In North Carolina, the Constitution is amended by a concurrence of legislative and popular action. First, the legislature passed a bill which substituted "district attorney" for "solicitor" and then submitted it to majority vote of the people in an election. The proposed amendment was passed by popular vote at the election of November 5, 1974. However, before the constitutional question was put to the voters, the legislature passed a law on March 5, 1973 that authorized the term district attorney to be interchangeable with the constitutional office of solicitor. That law has never been repealed and a bit of incongruity was created. The constitution refers to the Office as District Attorney but a statute refers to the constitutional Office of Solicitor and allows for the use of either District Attorney or Solicitor. All North Carolina prosecutors now call themselves district attorneys.

In 1985, the cupola atop the Madison County, North Carolina Courthouse began to visibly tilt to the right. Madison's old courthouse was built in the early 1900s. Lady Justice stands at its very top. As people on the street below noticed the tilt, the Madison County Commissioners kept assuring the people that the structure was sound and that no one using the building was endangered. After some months, the commissioners determined to repair the building. When construction crews began their work, the workers noticed the wooden timbers used to support the roof were separated and the steel rods used to join the wooden beams were sheared from their location. To have used the building at all was dangerous indeed. By then, seventy-eight years of weight pressing downward took its toll on the courthouse.

The top floor of the courthouse was vacated and workers removed Lady Justice and the cupola. Laminated wooden beams replaced solid wooden beams, and the renovated structure eliminated joints attached by steel pins. The building was restored after many months.

During her absence from atop the building, Lady Justice was housed in the grand jury room adjacent to the district attorney's office. Attorney Jim Baker (now Superior Court Judge) had his picture taken with her and so did others. Knowledgeable people recalled that the lady was once removed for a short time to repair a deteriorating base. Otherwise, she had remained on top of the Madison County Courthouse.

The Lady Justice was made of a type of plaster, and, at close range, she was not attractive because her features lacked detail. How much more pleasant she looked when she was far away as one looked upward from the street to her high berth! Most interesting, however, was the fact, that with the help of a curious State Bureau of Investigation agent, we discovered that she had three bullet entrance wounds and three bullet exit wounds. THE LADY WAS SHOT THREE TIMES!

She may be brought down again in the future. It may be interesting to compare the number of bullet wounds with our observations of 1985 and 1986. Shortly after the building was restored, arsonists broke into this grand old courthouse and set fire to the courtroom. The building was nearly destroyed but was eventually fully restored. Otis Lee Searcy was convicted of the arson and sentenced to prison. He was ordered to pay restitution for the uninsured amount of $42,178.54. North Carolina Speaker of the House of Representatives and Representative Liston Ramsey, from Madison County, used his influence to get a State of North Carolina appropriation to restore the courthouse.

As a lawyer and a prosecutor, this story allows me to make a point. At times during our history, justice pressed too hard on those who were weak. In retrospect, we can observe a noticeable tilt in the justice system. In our history, justice at times came under attack and may well have suffered wounds, and there were times when renovations to the system were required. It may be said that the system looks better from a distance than up close. Obviously, we have serious problems, but for me, it has been a salutary experience to have served as a prosecuting attorney in the mountains of western North Carolina.

TABLE OF CONTENTS

Case I

Spruce Pine's Race Riot

Case II

Murder During the God Praise

Case III

The Trouble with Hanging

Case IV

Law's Alternative

CASE I

SPRUCE PINE'S RACE RIOT

Introduction

Mitchell is a remote rural mountain county in North Carolina. Its residents, like those of the rest of Appalachia, faced hard times. Mitchell County's farms are small, communities are isolated, and its people are stout because of hard work. In mountain colloquialism, "stout" means "strong."

While traveling in this rural county, one sees well-kept cemeteries with many Civil War era headstones. Members of the Thirteenth Tennessee Cavalry, a Union cavalry which had mustered at Jonesborough, Tennessee, were buried in this county. Mitchell County owes its formation to the Civil War. People in the western end of Yancey County favored the South and fought for the Confederacy. Mitchell County was carved out of the eastern section of Yancey County to create a home for the county's Union supporters. Those who favored preservation of the Union became Republicans and those left in Yancey remained mostly Democrats.

To many folks in the mountains, politics is like religion— one is born into a faith and into a political party. Jobs were given or withheld based on political considerations. Although Democrats, who governed North Carolina most of the time, meted out better roads to those living in Democrat areas, travel was always difficult in most mountain counties. Those living now in these counties continue, as a rule, the politics and religion of their ancestors. Party switchovers are rare and when switching does occur, seldom does the person who switched become fully accepted by his new party.

To be a mountain Republican does not, however, mean that a person favors equality of ethnic groups. Northern Whigs who opposed any extension of slavery nationally formed the Republican Party. North Carolina provided no delegates to that party's earliest conventions, and there were no presidential electors in the state for either John C. Fremont, the first nominee, or for Abraham Lincoln. After the Civil War, North Carolina Republicans won some elections with large support from African Americans. Conversely, the Democrats gained power by excluding African Americans from voting. Some elder citizens remember how the

Republican Party, in decades after the Civil War and continuing into several decades of the Twentieth Century, was called, derisively, the "nigger" party.[1] Slavery did not exist to a great extent in Yancey and Mitchell counties, and African Americans owned no land in Mitchell County. Even now, not many African Americans live in Mitchell County.

Mitchell County citizens who know county history recall indignities sometimes inflicted on African Americans who ventured into the county. An African American who traveled with a white salesman was reportedly forced by local people to stay in a cage where he was brutalized. While these incidents may be true, they lack documentation. However, there are three documented racial incidents in Mitchell County in the nineteenth century.

The *Biennial Reports of the Attorney General of North Carolina* state that "Robert Chambers, colored," was lynched in Mitchell County on April 30, 1896. Chambers was charged with chloroforming and attempting to rape a white woman, and was lynched without a trial. This incident happened in Cranberry which was then a part of Mitchell County, later becoming a part of Avery County.

An earlier Mitchell County lynching happened near Bakersville, in the Cane Creek Section of the county on April 1, 1894. Bakersville is the county seat. Hol (Holland) English was taken from the county jail at Bakersville by a mob and hanged from an apple tree. English had been held in confinement after he was arrested for the murder and disfigurement of his wife, Ellen, on March 25, 1894. Mrs. English's badly damaged body was found in the Toe River in the Beech Bottoms section of the county. This section also is now a part of Avery County. Most of the members of the lynch mob were from the area that is now part of Avery County.

Coroner Prestwool determined there were thirteen wounds to Mrs. English's head. In addition, the deceased's skull was fractured just behind her ear, her nose was broken, and there were several cuts on her face and head. Apparently Hol English was tired of his marriage and wanted to marry another woman. There was some evidence that he previously tried to poison his wife.[2]

2

Descendants of Hol English were targets of racial discrimination over the years. Some dispute the idea that they are descended from an African American. However, at that time in the South, the white majority made its own determination of one's race, and English was considered to be Negro. Some Mitchell County residents who have heard the story all their lives continue to claim that English was indeed an African American.[3]

The Attorney General's *Biennial Report*, which was the only official record of this lynching, states that Hol English was a white man. The point of the matter, however, is that English was thought by the mob to be an African American. The *Marion Record* of April 6, 1894 stated, "English was said to be slightly tainted with negro blood, but his wife was white." The *Bakersville Enterprise*[4] of April 4, 1894, reported that Hol English was known as "Black Billy." Not all lynchings in the south involved race, but most did. In some instances thousands of people attended lynchings. Hol English was hanged by a mob estimated to be comprised of 100 or more people.

In modern times, the public is shocked by a mother killing her children, yet one of the earliest such recorded events took place in Mitchell County. Like the two incidents discussed above, this crime also had an Avery County connection. The murder actually occurred in what is now Avery County, again near the Beech Bottoms Section. This is an area that has historically held a small African American population. Mary Jane Crowson was identified in trial testimony to be 22 or 23 years old. Miss Crowson had a racially mixed four-year-old son. Witnesses who testified during the Crowson trial referred to the child, Rufus, as "colored." In the indictment, charging murder, drawn by Solicitor W. H. Bower, Mary Jane Crowson was shown to have an alias "Mary Jane Barrier." Likewise, the victim was called Rufus Crowson, alias Rufus Barrier. Obviously, the solicitor's use of the alias for the child signifies confusion as to the mother's last name. Little is known about this young mother. Public records consist of the official Supreme Court opinion and the Supreme Court's original papers that included the lawyer's narration of the testimony, the indictment, and the matters which occurred during the trial where error was assigned.

The testimony of the witnesses at trial showed Mary Jane's mother's name to be Mary E. Wiseman. Wiseman family researchers state that Mary E. (Crowson) Wiseman was the second wife of one of the early Wisemans. Mary's daughter, Mary Jane, was born before that marriage. Rufus, Mary Jane's son, was apparently born out of wedlock and given his mother's last name. To have had an illegitimate child in the late 1800s would have violated mores of that time. In law books, illegitimate children were called "bastards." Societies were intolerant of children born out of wedlock. Moreover, the fact the child had been the product of a white woman having had intercourse with a Black man would have created even more public contempt. White southerners generally maintained that segregation was necessary to protect white women. North Carolina law forbade interracial marriages through the miscegenation statute.

Mary Jane also was limited mentally. Her mother testified at trial that Mary Jane "did not have sense enough to wash a garment clean," and the witness, J. P. Thompson, testified that Mary Jane was of "very low order of intellect and with a very degraded character." It may be that modern persons would find Mary Jane Crowson to be mentally retarded. Confusion as to her name appears in the testimony of Brown Burleson who testified that he knew the defendant as Mary Jane Crowson but according to him he had heard her called Barrier "recently."

On January 10, 1887, the mother murdered her son known either as Rufus or Ellis Rufus. The child was missing about twenty days before his body was found in the Toe River. The murder trial of Mary Jane Crowson began in Bakersville, North Carolina, on April 18, 1887. The defendant was represented by two attorneys, with Esquire W. B. Council acting as lead attorney.

Mary Jane Crowson asserted a defense of insanity. This defense was supported by one of the witnesses, Ellen Cantrell, who testified, "I can't believe any sane woman would have committed this offense." J. S. McKinney testified that he saw the mother and young child on January 10, and when he later saw Mary Jane Crowson, she did not have the child with her. Pressed for an explanation, she told McKinney that she gave the child to a man named Woods. McKinney determined through his investigation that Woods denied receiving the child. McKinney also saw footprints in the snow near the river. Over time, four men questioned Mary Jane Crowson and emphatically told her that she "had better show up what she had done with the child." Deputy Sheriff W. H. Greer was one of the men who questioned the defendant, and he advised her that if she would take him to the last place where she had the child, then Greer would be able to use a crooked stick and with this instrument he could divine what had happened to the child. In time, Mary Jane Crowson took the men to the river where she at first "seemed brave, but when she got to the river she became agitated and looked guilty." At one time this young mother had stated "if anybody wanted their negroes drowned to bring them to me."[5]

Mary Jane Crowson was found guilty of murder and Judge J. C. McRae sentenced that she be hanged by the neck until dead on July 22, 1887, between the hours of 10 a.m. and 2 p.m. Mary Jane Crowson was the first person sentenced to death in a Mitchell County courtroom. She appealed her case to the North Carolina Supreme Court.

Chief Justice William Smith wrote the decision for the unanimous court. The decision reiterates an important principle which, historically, has been the law. The justices were concerned about the coercive nature of the interrogation by the four men. Essentially, the four men had demanded that she confess to what she had done and this was thought to be too much intimidation considering the mental state of the young mother. The court ruled that, under the circumstances, the trial judge was obliged to look for circumstances indicating that Mary Jane Crowson's statements were voluntary or otherwise. The trial judge, having failed in this responsibility, committed error, and the case was sent back for a new trial.

A second trial was begun on April 16, 1888, and Mary Jane Crowson was allowed to plead guilty to manslaughter and she was sentenced to 20 years in prison. Mary Jane Crowson was pardoned by Governor Daniel Russell on July 29, 1899.

Footnotes

[1] J.E. Holshouser, Sr. was a Republican Party stalwart. He served as United States Attorney and later as a North Carolina District Court Judge. He remembered, after his son was elected Republican Governor of North Carolina, the prevalence of this derogatory term.

[2] *Asheville Daily Citizen*, April 2, 1894; *The Comet*, Johnson City, Tennessee, April 5, 1894; *Tri-County News Journal* (Harvey Miller article), March 30, 1989; *Marion Record*, April 6, 1894.

[3] The writer has talked with citizens from the Beech Bottoms Section, Bakersville, former elected office holders, and a lineal descendant of a member of the lynch mob. This writer was repeatedly told that Hol English was an African American. There is no question that the lynch mob considered that they were dealing with an African American.

[4] Issues of the *Bakersville Enterprise* are not known to exist in archival or library settings. Roy Ollis has retained this old paper and provided a copy to the author.

[5] These words appear in the official report of the North Carolina Supreme Court. The fact that the highest court of North Carolina failed to capitalize the word "negroes" significantly shows the lack of esteem given to African Americans at the time.

Chapter 1: A New Railroad

Until the early 1900s, Mitchell County, like many North Carolina mountain counties, remained isolated from the booming expansion occurring throughout the continent. This would begin to change with the coming of the railroad.

Building a railroad from Cincinnati, Ohio to Charleston, South Carolina would necessarily traverse North Carolina's mountain terrain. After several attempts, costing many lives, the railroad became a reality in 1912. The Carolina Clinchfield and Ohio (C.C. and O.) follows the Toe River basin and passes through Spruce Pine in Mitchell County. Those who bought the right of way for the railroad could have elected to pass through Bakersville, the county seat, but instead chose Spruce Pine. Spruce Pine and Bakersville, although in the same county, are competitors. Although Bakersville was larger, Spruce Pine became the dominant commercial center. Before the county's high schools were consolidated, the schools from the two towns were arch rivals in athletic events. Politicians often express their affinity to one section or the other and in so doing, speak with disdain of those from the other section. The people refer to themselves as being from either the Spruce Pine or the Bakersville end of the county. In some areas, such as at Altapass, hotels were built alongside the railroad, which suddenly became a cherished mountain retreat for people living along the routes of the "C. C. and O." Toecane, where the Toe River and Cane Creek converge, developed into a significant depot town that contributed to development of other areas of Mitchell County. Toecane also had its hotel and stores. In 1923, this was an active commercial district.

The Spruce Pine Terminal flourished. Gradually, there was a demonstrated need for a second livestock area and the waiting room grew crowded. In early 1923, the *Toe River Herald*, a small newspaper serving Spruce Pine, alarmed the railroad by running a small ad: "A petition to the Corporation Commission regarding a new depot is being circulated this week. Get your name on it."[6] J. J. Champion, Vice President of C.C. and O. Railroad dispatched Industrial Representative D.C. Boy to Spruce

Pine to report on the need of a new terminal for this area. In a letter to Vice President Champion,[7] Mr. Boy responded:

> Of course Spruce Pine needs a new depot . . . .There is one point which the people of Spruce Pine will bring before the commission that might have some effect and that is, there is no waiting room for colored people. Up to last year a colored waiting room has been very little needed, because of the few negroes coming to that section. But the highway construction work in the last year or so has brought in a large number of negroes and this work is likely to go on several years. Another thing that will increase the business, both passenger and freight at Spruce Pine is the good roads now being built.

Mr. Boy's letter succinctly demonstrated the new phenomenon that was transforming the entire region around Spruce Pine and other mountain communities. Governor Cameron Morrison had been elected and his plan for growth in North Carolina was to build roads connecting all the county seats of North Carolina. Construction was well under way in Mitchell County on new roads, and to help accommodate this construction, a prison unit was situated west of Spruce Pine in an area near the mountain known as Chalk Mountain.[8] Inmates from this prison unit were utilized in road construction. Contracts had been awarded to large construction companies to build roads and to accommodate the new growth. Spruce Pine needed improvements to its water and sewer operations. In addition, the abundant mining operations in Mitchell County were operating at full-scale production. Native Mitchell County people were often disinclined to taking employment; their preference traditionally was to farm their small operations that were worked by numerous generations before them. In 1923, they were reluctant to leave their farms for industrial work, and jobs for factory workers went begging. African Americans were brought into Mitchell County to accommodate this need for construction and mining labor.

In 1923, North Carolina was a solid Jim Crow state. Segregation of races was written in stone as a cardinal rule. The rule forbade African Americans from using facilities provided for white patrons, and no facilities existed at all for the Black citizens at the depot. During segregation, Black citizens were at times forced to go all day without using a rest room. As long as there were only a few African Americans needing a waiting room, white persons felt there was little need for one, but as the numbers increased, the need became too critical to ignore. In early 1923, there appeared such large numbers of transient African Americans arriving in Spruce Pine that the need for a waiting room became only one indication that a larger depot would have to be built for all persons, especially for white patrons who would then not be forced into proximity with Black citizens.

In an area that had precious little knowledge of race relations, Mitchell County in 1923 was mixing all the ingredients for racial unrest.

Footnotes

[6] Issues of the *Toe River Herald* are not known to exist. The quoted portion of the paper was clipped by someone in the railroad organization. It is preserved among the archives of the C.C. and O. Railroad papers at East Tennessee State University (ETSU) in Johnson City, Tennessee.

[7] The C. C. and O. Railroad's papers and photographs are maintained as loose file papers at the library of East Tennessee State University at Johnson City, Tennessee. Subject headings have been assigned to the boxes of materials. This correspondence is in a box labeled "Spruce Pine."

[8] Albert Canipe, although a Democrat, won several elections in Republican Mitchell County. He served in the North Carolina General Assembly and served as a county commissioner. Before his death, he identified the location of the prison unit.

Chapter 2: A Kinder, Gentler Time

A visitor to the historic district of Wilkesboro, North Carolina cannot miss the Johnson J. Hayes United States Courthouse and Post Office. The imposing building stands prominently in the business district of this small town. Wilkes County, North Carolina, once the leading moonshine-producing county in the United States and the home of stock-car racing, provided substantial numbers of federal criminal cases pertaining to moonshine (non-tax paid liquor). Because of those cases, federal court was held for years in Wilkesboro. While the Federal Courthouse was under construction, a decision was made to move the federal court from Wilkesboro. Upon completion, the Federal Courthouse remained an empty shell. Later, the federal government leased the courthouse to the North Carolina District Court.

When a new county courthouse was built, the federal building sat idle once again.

Johnson J. Hayes played an important role in the development not only of Mitchell County but also all of northwest North Carolina. Appointed by President Calvin Coolidge as the first United States District Court Judge for the Middle District of North Carolina in 1927, Johnson J. Hayes served in that capacity until his death in 1970.

To be considered for appointment to the Federal Judiciary, one must demonstrate notable accomplishments. Hayes served as a North Carolina Solicitor for twelve years. He was elected solicitor in the Seventeenth District of North Carolina in 1914 for a term beginning January 1, 1915. In his autobiography,[9] Hayes wrote, "The seventeenth Judicial District was composed of Alexander, Avery, Catawba, Mitchell, Watauga, Wilkes and Yadkin counties, all then giving safe Republican majorities. The Legislature arranged it this way, hoping to make the other nineteen districts Democratic."

The North Carolina Legislature often created election districts to inhibit the growth of the Republican Party. In later years the seventeenth district was modified to include Avery, Mitchell, Wilkes, Yadkin and Davie Counties. These counties are not contiguous, as no law required them to be. Many years later,

Ray Braswell, a mischievous Republican legislator introduced legislation that would have created a district incorporating both North Carolina's westernmost and easternmost counties. Braswell simply wanted to poke fun at the legislative body willing to gerrymander districts for political advantage, a practice not by any means unknown today.

Hayes' autobiography points out the difficulty of travel in this mountain district in the early 1900s. In order for Hayes to be in Bakersville on a Monday morning, he had to leave his home in Wilkes County on Friday evening. He traveled by train from his home to Winston-Salem and from there to Barber Junction in Rowan County. His next leg took him to Newton and then to Marion where he transferred to the Johnson City train to Toecane. From Toecane he took a hack to Bakersville.

Hayes never drank alcohol. As a Federal Judge, Hayes often dealt with liquor cases. Ordinarily, he dealt with these cases harshly. Palmer Triplett, who lived in Watauga County, recalled a story that Judge Hayes once had his vehicle stuck in a creek near Darby. The road crossed a creek and traffic had to ford to pass from one side to the other. A resident helped the judge out of the creek; a man who later stood convicted of making liquor and awaited Judge Hayes to sentence him. Giving a probationary sentence, Judge Hayes recalled the help that this convicted man had provided him and considered that mitigation.

Judge Hayes told a story attributed to one of the lawyers who rode circuit in this area; later to be Lieutenant Governor of North Carolina and the namesake for the future county seat of Avery County, W.C. Newland. Presiding over court in Bakersville was a harsh judge particularly strict about courtroom decorum. On one court date a man from Roan Mountain, Tennessee came to court with a red bandana handkerchief tied around his neck. With his wide brimmed cowboy hat tucked under his arm, and with spurs on his heels, he reeled and rocked as he approached the bar. Thinking the man drunk, the judge ordered the sheriff to arrest him and bring him around so that the judge could conduct an inquiry. The Roan Mountain man insisted he was not drunk, "I hain't had a drap since before breakfast and only a small drap at that." Satisfied that he was setting a trap from which the cowboy could not extricate himself, the judge challenged him to walk along a crack in the floor of the aisle from the bench to the rear door and promised that if his foot did not miss the crack, then the judge would release him. "In his long strides of a least three feet at a step, he centered the crack each time. When he got within about four feet of the door, he gave a big leap and yelled as he went out the door, 'Whoopee, by God, I did it.'"

During Hayes' twelve years as a prosecutor in North Carolina, only two persons prosecuted by him were electrocuted. "It is my firm belief that these were the only two cases in my twelve years where the punishment was deserved." One of the death sentences involved a rape that happened in Catawba County and the other one was a rape prosecuted in Mitchell County. Of the latter, Hayes wrote, "An escaped convict chased a cow around in the pasture and then entered the farm house in which a 75 year-old woman was alone. He ravished her and was promptly caught by the officers. He was tried, convicted and electrocuted." Although he did not mention the name of this condemned man, Judge Hayes was writing of John Goss.

In 1923, there was no division of rape into degrees, and anyone convicted of this crime faced a mandatory sentence of death by electrocution at the state prison in Raleigh. John Goss, who was prosecuted that year by Solicitor Johnson J. Hayes, became the only man executed in a case from Mitchell County.

Julie Thomas McClellan is the granddaughter of rape victim Alice Thomas.[10] She remembers the rape incident. When informed that her grandmother was raped in 1923, Mrs. McClellan thinks that it happened later, because she remembers when her Aunt Vine, or as the children called her, Aunt Vinney, crawled up the steps to seek help. During conversation, she questioned her memory. "How could a child three years old have a memory?" McClellan said, "Maybe I remember it because I have been told about it all my life. But I do remember it. Maybe it's because when a very terrible thing happens, children take special note of it and remember it."

Mrs. McClellan continues to live where she has resided almost all her life, surrounded by family who have done the same. The McClellan Road, a narrow dirt track, was named for Mrs.

McClellan and her husband. Further down Gouges Creek Road is another dirt road named Thomas Road. Living in the area are grandchildren, great grandchildren, and adult great-great grandchildren of Mack and Alice Thomas. Monroe Thomas, Mrs. McClellan's brother, lives with his wife in the same area. Mrs. McClellan remembers families who lived there named Thomas, Buchanan, and McClellans.

Mrs. McClellan's grandmother, Alice Thomas, was walking to visit her neighbor, Vine Silver. Mrs. Thomas was confronted near the Gouges Creek Church by a Black man holding a long knife; he held it to Mrs. Thomas' throat. She began praying, and the armed man said, "It's all right if you pray, but don't pray too loud or I will kill you." Mrs. Thomas later said her prayers saved her. The black man raped Mrs. Thomas in a rhododendron thicket. (Mrs. McClellan referred to it as a "laurel" thicket, but rhododendron is more prevalent and is frequently called laurel.)

According to Mrs. McClellan, the Black man had earlier appeared at the residence of Vine Silver. He had chased the cow in the yard, and took the bell from the cow's neck. He rang it incessantly, and Vine Silver appeared at the door and asked what he was doing. He told Mrs. Silver that he wanted water. She gave the man a glass and told him where the spring was. Mrs. Silver, frightened, left the house, running toward the home of Wilburn Thomas, Alice Thomas's son. When she reached the house, Vinney crawled up the steps in obvious distress. Wilburn Thomas went searching for his mother, and he found her after she was raped. "Nothing like this ever happened. Back then things were not like they are today."

Sons of Mack Thomas went on foot looking for this unknown Black man. Word of the rape rapidly spread through this little community and all the men in the community, including Mack Thomas, armed themselves. They went to Dogwood Mountain, one of the taller mountains in the area, the site for one of the region's feldspar mining operations. Some local people had worked in mining, but for the most part, the company had to bring in Blacks to work as laborers. The Black population lived on the mountain in shacks. Mrs. Wilburn Thomas had employed some of the women to do household chores. According to Mrs. McClellan, after the birth of her younger brother, Monroe, in 1923, some of the Black women who were the wives of the laborers in this mining operation had washed clothes and done ironing for Mrs. Thomas. There was harmony and peace, and no ill will shown prior to the rape of Mrs. Alice Thomas.

The white men of the Gouges Creek community, armed with long guns, forced the Blacks to remove their belongings and then forced them at gunpoint to walk several miles to the Spruce Pine Railroad Terminal. There they were forced to board the train and leave Spruce Pine. The Blacks at this particular mining operation never returned. Mrs. McClellan commented: "That's why there are no Blacks here today. Back then, things were not like they are now." Mrs. McClellan has never heard that there was any actual violence inflicted upon the Blacks, but she emphasized that there would have been violence if they did not do what they were told. Mrs. McClellan does not remember the names of any of those who were forced to leave. She does not know how many of them were forced onto the train that day. Her father, Wilburn and her grandfather, Mack, "were involved in it."[11] The Dogwood mine later operated with only white citizens who lived in the area. Many years later the mine shut down altogether.

Mrs. McClellan remembers that her grandmother suffered greatly as a result of the rape. After the rape, Mrs. Thomas was afraid. She often sat quietly alone with her thoughts. After the death of her husband, Alice Thomas was afraid to be alone, and a grandchild had to stay with her. Mrs. McClellan's face saddened measurably as she talked about the impact that this crime had had on this elderly lady. Mrs. McClellan recalls that shortly after the rape, the sheriff brought Mrs. Thomas a gun and told her to use it if anyone threatened her. Mrs. Thomas told him that she could not kill anyone. Mrs. McClellan remembers that Mrs. Thomas chose not to go to Raleigh to witness the execution of John Goss. She does not know whether Mr. Mack Thomas went or not, but she does remember that both Mack and Alice Thomas were pleased when Goss was electrocuted. Mrs. Alice Thomas said, according to Mrs. McClellan, "he got what he deserved."

Alice Thomas died July 13, 1957. According to her daughter-in-law, Mrs. Monroe Thomas, she never fully recovered from the experience of having been raped on September 26, 1923.

Footnotes

[9] *Autobiography and Additional Hayes Family Data* by Judge Johnson J. Hayes shows no publisher and no date of publication. It appears to have been written for family members. This author was given a copy by Attorney Kyle Hayes on April 29, 1982.

[10] The conversation between the author and Julie Thomas McClellan occurred at her residence on July 22, 2002.

[11] Wilburn Thomas was a part of the posse formed to seek the then unknown assailant. This role took him eventually to a railroad overpass in Burke County. Wilburn Thomas and his father Mack Thomas later were to be targets of the grand jury inquest among others. Mack and Wilburn Thomas were indicted by the Mitchell County Grand Jury for riot in connection with the forced removal of Black citizens, and Mack Thomas pleaded guilty in October, 1923. Wilburn Thomas pleaded guilty to the same charges on November 12, 1923.

Chapter 3: The Trial and Execution of John Goss

Progressive prison administrators have long maintained that they must be allowed to reward prisoners for good behavior and punish their misbehavior. North Carolina often has been at the forefront of developing incentives for rewarding prisoners for good behavior. By 1923, North Carolina instituted the "trusty" system. Prisoners who served a significant portion of their sentence and were well behaved were designated as trustees and were given more liberties than other inmates. A serious crime in eastern North Carolina in early 1923 by a prison trustee, however, brought the trusteeship program under the public spotlight. Many thought that another incident by a prison trusty would end the program. This second incident would take place in Mitchell County, and the trusty was John Goss.

John Goss lived in New Hanover County, North Carolina. Goss's grandparents were slaves who were freed at the end of the Civil War. He was illiterate; his last name was sometimes spelled "Gause." He was sentenced to the state prison on January 20, 1913 and had served over ten years of his fifteen-year sentence.

In 1923, he was held in the Mitchell County prison unit. John Goss had no prison demerits and was allowed to be a prison trusty. Trusty prisoners were assigned work for a construction company then working on Mitchell County roads. The trusteeship program allowed prisoners an opportunity to show responsibility and have some liberty from the structure of the prison.

Mrs. Alice Thomas was alone in her neighborhood on September 26, 1923. She reported to her family that she was raped by a Black male. The events following this accusation set forth a chain reaction unparalleled in regional history.

Within days, this unassuming rural matron appeared in the *Asheville Citizen*, and the State of North Carolina sent her and her husband on a train trip to Raleigh, North Carolina. Angry white men forcibly expelled Blacks from Mitchell County. The Town of Spruce Pine became an armed military encampment, and the news stories with a dateline "Spruce Pine" became front page material for several weeks. One of the largest crowds ever to witness a term of court in the county assembled for the trial of John Goss.

On September 26, 1923, a small posse was formed consisting of Deputy Sheriff Mack Buchanan and Mrs. Thomas' relatives and neighbors. It began searching for the fugitive known then only as a Black man. These men traveled on foot and covered an estimated 75 miles over rough terrain. This group operated on the assumption that their fugitive would travel east and was able to follow clues ultimately leading them to a railroad overpass near Drexel in Burke County. In Burke County, the posse was joined by Burke County Sheriff Michaux and one of his deputies. Following the group's hunch, Deputy Sheriff Halliburton boarded the next train going east, reaching Hickory, North Carolina, on September 29, 1923.

On the night of Saturday, September 29, 1923, Hickory Chief of Police E. W. Lentz saw a Black man coming out of a house in town, eating cheese and crackers. Lentz arrested this man and determined his name to be John Goss. Lentz told a newspaper reporter that, upon interrogation, Goss had confessed that he lured a woman out of her house in Mitchell County, insisting that he did so to get a pair of shoes.[12] Since Goss was an escapee from prison, Hickory officials took him without delay to the state prison in Raleigh.

In Mitchell County, word spread that a Black man who had escaped from the convict camp was probably the rapist. Crowds, emboldened by whiskey and driven by fear of an unknown assailant at large in the community, began a roundup of all Blacks in the area around Spruce Pine. The mob, estimated at 200 armed and rowdy people, corralled 150 to 200 Black citizens and marched them to the railroad depot in Spruce Pine.[13] The mob stopped a south-bound train and forced the Blacks into five freight cars, sending them against their will to Spartanburg, South Carolina. The mob then delivered an ultimatum that all Blacks leave Spruce Pine the next day.The supervisors of the work camps readily delivered the ultimatum to their Black employees. On September 27, 1923, the Blacks still in the area fled under the threat of white retaliation. Some Blacks escaped over the state line into Tennessee. At the end of September 27, 1923, all Black residents with the exception of one elderly lady in Spruce Pine either were forcibly removed or left the area under threat. Spruce Pine now was a whites-only town.

The *Spartanburg Journal* of Spartanburg, South Carolina, reported on September 28, 1923:

> The forced exodus of black laborers was reported completed today by Mayor A.N. Fuller. The crowd of citizens who collected nearly 100 negroes from construction gangs in the city and placed them aboard freight trains yesterday declared that they will never have another negro in their town. Mayor Fuller said today that while this sentiment will probably die down within a few days, it is necessary, that the improvements go forward. There is no white labor available, he said, and it is necessary that negroes be brought back.[14]

The *Spartanburg Journal* reported on September 29, 1923:

> "There was no evidence of mob spirit here [Spruce Pine] since Wednesday afternoon [September 26], when the last of the negroes, a party of about 25 women, were rounded up and marched through the streets to the railway station, put aboard a box car and carried out of town."

The *Journal* reported that between 150 and 200 Negro laborers were driven from the Spruce Pine vicinity on Wednesday, September 26.

Spartanburg had a natural interest in Spruce Pine since the Fisk Carter Construction Company of Spartanburg had a contract for installing a water and sewer line in Spruce Pine. The company brought Black laborers from South Carolina to Spruce Pine. When the laborers were forced to leave Spruce Pine, they ended up in Spartanburg and camped out along its river. Second, Spartanburg area residents frequently visited Altapass, a resort near Spruce Pine, to escape the South Carolina summer heat.

The railroad brought booming growth to the Spruce Pine area. Ambitious infrastructure projects were underway involving improvements to the sewer and water lines. Governor Cameron

Morrison promised North Carolinians more and better roads and several road projects were underway in Spruce Pine and Mitchell County. The Fisk Carter Construction Company had a contract with the state to build approximately five miles of concrete road from an area west of Spruce Pine to an area near Yancey County at Crabtree Creek. Sand and gravel were brought in over the railroad for this construction. A separate road was under construction into the Plumtree section and a road was being built toward Bakersville. Additionally, the mining operations in Mitchell County were prospering and labor was in great demand.

The Town of Spruce Pine offered a $200 reward for the capture of the person who assaulted Mrs. Mack Thomas. The Mayor of Spruce Pine, A.N. Fuller, notified Governor Cameron Morrison of the forcible evacuation of all Black citizens from Mitchell County. That brought the State of North Carolina into the act as Spruce Pine deteriorated into chaos. On September 27, 1923, Governor Morrison in Raleigh issued a news release:

> A serious situation has arisen at Spruce Pine, in Mitchell County, which caused the Governor to dispatch Adjutant General Metts[15] there by the first train. He is instructed to keep in touch with developments and advise the Governor immediately if any assistance is needed in maintaining law and order. The Governor late this afternoon received a telegram from local authorities indicating that there has been some movement started toward driving colored labor away from the place. He immediately informed the authorities that he would afford the community ample protection, in order to safeguard the rights of all its citizens, both white and colored.

On the same day, Governor Morrison telegraphed the Spruce Pine officials:

> Hon. A. N. Fuller, Mayor, Spruce Pine, N.C., T.W. Deyton, Sanitary Officer, Spruce Pine, N.C., Dr. Charles A Peterson. Spruce Pine, N.C., Dan W. Adams, Spruce Pine, N.C. Please call on local authorities to

> uphold the law and protect everybody in their rights,
> including the colored people. I am directing Adjutant
> General Metts to leave for Spruce Pine tonight. I will
> afford all protection the local authorities may require.
>
> CAMERON MORRISON

North Carolina National Guard troops were dispatched to Spruce Pine with a mission to prevent further violence and to provide safety to any Black citizens who returned.

When John Goss was arrested in Hickory on Saturday, September 29, 1923, he was not charged with any crime. In fact, no warrant for rape was ever issued in Mitchell County. Instead, the Solicitor simply obtained a bill of indictment from the grand jury charging rape. Goss was a prison escapee and could be taken back into custody without new charges. On October 1, 1923, Governor Morrison directed General John Van B. Metts to see if Mrs. Mack Thomas could come to Raleigh at state expense "to identify prisoner charged with assault upon her."[16] On the same day, the Governor telegraphed the Mitchell County Sheriff,

> Please consult County Commissioners and let me know
> if they do not think special term of court should be
> called to try John Goff (sic) As I see situation this should
> be done speedily as possible Consult lady assailed and
> see if she can come here State's expense to identify
> prisoner.

Under normal circumstances, criminal investigations are conducted in-house by county or other local officials. The Governor's intrusion into the case of John Goss, while extraordinary, was probably necessary under the circumstances. These telegrams show North Carolina's chief executive was eager for a prompt trial even before the victim could identify her assailant. Under the law, the Governor had the power to commission Superior Court Judges to hold a term of court as well as to commission special terms of court. Governor Morrison had the authority to determine when Mitchell County got a special term of court and who the presiding judge would be. Governor

Morrison, early on, determined that Judge Thomas B. Finley would be the presiding judge.

Mrs. Thomas and her husband agreed to travel to Raleigh on October 2, and, upon observing John Goss at the state prison, Mrs. Thomas identified him as her assailant. Almost immediately, Governor Morrison ordered a special term of Superior Court to be held in Bakersville on October 22, 1923. Both Solicitor Johnson J. Hayes and Judge Finley protested this date because it required a cancellation of an existing term of court in Avery County. Judge Finley proposed a trial during the regular term of Superior Court for Mitchell County on November 12 or a special term on October 29, which would not have interfered with any other term. Governor Morrison was insistent, and on October 5, 1923, sent a telegram to Judge Finley:

> Do hope you and Solicitor will comply with my request about Mitchell court. Keeping troops there immensely costly to State. Absolutely necessary to keep troops there until court convenes as it now appears. Please let me hear from you and I hope very much that you and Solicitor Hayes can comply with my request.

Governor Morrison said nothing about protecting the rights of the accused. In 1923, people were less concerned about legal rights for the accused.

The Mitchell County commissioners also objected to a special term on October 22, 1923. Despite objections from the county commissioners, the judge and the solicitor, the Governor set in stone the time of John Goss' trial: October 22, 1923.

Daily news stories from Spruce Pine were making front page throughout North Carolina. The photograph of Mrs. Thomas appeared in the Asheville newspaper. Newspaper coverage of a rape victim can be pitiless and worsen the suffering of victims, but in 1923 it was routine for crime and court reporting.

On October 2, 1923, the Tri-County Fair began in Spruce Pine after its Black labor had been compelled to leave town. The Town of Spruce Pine adopted two ordinances, one prohibiting the sale of firearms or ammunition, the second requiring all stores and restaurants to close at 10:00 p.m. A joint county and town proclamation declared,

> No one unusually or dangerously armed openly or concealed would be permitted to enter the town of Spruce Pine.

These proclamations were deemed necessary with feelings still running high throughout the community, and

> in view of the riotous conditions due to recent unlawful acts on the part of certain citizens of Mitchell County and Spruce Pine and parading of unauthorized armed bodies necessitating the ordering by his Excellency the Governor of North Carolina of state troops into this county.[17]

The Tri-County Fair was not well attended, but it provided some opportunity for the military to bolster its relations with the local population. Members of the cavalry from Buncombe County put on a show and its well-trained horsemen won praise from the townspeople. On October 6, 1923, the *Raleigh News and Observer* reported,

> Spontaneous applause greeted the demonstrations and the ice was broken. It was a thriller for these mountaineers to see one man ride four horses at one time. This morning a man went very diffidently to the camp of the Asheville lads (some military troops were from Asheville) leading behind him a refractory mare. She would not be ridden on any account and her owner wanted to know if any of the boys could tame her. They tamed her, though it took off some skin. The mountaineer was thrilled but not convinced of any reformation on the part of the mare.

General Metts ordered a small contingent from the National Guard unit at Lincolnton to report to Spruce Pine, so that troops from Lincolnton, Concord, Asheville and Morganton were now a part of "Camp Mitchell." The military began immediately to escort the returning Blacks. The presence of the Guard prevented further outbreaks of violence.

A Mitchell County Justice of the Peace issued warrants against fourteen Mitchell County citizens for unlawful assembly, committing a riot, and conspiracy to unlawfully assemble, riot and committing assaults.[18] These warrants were issued against those alleged leaders in the September 26 and September 27 events. Sheriff R.B. Forbes quickly arrested some of these fourteen men. On October 10, 1923, Justice of the Peace Frank A. Carr held a probable cause hearing and bound over those cases for trial. All but two were released on $1,000 bonds. The other two were locked up in jail.[19]

Mr. J.E. Burleson was a wealthy citizen of Mitchell County. His letter to the Governor dated October 8, 1923, suggested some mutual familiarity:

> What I am writing you is confidential and my view of the situation with other good citizens. Now, I think that these men ought not to escape prosecution, because if they do they will try the same thing over again...it has hurt the industry there a great deal and it is going to keep men from investing in the mines and all on account of this move. If these people are prosecuted, this will stop it and anyone can take labor and work in peace, but if not, they will do the same thing again.[20]

Walter F. White, assistant secretary of the National Association for the Advancement of Colored People, sent a telegram to the Governor on September 28, 1923:

> Press dispatches report that an armed mob of two hundred citizens of Spruce Pine North Carolina are today rounding up all male Negroes in Spruce Pine and vicinity and deporting them on freight trains because of an alleged attack by a Negro on an aged white woman National Association for Advancement of Colored People is requesting of you information regarding correctness of this report and is also asking that you as

governor of the state use all power at your command to protect the civil and constitutional rights of colored citizens who are being driven from their homes and jobs regardless of their innocence or guilt.

Governor Morrison sent back a curt reply the same day:

My actions in matter referred to by you are being given to Associated Press as quickly as can be done to prevent action of State being prematurely made known to the lawless from whom we seek to protect the State. You can get information through the news sources as the rest of the public acquire it.

Governor Morrison was interested in building roads connecting all the county seats of North Carolina and wanted to be fondly remembered for this legacy. The incident in Spruce Pine represented a distraction, and compounded by the racial attitudes of the day, was less sympathetic to "the civil and constitutional rights of colored citizens."

Back in Mitchell County, Sheriff R.C. Forbes felt uncertain of his role. Ordinarily he would have been responsible for the investigation of the crime and the safekeeping of prisoner John Goss, but he saw the Governor make all the key decisions. It was the Governor who decided to have Mrs. Mack Thomas come to Raleigh to identify the prisoner. It was the Governor who decided that the prisoner would be tried on October 22, 1923 and who decided that the presiding judge would be T.B. Finley. Sheriff Forbes inquired of the Governor, "Shall I come to Raleigh to receive John Goss negro prisoner for Mitchell County for special term of court If so on what day shall I arrive there."

Governor Morrison had no intention of entrusting John Goss to local authorities. When the time came for preparation for the October 22, 1923, trial, Goss was taken by state prison authorities by train to Hickory and there they met National Guard troops from North Wilkesboro who formed an entourage and accompanied Goss to Toecane.

Bob Hughes, a man who held an elective office in Mitchell County, remembered that Goss was the "least little man I have ever seen."[21]

An estimated 600 people were present in Bakersville[22] as Goss' short frame, exaggerated by the bulk of the chains wrapped around him, was presented. Armed military troops stood guard as far as the eye could see. Goss rode on a flatbed truck brought in by the military to Bakersville. When he was taken into the Mitchell County courthouse on October 22, 1923, he was not yet legally accused of rape or anything else, and had not been appointed a lawyer.

Judge Finley ordered all persons under 16 and all women from the courtroom. Two panels of jurors were summoned that day. From the first panel was selected the Grand Jury. Bakersville attorney S.J. Black was appointed to represent John Goss. Solicitor Johnson J. Hayes submitted a bill of indictment to the Grand Jury charging John Goss with rape. Solicitor Hayes, as was his practice in all cases, signed the bill with only the word "Hayes." Judge Finley apprised the grand jurors of the meaning of the charge and advised them in forceful language that they should give their best to their country to aid in law enforcement. He criticized the Ku Klux Klan.[23] His charge was said to be masterful.

When the court resumed after a recess, the Grand Jury returned a true bill of indictment and Citizen John Goss was now charged with rape. It took only a few minutes for the Grand Jury to return this true bill.

The sheriff was earlier directed to summon additional jurors from whom the trial jury would be chosen. Some of the prospective jurors were excused either by the defendant John Goss or by the state. Several did not believe in the death penalty. Some stated that they had formed an opinion relating to guilt or innocence. At least one of the jurors stated that he had a prejudice against Black people. About 3:00 p.m., the jury had been selected and empaneled.

Three witnesses testified for the state. Captain J.B. Holloway, the superintendent at the convict camp, testified that Goss was a prisoner who went to work with the road construction crew on the morning of September 26, 1923. Holloway said that

Goss did not return to the camp and he had not seen Goss again until the day of the trial.

Alice Thomas testified that on September 26, 1923, just after 12 o'clock noon she was near Mrs. Melvira Silver's[24] home approximately one-half mile east of her home. Goss suddenly confronted her and asked for milk. Brandishing a large pocketknife, he forced Mrs. Thomas to have sex with him against her will. Defense lawyer Black asked Mrs. Thomas if she could be mistaken in her identification of defendant, to which she responded that she could not be mistaken and that Goss was the man. Cross-examination took little time and generated less impact.

Mrs. Melvira Silver testified that she saw the defendant, John Goss, at her house a few minutes before the incident. When asked if Goss was the one she had seen, she replied, "That's the jock."[25]

Within thirty minutes, the presentation of evidence was over. The entire trial lasted only a couple of hours. After about five minutes of deliberation, the jury found Goss guilty of rape. Judge Finley was ready for the sentencing.

> The jury having returned a verdict of guilty of rape as charged in the Bill of Indictment, and the prisoner, John Goss, (colored) being at the Bar of the Court:
> The judgment of the Court is, that the Defendant, John Goss (colored) be put to death by electrocution, and to this end, the prisoner, John Goss (colored) is committed to the custody of the Sheriff of Mitchell County, and to be by him, or some one by him lawfully authorized, and another deputy, conveyed to the state's prison and delivered to the Warden of the Penitentiary, and said John Goss (colored) shall be by him kept securely in the death Cell until on the 30th day of November, 1923, between sunrise and sunset, when the warden or Deputy Warden (in case of the death or disability or absence of the Warden) shall cause to pass through the body of John Goss (colored) a current of electricity of sufficient intensity to cause death, and the application of said current must be continued until the said John Goss (colored) is dead, dead, dead.[26]

Imposition of the death penalty in those days carried far less weight, moral as well as legal, than it does now. When John Goss was tried, the death penalty was mandatory for those convicted of capital crimes. At that time, an appeal was not automatic and the defendant would have to decide to appeal. John Goss decided not to appeal, and the matter ended. Goss's only hope rested with executive clemency from Governor Morrison. Goss never sought such relief.

Goss was taken by military escort to Hickory by train.[27] There the military consisting of 43 men and three officers left to return to North Wilkesboro and Goss continued by train in custody of state prison guards. Mitchell County Deputy E. B. Hensley accompanied this group and on October 24, 1923, he delivered Goss to the warden of Central Prison.

When November 30, 1923, arrived, Goss took no legal steps to delay his execution and the news media had gathered expecting to observe a death sentence carried out. Mack Thomas may have been there.[28] However, no execution took place, because Governor Morrison was out of state, and according to his orders, no executions should occur when he was not in the state.

Stays of execution became commonplace generations later but, on November 30, 1923, John Goss was granted an extraordinary stay that he did not request. His electrocution on Friday, December 7, 1923 was witnessed by several North Carolina State College students who faked their ages to witness the execution. Fridays were favored days for executions and at one time the law required that executions must occur on this day of the week.

It was widely reported in the statewide news media that before he was electrocuted, John Goss confessed to a minister that he committed the assault on the white woman.[29]

On December 8, 1923, the *Asheville Citizen* editorialized:

On Goss's arrest, the people of Mitchell quieted themselves and the law proceeded to establish another record for speedy trial and prompt punishment. It is such triumphs of law over tendencies to lawlessness and such records for dispatch in Court procedure in aggravated criminal cases that have done so much to give North Carolina a good name as a law-abiding State.

The execution took place forty-six days after the conviction and on the seventy-third day after the crime.

The trial of John Goss was unremarkable for its courtroom tactics and it is not cited for any legal precedent. Proceedings were not recorded in any appellate court records and it left behind only the barest of archives. Indeed, the only legal significance of the trial was its rush to judgment. Records for expediency are generally not indexed, but it is difficult to imagine that due process of law could ever be meted out more quickly.

The *Raleigh News and Observer* reported the execution on page nine on December 8, 1923. Executions were not sufficiently newsworthy to be placed on the front page, but what is truly startling is the patently racial coarseness of this article:

> John Goss met death with a stolid face when they led him into the execution chamber yesterday morning to pay with his life for a criminal attack on a aged white woman in Mitchell County late in September after he had escaped from a convict camp where he was serving the last month of a sentence for a similar crime committed in Wilmington 15 years ago.
>
> John Goss died hard. Full five minutes the current played through him, and the air of the room grew heavy with the odor of burned flesh before the attending physician finally nodded his head to the warden, indicating that the heart under the black breast was still.
>
> Goss looked the part of the picture that 'mean nigger' conjures up. Short, squat, thick bodied, and with the face of a gorilla. Even the eyes were muddy with a diffusion of the color of his skin. He held them steadfastly open as death came steadily toward him, and when he was dead, he stared with solid indifference toward the ceiling.

Four shocks were required to take the life out of him.
The steady pumping of his heart against the black thick
breast was perceptible after the first. The second had
weakened it but slightly, and the third a little more.
After the forth the stethoscope could find no trace of
life in the black carcass and he was dumped into a basket
to be sent to one of the medical schools of the state.

John Goss is the only person ever to be executed in a case
originating in Mitchell County. Modern attorneys can find a score
of ways to challenge the trial and the skill of the attorney who
represented the defendant. There was almost no time allotted to
the defense attorney for preparation, the tense community and
military atmosphere surrounding the event could have been argued
to have created a prejudice against the defendant, and the possibly
suggestive circumstances preceding the identification of defendant
by the victim most assuredly would have been challenged in any
modern trial. Many constitutionally protected rights taken for
granted now, but not yet in existence, were ignored. Larger legal
ramifications are beyond the intended scope of this book, but it
should be noted that in 1966, in the Doctor Sam Sheppard Case,[30]
the United States Supreme Court recognized that due process of
law requires an atmosphere of "judicial serenity and calm."

North Carolina law curently endows persons accused of
capital crime with extraordinary legal rights. There is an automatic
appeal to the Supreme Court of those sentenced to death. Persons
accused of capital crimes are now entitled to representation by
two attorneys. There can be no time restrictions on the attorneys'
arguments to the jury. The defense attorney is always entitled to
the final argument. No part of the trial may be conducted in the
defendant's absence. The North Carolina Supreme Court has, for
generations, operated under a self-imposed rule that in capital
cases the justices would screen the entire record looking for trial
errors even though specific objections were not made at trial.

It is fruitless to compare modern trials with those that took
place at different times under vastly different social circumstances.
The Goss trial did not depart from the circumstances of many
trials conducted during that time. In another era or in another

place, Defendant John Goss might have contributed to the development of the law, and his name might have become infamous like Miranda, Gideon, or Sheppard. But, in 1923, the judges had not yet begun patching some of the cracks in the justice system.

Footnotes

[12] *Asheville Citizen*, September 30, 1923 and *Hickory Daily Record*, October 1, 1923.

[13] *Atlanta Constitution*, September 29, 1923 and *The Spartanburg Journal* September 28, 1923.

[14] In 1923, the word "negro" was often not capitalized. Later practice of capitalizing the word signifies a milestone in the recognition of the civil rights of all persons.

[15] John Van B. Metts

[16] Cameron Morrison's loose papers in the North Carolina Archives, telegram to General Metts: "Please see if assailed lady can come here at State's expense to identify prisoner charged with assault upon her If she can come get transportation for her and male member of family to accompany her and charge to expense account It seems to me special term of court should be held quickly as possible."

[17] *Charlotte Observer*, October 2, 1923.

[18] Justice of the Peace J. W. Bennett issued the warrant based on an affidavit of Spruce Pine Town Marshall, L. H. Wright. Those charged were Stokes McKinney, Peter Biddix, Heap Greene, Jr., Fayett Ward, Dot Buchanan, John Pitman, Logan Ward, P. E. Jackson, Mac McMahan, D. H. S. Tappan, Molton Buchanan, Andrew Green, Lane Buchanan, and Roby Buchanan.

[19] Molton Buchanan, Pete Biddix, and C. A. McMahan objected to W. J. Bennett, the original Justice of the Peace, presiding over the probable cause hearing and moved that the case be heard by another justice of the peace. The case was removed to Justice of the Peace Frank A. Carr who heard testimony from Coleman Riddle, L. H. Wright, Paul Silvers, D. W. Adams, Sam Burleson, Phillip Stewart, and E. A. Ellis, and found probable cause. All defendants except Dot Buchanan and Stokes McKinney were allowed to make bond. Stokes McKinney and Dot Buchanan were held in the Mitchell County Jail until the special session of court on October 22, 1923. Defendant Logan Ward was not present at the hearing and his whereabouts not known. Many years later, reminiscing about this affair, Molton Buchanan confided to Attorney Lloyd Hise that one of the witnesses had mysteriously disappeared, and the state's case was diminished. Eventually, Logan Ward was indicted by the Mitchell County Grand Jury and in November, 1923 he pleaded guilty. The Justice's notes of the hearing were located in the Mitchell County Clerk of Court's office, but the writing was

undecipherable. Clearly, however, Stokes McKinney was portrayed as spokesman and prime actor for the angry mob.

[20] Governor Cameron Morrison's loose papers, maintained and indexed under 'Governor Morrison papers' at the North Carolina Archives, are the source of this and Walter F. White's letter. Numerous telegrams and letters are preserved in the Archives, and they proved invaluable.

[21] Conversation with writer. Goss was sentenced to prison from New Hanover County under the name John Gause. This misspelling was often repeated in newspaper accounts of Mitchell County events. It probably occurred because he was known by this name to prison authorities. Volume II of the Descriptive index for prisoners in the North Carolina Archives shows that John Gause was sentenced for second degree burglary in New Hanover County on January 20, 1913. He received a fifteen year sentence and was received in prison on April 2, 1913. He was eighteen years old, five feet four inches tall, and weighed 145 pounds.

[22] *Raleigh News and Observer,* October 23, 1923.

[23] A *Raleigh News and Observer* reporter, Ben Dixon McNeil, wrote on October 23, 1923, that civil and military authorities were looking for a Ku Klux organizer. In Governor Morrison's papers there are two interesting telegrams. The first is from Adjutant General Metts to Governor Morrison which in part states, "McNeil had no such knowledge or right to so state." Governor Morrison's telegram of the same date states simply, "Don't fool with Ku Klux None of our business." What role, if any, the Ku Klux Klan had in the Spruce Pine riot is beyond the scope of this book. References to the Klan sometimes appear in the research. Obviously, Judge Finley thought the Klan had a role in light of his instructions to the Grand Jury.

[24] Melvira Silver is the same person to whom Mrs. Julie Thomas McClellan referred when she called her "Aunt Vine" or "Aunt Vinney." There was no relationship between Wilburn Thomas' family and Mrs. Silver; "Aunt Vinney" was a term of respect.

[25] Judge Finley's notes, preserved in the Clerk of Court office, are hurriedly and poorly written, but nevertheless a source for this book. This quotation has not been deciphered in those notes, but is attributed to an article in the *Raleigh News and Observer* October 23, 1923.

[26] Minute Docket 15 page 42, Mitchell County Clerk of Superior Court, Bakersville, North Carolina.

[27] "Tuesday, at 12:30 p.m., troops proceeded to Toecane, N.C. with the prisoner, and entrained at 1:30, arriving at Hickory at 6:35, had supper at a cafe, and at 8:00 o'clock, proceeded by auto to home station at North Wilkesboro, N.C., arriviing at 11:0.m. Equipment was checked and men dismissed. It was not deemed necesary to send a squad of troops on to Raleigh with the prisoner," E.P. Robinson, Major C. E., Commanding, *Biennial Report,* The Adjutant General, 1923.

[28] Joe Snyder, late of Cane Creek, spent many hours with the writer giving the history of Mitchell County. His long involvement in Mitchell County

government and politics and interest in history made him a most knowledgeable source. Mr. Snyder maintained that Mack Thomas walked to Raleigh to witness the execution. If this is true, then he could not have had an advance notice of the stay of execution. He may have stayed in Raleigh until December 7, 1923 when the execution took place. Neither Mack Thomas' granddaughter, Julie Thomas McClellan, nor his grandson's wife, Mrs. Monroe Thomas, knew anything about this. Those women have said that Mack Thomas was pleased after Goss was electrocuted.

[29] Joe Snyder's father sat on the jury that convicted John Goss. Snyder told the writer that his mother was disturbed by the verdict and sentence of death until she heard that Goss had confessed. Thereafter, according to Snyder, his mother was satisfied that the verdict was correct.

[30] *Sheppard vs. Maxwell*, 384 U.S. 333 (1966).

Chapter 4: Camp Mitchell

By 1923, racial violence and intimidation became commonplace throughout the United States. The summer following the end of World War I was called the "Red Summer" meaning the bloody summer, and from 1919 to 1925 race riots exploded across the country. Chicago, Illinois endured a major race riot in 1919. Tulsa, Oklahoma erupted in a violent racial conflagration in 1921.

In the south, the Ku Klux Klan revived its activities, and the number of lynchings increased. The year 1919, saw 83 recorded lynchings in the United States. Riots occurred that year in Washington, D.C., Knoxville, Tennessee, Longview, Texas, Phillips County, Arkansas, and in Omaha, Nebraska as well as the one in Chicago.

In 1923, Governor Cameron Morrison of North Carolina was compelled five times to order troops from the North Carolina National Guard to various towns to provide protection for Black citizens awaiting trial. On January 25th, troops mobilized from Goldsboro to Kinston to protect a man on trial in criminal court from mob violence. On January 28th, troops went from Wilmington to Whiteville to provide protection for a Black man on trial. On November 9th, Company M of the National Guard stationed at Wilson was ordered to Nashville to protect a prisoner in custody. Upon arriving at Nashville, the guard learned that the prisoner was sent to the state prison for his safekeeping, and the guard returned to its base. On November 30th, the unit was ordered back to Nashville to protect the same prisoner who was being tried in court in Nashville. On October 20, 1923, troops were sent from North Wilkesboro to meet officials of the state prison at Hickory, and then to proceed with those officials to Bakersville for the purpose of guarding prisoner John Goss.[31] After the two incidents at Nashville, the Nash County Commissioners adopted a resolution criticizing the Governor for sending troops to Nashville to protect the Black prisoner Lee Washington. Governor Morrison responded in a statement issued on December 9, 1923, that he intended to use "every particle of power given to me by the Constitution of the State to prevent lynchings" in North Carolina.[32]

In addition to ordering troops to guard John Goss during his trial, Governor Morrison had previously ordered troops of the North Carolina National Guard to Spruce Pine to restore order, repatriate the Black citizens who were forced to leave, and for investigating the identity of those involved in the uprising.

On September 27, 1923, Governor Morrison ordered the Adjutant General, Brigadier General J. Van Metts, to Spruce Pine to investigate and report conditions to the Governor. When Metts arrived on September 27th, he found a tense and confrontational situation. On that very day he ordered units from the 109th Cavalry at Asheville and the 105th Engineers at Morganton to "proceed to Spruce Pine with the least practical delay for the purpose of maintaining law and order, and cooperating with the civil authorities of Mitchell County." On September 28th, troops began arriving in Spruce Pine. Initially, there were 145 men. The troops encamped on the south side of the Toe River and fortified that area. Machine guns were trained on the business section of the town.

On October 1, 1923, General Metts ordered even more troops to Spruce Pine. Troops from the 120th Infantry at Concord were ordered to join the others already dispatched. When this unit joined the others, a total of 250 troops were at the fortification which was popularly known as "Camp Mitchell."

Albert Canipe, who served Mitchell County in the North Carolina General Assembly and as a county commissioner, was a respected and popular man who won elections in Republican Mitchell County in spite of being a Democrat. Before he died, he shared his recollections of Camp Mitchell. At the military base, now the site of the First Baptist Church, Mr. Canipe recalled that the weapons were positioned to face the main part of Spruce Pine, but they looked outdated. He sensed that the military presence was needed only for a short time.

A palpable sense of urgency, however, existed in Governor Morrison's September 29th telegram to General Metts:

> Prison camp near Spruce Pine must be protected at every cost Notify Sheriff of County you are ready to uphold law and sustain him and protect Negro laborers in their

right to work in County. If Sheriff will not do his duty in your opinion notify me Assemble adequate forces beyond all doubt to uphold the law and protect this State from being overcome by mob.

Cameron Morrison
Governor of North Carolina

The prison camp was never threatened although there was concern that it might be placed under siege. The Black prison inmate population, which numbered thirty-three, was never removed from the Mitchell County Prison although some of the convicts who worked on road construction were subjected to intimidation by the white mob.

Governor Morrison received abundant correspondence on the Spruce Pine situation. R. Fred Brewer, general manager of Clinchfield Products Corporation wrote on September 28, 1923:

> This corporation had approximately forty five negro laborers, a good many of them had their families with them, these laborers were all driven from their homes and forced to leave the community because someone committed a crime. It has been utterly impossible to secure sufficient labor in this section to operate our mines therefore it has been necessary for us to bring this labor in, some of the men we had have been with us for a number of years and the writer knows that they were reliable and law abiding citizens.

The president of P.H. O'Brien Construction Company of Birmingham, Alabama wrote the chairman of the State Highway commission on September 27, 1923:

> This evening at three o'clock one hundred and fifty armed men with Winchesters and shot guns and pistols came on our work in Avery County Project 800 and ordered all our colored labor to leave and get in front of them and march them to Spruce Pine, N.C. a distance of five and one half miles: I begged and pleaded with them and told them that our negroes were law abiding citizens and did not go out of our camp at night and

absolutely they knew nothing of a rape committed on an old white lady by a negro yesterday in Mitchell County. I begged with this mob to please let our labor alone and told them that our negroes were quite law abiding negroes that I brought from Alabama, and they gave me until tomorrow at noon to get them out of the State which I intend to do. Fifteen of the negroes ran away when they saw the mob coming and we only have between 25 and 30 in camp tonight as best I can check them over. We will not have a man to bridle a mule tomorrow at noon and both of our steam shovels are shut down tonight. They loaded at Spruce Pine, N.C. today 2 box car loads of negroes and run them out of here and three more car loads of them went out from Spruce Pine, N.C. today on the passenger train.[33]

Once the Black residents left the county and the troops began arriving, the situation quieted. General Metts telegraphed the Governor on September 29th, "Troops here things quiet at present though atmosphere charged Convict camp has not been molested."[34] Newspapers not only in the region but across the state made Spruce Pine a front page story and household name. When John Goss was arrested in Catawba County, it was reported that the Hickory Police Chief, E. F. Lentz, was concerned that the posse consisting of relatives of Mrs. Thomas might be eager to dispense justice themselves. Mrs. Thomas' sons were quoted as saying that they were content to let the law run its course, but in the end they wanted to see Goss electrocuted if he were guilty.[35]

On October 1, 1923, General Metts telegraphed the Governor: "11:15 a.m. Sunday quietness prevails Many rumors afloat conditions very unsettled convict camp quiet with detachment of troops there I have today talked with camp foreman Troops on alert day and night with patrols in the town."

General Metts' assurance to Governor Morrison came the day following an apparent outbreak of gunfire in Spruce Pine. The *Washington Post* of October 1, 1923, reported that during the night of September 30th:

This little mountain city, in turmoil last week following an attack by a Negro on an aged white woman, was again thrown into a state of great excitement at 10 o'clock tonight when twenty shots were fired by unidentified persons in the northwest section of the city. State troops were searching the mountainside for persons who fired the shots.

The *Atlanta Constitution* on October 2, 1923 reported:

Spruce Pine, N.C. October 1 the arrival by special train late today of company E, 120th infantry from Concord, the return of eleven Negroes who were driven out of the community by armed men last week and conference between military and civil authorities to perfect plans for the handling of the crowds expected to attend the tri-county fair, which opens here tomorrow, were among the outstanding developments in the Spruce Pine situation here today.

The Christian Science Monitor on October 1, 1923, both praised Governor Morrison and wrote of another controversy raising racial questions:

While the Governor of North Carolina is throwing every effort toward the maintenance of law and order and has troops stationed in Mitchell County for protection of its Negro laborers, the Attorney General of this State is in a northern capital arguing for the return to this State of a Negro charged with a capital felony whose return is being contested on the ground that he 'would not get a fair trial.'

Trouble may occur today, when Negro laborers are to report again for duty. But those who seek to cause any disturbance will be met with stern force. Soldiers are on hand and no disorders will be tolerated. If necessary more will be sent.

> While other southern states are grappling with the Negro problem and are losing many of their Negro laborers in the migration wave, North Carolina is holding its Negroes; educating them and is affording them protection in the courts and in pursuit of their honest undertakings it is pointed out.

General Metts returned to Raleigh in early October, and Major E.P. Robinson was the commanding officer over the troops in Mitchell County. On October 10, 1923, a decision was made to withdraw the troops despite some dissension among local officials.[36] By withdrawing the troops the Governor showed confidence in the local civil authorities and in the local population. This confidence was not misplaced. Sheriff's deputies in Avery and Mitchell Counties were assigned by their superiors to protect Black citizens working for construction companies. Mitchell County remained quiet after the troops were gone.

Because John Goss was a trusty in the North Carolina Prison System, there was an outcry from many North Carolinians, that the system be revised. Eventually the public outrage subsided and the trusty system remained in place.

After John Goss was indicted, tried, and convicted on Monday, October 22, 1923, the Grand Jury returned for additional work on Tuesday, October 23, 1923. Solicitor Hayes submitted a single bill of indictment[37] against eighty-five persons for their suspected conduct in the forced removal of the Black citizens.[38] The indictment had four counts similar in wording to the original arrest warrant for the first fourteen who were charged. The Grand Jury returned true bills against approximately seventy-seven persons.[39] Confusion in the court minutes cannot altogether be reconciled and this number reflects a comparison of several entries within the court minutes together with a news account appearing in the *Johnson City Chronicle* on October 24, 1923.

Some of the defendants were previously arrested and most were allowed to make bail. Of the original fourteen charged, twelve pleaded guilty on October 23, 1923, and judgment was continued to November 12, 1923. On November 12 and 13, 1923, the remaining defendants pleaded guilty to two misdemeanors and all were sentenced. A total of sixty-four persons pleaded guilty (this number excludes the name Columbus Thomas which was used twice in the court minutes). S. J. Black, John Goss' former attorney, represented most of the men who were charged with rioting.[40] Four of the defendants were required to pay a fine of $25.00 and court costs. One defendant had to pay a $10.00 fine and court costs. Most of the defendants were required only to pay court costs and be law abiding citizens.[41]

Prior to 1932, a state was not obligated under the United States Constitution to appoint an attorney for indigent persons accused of capital crimes. In that year, the U. S. Supreme Court ruled that the Constitution required that states provide an attorney in capital cases.[42] North Carolina acted earlier to provide this basic right. On March 7, 1917, the General Assembly of North Carolina passed "An Act Relating to the Compensation of Counsel Appointed by the Judge to Defend Persons Charged with Capital Crimes." The statute provided that in cases where the judge appointed an attorney to represent on accused of a capital crime, the county was obligated to pay a fee but not to exceed $25.00. Even before the enactment of this statute, most if not all of the capital cases tried in North Carolina involved a defense lawyer at the trial level. In one case a former slave was charged in Yancey County with a capital crime shortly after the Civil War and when the case was tried in Buncombe County, the defendant had an attorney represent him at trial.[43] The practice seems to have been that attorneys were appointed for trial, but there was no provision for representation in the appellate court. Much later, the United States Supreme Court ruled that the right to counsel is the right to effective assistance of counsel.[44] In 1923, there were no standards for effectiveness of an attorney's performance, and no body of law giving any right to the defendant other than the statutory right to have an attorney. Developments in law assuring attorneys sufficient preparation time also occurred after 1923.

At the conclusion of the Goss trial, Judge Finley, in an effort to help the attorney collect a larger fee than mandated by statute, ordered that the attorney, S. J. Black, be allowed a fee of $25 to be paid by the Commissioners of Mitchell County, but also he "respectfully recommends the county Commissioners allow him a further sum of $75.00, which the Court considers reasonable and just."[45] Meeting in regular session on November 5, 1923, the Mitchell County Commissioners awarded Mr. Black, Esquire, $25, and ignored the judge's recommendation for an additional $75 fee.[46] The Commissioners awarded their chairman, J.H. Griffith, $6, for his having presided over the special meeting of the Mitchell County Commissioners necessitated by Governor Morrison ordering the special term of Superior Court and at which the commissioners drew names of jurors to be summonsed for that term. Sheriff R.C. Forbes was to be paid $10 for car hire required in fulfilling the orders of the court during the special term.

The amount paid S.J. Black pales by comparison to an amount of money approved as a fee to pay the Town Attorney of Spruce Pine. On October 10, 1923, at a special meeting of the Alderman of Spruce Pine, a majority vote of the aldermen guaranteed a fee of $500 to Attorney E.F. Watson to prosecute all the defendants previously arrested for rioting through all the courts.[47]

Hickory Chief of Police Lentz sought to collect the reward of $200 that the Town of Spruce Pine had offered. No public policy at that time prevented a law enforcement officer making a claim for a reward. Mayor A.N. Fuller wrote Chief E.W. Lentz on October 2, 1923:

> The Spruce Pine reward was written to read that when the man was captured that the reward was to be divided between the parties who participated in the capture as their several interests might then appear. A Deputy Sheriff from Mitchell County, four sons of Mrs. Thomas and her nephew, it appears literally drove the prisoner into the arms of the men who captured him, since they trailed him off the mountain country on into the point of capture. We strongly feel, therefore, that the 6 above men should participate in the rewards.[48]

Records do not reveal any further activity regarding the reward and the matter most probably ended there.

The North Carolina National Guard left Spruce Pine on October 10, 1923. The Guard was to return later to protect Goss during the trial. At the time of their departure, their Adjutant General made this statement concerning their performance:

> Though this was a very unusual and difficult situation, as well as very perilous for a few days, the officers and men conducted themselves in such a manner as to bring credit upon themselves and the State.[49]

John Goss was taken by military troops from Toecane on October 23, 1923. The day earlier, after he was convicted, news reporters questioned him about his reaction to the trial. He thanked Governor Morrison for taking steps to protect his life. He stated that he had considered pleading guilty to assault with intent to rape, but his attorney advised against it. He also said that he had made things right between him and God.[50]

When the troops left Spruce Pine on October 10, 1923, the news reporters also left. After Goss' conviction, the state media lost interest altogether in the events of Mitchell County. There was little coverage of the white citizens who pleaded guilty to rioting. The relatively small fines levied on the perpetrators, the attendant disinterest of the news media in their trials, and the fact that no one ever seriously attempted to identify or enumerate the Black citizens who were forced at the point of a gun to leave their homes and jobs speak of the attitudes of the time.

The Black citizens were, in fact, kidnapped. The kidnap law of the time made it illegal to forcibly remove any person from one place to another. Kidnapping remained a misdemeanor charge, but, for every victim the possibility existed to charge a separate crime. To charge kidnapping would have required the solicitor or the military or the law enforcement officers to identify the victims by name. This was not done. The victims numbered nearly two hundred. Not all of the white men took part in each kidnapping, and the screening of the facts as they connected one defendant to each victim would have been extremely difficult. The decision not to charge kidnapping instead of a single act of rioting would have been made easier by the racial makeup of the accused and the victims. Newspapers reported the forced departure of the Black citizens, and they photographed the return of some of those citizens, but no newspaper sought to identify any Black citizens by name. No newspaper asked any victim, "What went through your mind as you were being forced against your will to board a freight train?" The names of the victims are lost to history.

Governor Morrison, however might have been encouraged to take the matter to heart after receiving the following letter which was found in his papers:

> Hon Mr. Morrison, Gov I noticed in reading from the daily press of our city and state, Birmingham, Ala. According to the press that a crime was committed by a member of my race, Negro, at Spruce Pine, N.C. in your good state and according to newspaper report the Negro made an attack upon an aged white woman which has caused excitement and bad feelings of the white citizens against the Negroes in that vicinity. It is reported that the ill feelings of the white people has run so high that innocent colored people of Spruce Pine have to flee to save their lives. I deplore such an attack by a man of my race on a member of your or any other race and feel that the guilty party should be brought to justice and dealt with according to the full extent of the law and that every law abiding citizen regardless of color, should assist in running down and capturing those who are guilty of such outrageous crime, and yet I feel that the respectable and law abiding Negroes of that and any other community should not suffer and be driven away from their homes on account of what one bad member of his race does.
>
> I feel safe in saying that if the good white people in the state of North Carolina and in the said community where the crime is reported to have been committed were to follow your instructions and effort to protect all citizens regardless of color that no one would be molested other than the guilty party. As a humble colored preacher who has the interest and welfare of all the people at

heart, I want to thank you for the effort you have displayed in this matter in trying to protect the lives of the humble and innocent people who dwell in that community.

I trust that the good relationship between the two races of the said community will soon be restored to normalcy.

Thanking you for your effort and consideration in this matter, I am,

Your humble servant, Rev. W. H. Hunt

Governor Morrison and other North Carolina Governors acted to prevent lynchings in their state. In Rowan County, in 1906, crowds estimated in the thousands, stormed the Salisbury jail and lynched three African-American inmates who were held for the murder of the Lyerly family. Governor Robert B. Glenn ordered the National Guard to Salisbury to restore order and investigate the event. One person, George Hall, was convicted of breaking and entering into the Rowan County Jail with the intent to kill confined prisoners. He was sentenced to long hard labor. This case has the interesting twist in that Governor Glenn was in Atlantic City, New Jersey when he commissioned the term of court at which Hall was tried. Hall's attorney contended that Governor Glenn's actions in setting up the court were void. Governor Glenn was actually called as a witness on this motion. At his appearance in Salisbury, Governor Glenn testified, "I got this telegram at Atlantic City, and as it needed attention at once, I ordered the Commissioners to hold this special term of court, *because I wanted to stop this lynching in North Carolina* (emphasis added)." [51]

The decision to hold John Goss' trial in the county when military troops were present and when the population was angry may not have, according to today's standards, provided due process of law to the accused. Lawyer Black made no motion for a change of venue, although that motion had already developed and was sometimes used. The inordinate interest that the community had in this defendant and his trial is vividly pointed out in Major Robinson's report to Adjutant General Metts:

The detachment entrained at 8:05 a.m., Sunday, October 21st, and proceeded to Toecane, N.C., and from Toecane to Bakersville by truck, arriving at 4:35 p.m. 21st, with the prisoner, John Goss, all precaution for protection of prisoner being observed. A heavy guard with fixed bayonets was quickly thrown around the prisoner and maintained throughout the three-mile trip to the jail. Guard was immediately posted around jail and in the jail the prisoner was guarded to and from the courthouse and while in court. Guard was maintained day and night. The train was met by several hundred people who were quiet and orderly, but curious to see the prisoner and troops. A cordial welcome was extended the troops, and had not Bakersville been partially burned a reception would have been given for troops (few of whom should have been permitted to attend by reason of duty.) Close watch of the crowd and the situation in general was maintained at all times by the writer.[52]

In early life, Cameron Morrison was a Republican and attended the Republican State Convention in 1890. During the decade of the 1890s, African Americans voted with the Republicans and won some elections including that of Governor Daniel Russell in 1898. Shortly after 1890 Morrison joined the Democrats. He spoke to the Democratic State Convention in 1892 and campaigned actively in opposition to the Republican and Negro rule. Morrison became a leader of the "Red Shirts," a militant movement advocating white supremacy. Morrison, together with Robert B. Glenn, made efforts to eliminate lynchings in North Carolina. They, however, worked together with Charles Brantley Aycock to disenfranchise Negro voters. The poll tax and the literacy tests were enacted as means to insure the least possible number of African American votes. Aycock said in 1905, "We disfranchised the Negro on the distinct ground that with him as a voter we could not preserve peace, quiet and order."[53]

In 1932, the citizens of North Carolina gave a bronze statute of Charles B. Aycock to the United States Capitol to be permanently displayed in statuary hall as a North Carolinian with notable accomplishments.

Spruce Pine and Mitchell County went off the state radar, where they remain today.

Footnotes

[31] Adjutant General's Biennial Report for the year 1923.

[32] *New York Times*, December 9, 1923.

[33] Governor Morrison loose papers North Carolina Archives.

[34] Governor Morrison loose papers North Carolina Archives.

[35] An attitude that citizens will let the law run its course is commendable. Every criminal court prosecutor has encountered instances when hurt and angry victims or their families want to inflict violence on the suspect. The possibility of the death sentence has been used by the author on occasion to dissuade acts of violence by the victim toward the suspect. At times is was effective to say, "Don't do any thing foolish; let the law take care of this."

[36] Among Governor Morrison's papers is this telegram from D. W. Adams, a Spruce Pine official dated October 8, 1923: "GOVERNOR CAMERON MORRISON AFTER CONFERENCE WITH GENERAL METZ AND CIVIL OFFICERS SPRUCEPINE WE STRONGLY RECOMMEND YOUR LEAVING ONE HALF COMPANY CONCORD TROOPS SPRUCEPINE UNTIL AFTER BAKERSVILLE TRIAL FOLLOWING REASONS FIRST OPEN THREATS AGAINST LIVES OF CIVIL OFFICERS SECOND NEGRO LABORERS WILL LEAVE OR BE DRIVEN OUT THIRD EXPENSE WOULD BE LESS TO RETAIN HALF COMPANY CONCORD TROOPS IN ESTABLISHED CAMP THAN TO RETURN THEM FOURTH CRIMINAL PROCESS COULD PROCEED AND CONCLUDE AT SPECIAL TERM UNDER MILITARY PROTECTION WHICH WILL BE GREATLY NEEDED TRUST YOU MAY GRANT THIS REQUEST AND TREAT THIS WIRE CONFIDENTIAL BEST WISHES AND THANKS FOR YOUR PROMPT ACTION   D. W. ADAMS. Also among Governor Morrison's papers is this telegram October 9, 1923, "OUR FIRM DOING SEWERS AND WATER SPRUCEPINE AND RESPECTFULLY REQUEST PORTION OF TROOPS BE LEFT THERE A LITTLE LONGER WILL BE VERY DIFFICULT TO OBTAIN LABOR IF ALL TROOPS REMOVED. FISK CARTER CONST CO."

[37] Solicitors, under the existing procedure, were encouraged to use a single instrument to indict multiple defendants for the same crime. This helped reduce court costs. Current North Carolina procedure forbids the practice and each defendant must be indicted on a single indictment.

[38] The actual indictment was not found and may no longer exist. The *Johnson City Chronicle* of October 24, 1923, reported that the charge to which the first group of people pleaded guilty was "With force and arms did willfully and unlawfully conspire, confederate and agree among

themselves and with others to the jurors unknown, to unlawfully assemble themselves together, and arm themselves with pistols, rifles, shot-guns and other deadly weapons, and to unlawfully assault, intimidate and drive away negroes being employed at Spruce Pine and nearby points." This constitutes a single charge, and court minutes reflect that the indictment charged four counts, and that the defendants pleaded guilty to counts one and four. Attempting to determine what it was precisely the defendants pleaded guilty to, the original warrant was examined. In this case, the warrant by a justice of the peace preceded the indictment. The warrant has three charges: Count 1: "The defendants did unlawfully and willfully create, constitute and commit an unlawful assembly, they being more than three persons and together with others being a multitude of persons, and did assemble themselves together to do and commit an unlawful act, to wit: To drive a multitude of colored people being without fault and not charged with the commission of any crime, and the said defendants, not being armed with any process of legal authority and not pretending to act under color of authority, them, the said Colored people did unlawfully and willfully drive away from their places of employment, and did them, the said colored people, force to leave the County of Mitchell and State Aforesaid." Count 2 "The defendants being more than three persons and together with a multitude of other men did engage in a riot and did unlawfully and willfully by means of said riot, drive from their peaceful employment a multitude of colored people for no reason other than that they were colored people and these the said defendants did so drive away from the several places of employment." Count 3 "Defendant and a multitude of other persons did conspire, confederate and agree together to commit an unlawful assembly and to commit a riot, and to drive away from the County of Mitchell a large number of colored people, some of whom were then engaged in building public highways in the County of Mitchell, some of whom were engaged by different persons and corporations in mining in Mitchell County and others of said colored people being engaged in putting in a system of water works for the town of Spruce Pine, and all of which were engaged in peaceful pursuits, not charged with the violation of any law and that pursuant to said unlawful and wicked conspiracy the defendants did drive away from the various mines in Mitchell County and from the public highways a multitude of colored people, the conspirators being heavily and dangerously armed with guns, pistols and other weapons did force said colored people, in many instances, and at the point of said weapons, to board the trains and to leave the said County of Mitchell against their will." The Spruce Pine Town Attorney Watson is likely author of this warrant, since Solicitor Hayes lived at a distant location and usually was in Mitchell County only during court weeks or the days immediately prior to court. It is possible that the final four count indictment incoporated these three counts with the one quoted earlier.

[39] This writer previously wrote in a newspaper article that forty-two persons were indicted. This is in accord with a strict reading of the court minutes. Those indicted by the Grand Jury (as shown by the court minutes) were John Buchanan, Ralph Willis, Charley Sullins, Landon Young, Buddie Willis, Jon Buchanan, Will Ledford, Deck Buchanan, Munsil Greene, Coleman Pitman, George Pearson, Burt Pendley, Alvin Gunter, Andy Pitman, Charlie Duncan, Will Buchanan, Mack Buchanan, Jim Sullins, Newt Willis, Clyde Ledford, Mack Thomas, Columbus Thomas, Elsie Woody, Earl Ward, Hobart Pitman, Stokes Stafford, Waits Pitman, Willie Gunter, Stokes McKinney, Peter Biddix, Heap Greene, Jr., Fate Ward (the warrant issued by the Justice of the Peace used the spelling Fayett Ward), Dot Buchanan, John Pitman, Logan Ward, P. E. Jackson, Mack McMahan (the warrant issued by the Justice of the Peace used the spelling Mac McMahan), Molton Buchanan, Andrew Greene, Lane Buchanan, Roby Buchanan, and Columbus Ledford. (D.H.S. Tappan, who earlier had been charged in the warrant was not among those named in the indictment). Minute Book 15 page 43, Clerk of Court Mitchell County. The Court minutes are inaccurate in many details. The minutes show 42 people were indicted. Of those 12 pleaded guilty on October 22, 1923. The minutes show that 48 people pleaded guilty on November 13, 1923, which if correct, would mean that a total of 60 people pleaded guilty yet the minutes show that 65 people were sentenced by the judge, and even then one case was dismissed by the prosecutor and some defendants failed to show. Part of the difficulty in maintaining accurate records is attributable to the fact that all 77 originally named defendants were indicted in a single bill of indictment. The Grand Jury of October 22, 1923, returned three indictments—one against John Goss, one against 77 defendants charged with rioting and one unrelated to this occurrence. One would not be sentenced unless he had pleaded guilty and one would not plead guilty unless he had been indicted. Those who were given a sentence or a prayer for judgment continued upon a plea of guilty are Stokes McKinney, Fate Ward, C. E. McMahan, Peter Biddix, Lane Buchanan, Willis Gunter, George Pearson, Steve Pitman, Burt Pendley, Alvin Gunter, Arby Pitman, Spence Autry, Forest Fisher, James Sullins, Kim Bartlett, Dave Pitman, John Buchanan, Will Gouge, Charles Duncan, Doss Buchanan, George Stamey, Ralph Willis, Homer Buchanan, Mack Buchanan, Taylor Boone, Charles Sullins, Ed Sparks, Stokes McClellan, Sherman Hicks, Fonzer Buchanan, Wilburn Thomas, Nellis Thomas, David McClellan, Herbert McClellan, Elzie Woody, Landon Young, Muncil Greene, Vance Buchanan, Will Buchanan, Charles Buchanan, George Buchanan, Ervin Reid, Logan Ward, John A. Buchanan, Troy Ledford, Bela Wilson, Herbert Stafford, Coleman Pitman, Earl Ward, Columbus Thomas, Hobart Pitman, Stokes Stafford, Waits Pitman, Buddie Willis, Will Ledford, John Pitman, Andrew Greene, Roby Buchanan, Deck Buchanan, Mack Thomas, Dot Buchanan, Molton Buchanan, Columbus Thomas (This name twice

appears indicating a mistake), Jesse Childers, and Clyde Ledford. To account for the fact that 65 people were given a sentence, this writer considers it appropriate to go beyond the inaccurate court minutes. The *Johnson City Chronicle* covered this event more accurately and with less flair for emotion than did other newspapers.

[40] Attorney Charles Hutchins represented some defendants. Some defendants were not represented by any attorney.

[41] Minute Book, 15 page 51, Mitchell County Clerk of Court. The numbers of defendants obviously made recording of the pleas, sentences, and proceedings difficult for the then clerk of court. Mistakes appear in the official minutes, and some entries do not reflect accurately what happened. As an example, the court minutes show that not a true bill was returned for Wilburn Thomas on October 23, 1923,which should have been the termination of his case. Later minutes show that he pleaded guilty on November 12, 1923. Other errors exist in the official court minutes which do not account for all defendants. In some cases where defendants pleaded guilty, the judge *continued prayer for judgment* upon condition the defendant pay a fine. A continued prayer for judgment is a judicial device allowing some immediate punishment, but, in technical effect, even though the defendant pleaded guilty, he is not legally thereafter regarded as guilty.

[42] *Powell vs. Alabama*, 287 U.S. 45 (1932)

[43] *State vs Columbus Penland*, 61 N.C. 222 (1867)

[44] *McMann vs. Richardson,* 397 U. S. 759 (1970)

[45] Minute Book 15, page 44 Mitchell County Clerk of Court.

[46] Minutes of Mitchell County Commissioners, Mitchell County Register of Deeds, Bakersville, North Carolina.

[47] Town of Spruce Pine Archives, Town Hall, Spruce Pine, North Carolina: "Board of Alderman met in special session called by the mayor with W.E. Laughridge, Dr. T.W. Deyton, W.B. Kester and Mayor A.N. Fuller present. We all discussed and talked the arrest of the Rioters which occurred here some days ago, and by a majority vote it was ordered that the Town of Spruce Pine guarantee a fee to E.F. Watson of $500.00 to prosecute all the defendants in the case through all the courts and it was further ordered that the Town Counsell take the matter up with the District Counsell or Solicitor and see if the State or County would not pay the attys fee in the case.(Signed by all)"

[48] Town of Spruce Pine Archives, Town Hall, Spruce Pine, North Carolina.

[49] Adjutant General's Biennial Report, for 1923, North Carolina Archives, Raleigh, North Carolina.

[50] *The Asheville Citizen*, October 22, 1923.

[51] *State vs Hall*, 142 NC 710 (1906).

[52] Adjutant General 1923 Biennial Report, North Carolina Archives.

[53] North Carolina Public Documents 1905, Volume I, Document 1, page 23.

Chapter 5: Discomfort with Electrocutions

Witnesses who observed electrocutions saw the bodies of condemned persons heaving and straining against restraints, often accompanied by vigorous shaking and the smell of burning flesh.

Few neutral observers could have enjoyed the experience. But not all witnesses found them necessarily cruel and unusual. The Honorable Jerry M. Blair, District Attorney of the 3rd Judicial Circuit of Florida, witnessed three of Florida's electrical executions, including that of the serial murderer, Ted Bundy, and was not disturbed by what he saw. Florida continued to use electricity for the death penalty until 2000, when that state allowed condemned persons to choose between electricity and lethal injection. According to Blair, the executioner in Florida puts a hood over the head of the condemned, thus preventing witnesses from observing facial contortions.

District Attorney Blair relates that the recipient of the electricity tenses and then relaxes. Sometimes, smoke comes from the calf of the dying person. In Blair's judgment, 2,000 volts of electricity immediately brings about brain death. Others said that in electrical deaths, the cause of death is asphyxiation, and the person suffers until death results. Blood temperature rises extremely high and the physical features of the body are damaged. In Florida, two recent electrocutions resulted in an eruption of flames from under the headgear.[54]

Before lethal injection, most states used electrocution, considered by many as humanitarian. It was hoped that death in this manner was painless. But whether the deceased suffered or not, some witnesses did.

On March 29, 1889, William Kemmler used an axe to send the woman he lived with, Matilda Ziegler, into eternity. This murder happened in Cayuga County, New York, shortly after the State of New York had changed its method of execution from hanging to electrocution. New York's chief executive, in his annual message on January 6, 1885, told the legislature,

> "The present mode of executing criminals by hanging
> has come down to us from the dark ages, and it may

well be questioned whether the science of the present
day cannot provide a means for taking the life of such
as are condemned to die in a less barbarous manner. I
commend this suggestion to the consideration of the
legislature."

A commission was appointed by the legislature and Thomas
Alva Edison, working with the commissioners, began to study
whether electricity could be a reliable and painless way of executing
prisoners. Edison had envisioned a direct current system. George
Westinghouse worked with alternating current that had higher
voltage and could travel longer distances.

The two men competed fiercely to see which system would
dominate the new business of electricity. Edison announced that
he felt electricity could kill a human, but cautioned that it had to
be of the variety known as alternating current. Edison hoped
that tying executions with alternating current would create a
negative image for alternating current and strengthen the use of
direct current. He even coined a word and favored its use,
westinghoused, which he hoped would become synonymous with
electrical executions.

Tests on a large mammal indicated that electricity passing
through the body of a person constituted a quick and painless
manner of taking a life. Kemmler was the first person to await
death by electrocution. Financed by George Westinghouse,
Kemmler's death sentence by electrocution was challenged in New
York courts on the ground that such punishment would be cruel
and unusual and therefore in violation of the New York and the
United States Constitutions. The New York Court of Appeals
ruled: "that the application of electricity to the vital parts of the
human body, under such conditions and in the manner contemplated
by the statute, must result in instantaneous and consequently
painless death." Kemmler sought relief from the United States
Supreme Court which on May 19, 1890, denied the relief that
Kemmler sought.

"In order to reverse the judgment of the highest court
of the State of New York, we should be compelled to

hold that it had committed an error so gross as to amount in law to a denial by the state of due process of law to one accused of crime, or of some right secured to him by the Constitution of the United States. We have no hesitation in saying that this we cannot do upon the record before us."[55]

On August 6, 1890, William Kemmler was the first man to be electrocuted.

The first shock of electricity did not kill Kemmler, and a second shock was required. Kemmler's body smoked. His flesh and hair were singed. The *New York Herald* [56] reported under caption *Kemmler's Death by Torture*, "The spectators grew faint and sick. Men who had stood over dead and dying men and had cut men to pieces without an emotion grew pale and turned their heads away." Even so, the executioner's assistant said, "The man never suffered a bit of pain." George Westinghouse fumed, "They would have done better with an axe."

At Kemmler's execution, the State of New York had assembled electricians and doctors to give expert opinions as to the effectiveness of electrical execution. The *New York Tribune* reported,[57] "It is agreed, apparently that the electrical current produced unconsciousness instantly and therefore immediate release from all pain and suffering." Interesting were the comments of Doctor E.C. Spitzka:

> I have seen hangings which were far more brutal than was this execution, but I have never seen anything more awe inspiring. The execution was a success, for the man is dead. But the method is not a success for it has not performed what was promised of it. That was to rid the execution of the feature of barbarity and cruelty.

Continuing, the *Tribune* reported that Doctor William T. Jenkins:

> . . . was shaking like a leaf when the Tribune correspondent saw him a few minutes after the execution. Dr. Jenkins has seen many executions, but none ever unnerved him as this did. He thought that

Kemmler did not suffer, but he would not say whether the execution was satisfactory to him.

The country could now boast an alternate method of execution and other states began its use. A decade after the New York governor's pronouncement that hanging was barbarous, North Carolina's governor also came to the same conclusion. But North Carolina Governor Robert Glenn's decision that hangings were barbarous would come only after additional hangings had taken place.

The execution of Peter Smith (which will be discussed later) seems to have been the seminal event contributing to Governor Glenn's conclusion. In 1909, North Carolina began its use of electricity to take the life of condemned persons, and those executions were set up to take place at Central State Prison in Raleigh.

North Carolina has changed its methods of execution more often than most states. Each change has been precipitated by a stated concern for the pain of the condemned, but seems to have been motivated equally by witnesses' accounts of grisly and agonizing deaths.

North Carolina's experiment with executions by electricity ended October 5, 1935, when Robert Thomas, Ories Gunter, and Arthur Gosnell were electrocuted, in that order, at the state prison death house in Raleigh. These men together committed a murder in Madison County. They were tried ten days after their capture and sentenced to death in February, 1935. Gosnell was the one hundred sixtieth person to be electrocuted in North Carolina. The next day the electric chair was dismantled to make room for a new lethal gas chamber. Gunter and Thomas were said to be afraid of execution, while Gosnell went to his death grinning. The Justices of the North Carolina Supreme Court unanimously wrote in a disturbing and ominous manner:

> Out of the many tragedies of the hills, this is perhaps one of the saddest. It is full of moving pathos. Three mountain boys, poor, unlettered, and with nothing to do, set out to take what they can by hold-up and robbery.

A murder ensues. The community is aroused to indignation. They are quickly overtaken by the law, tried, convicted, and sentenced to death. Such are the wages of sin, and sin pays in wages. To the extent, however, that the judgments imposed are sacrificial in nature, or deterrent in purpose, a civilized State might well pause and ponder their plight. Are there no preventives for such crime?[58]

The Georgia Supreme Court, on October 5, 2001,[59] may have ended for all time the executions by electricity. Noting that, "Time works changes, brings into existence new conditions and purposes. Therefore a principle to be vital must be capable of wider application than the mischief which gave it birth." The Georgia Supreme Court declared unconstitutional under that state's constitution, the statutory method of execution using electricity. A large body of evidence consisting of opinions expressed by electrocution survivors, prison officials, autopsy reports, and post-mortem photographs were considered at the trial court stage. A witness for the condemned defendant testified that

> although very high voltage is applied in the first two portions of the three-stage, two-minute electrocution process, the brain is shielded from much of the electricity by the skull . . . and that the alternating current used in electrocutions could repetitively activate the brain, causing the perception of excruciating pain and a sense of extreme horror.

The Georgia court determined after a consideration of all evidence, "that it is not possible to determine conclusively whether unnecessary pain is inflicted in the execution of the death sentence," but the court was disturbed that death by electricity unnecessarily mutilates and disfigures the condemned person's body. Autopsy reports show that the dead bodies were burned and blistered, there was skin slippage, and the brains were cooked. Because of this mutilation, execution by electricity violated the Georgia constitutional mandate that no punishment be cruel and unusual.

Persons may yet die as a result of execution by way of electricity, but now the states allow the condemned the choice of lethal injection.

Footnotes

[54] Jesse Tafero on May 4, 1990 and Pedro Medina on March 25, 1997.
[55] *In Re Kemmler*, 136 U. S. 436 (1890)
[56] August 7, 1890.
[57] August 7, 1890.
[58] *State vs. Gosnell, Gunter, and Thomas*, 208 N.C. 401 (1935)
[59] *Dawson vs. State, Moore vs. State*, 274 Ga. 327 (2001)

CASE II

MURDER DURING THE GOD PRAISE

Chapter 1: Inhalation of Lethal Gas

On July 9, 1936, Superior Court Judge John H. Clement sentenced Ernest Reid Coffey to death, saying:

> The prisoner, Reed Coffey, having at this term of Superior Court of Avery County been convicted of murder in the first degree, it is therefore ordered and adjudged that the sheriff of Avery County in whose custody the prisoner now is forthwith convey to the State's Prison at Raleigh, North Carolina, such prisoner, Reed Coffey, and deliver said prisoner to the Warden of the Said State's Prison, who the said warden, on the 11th day of September, 1936 shall cause the prisoner, Reed Coffey, to inhale lethal gas of sufficient quantity to cause the death of the said prisoner, Reed Coffey, and to continue the application and administration of such lethal gas until the said prisoner, Reed Coffey, is dead.[60]

Inhaling lethal gas results in death by asphyxiation. The prisoner is strapped to a wooden chair and a cyanide pill on the bottom of the chair is dropped into a pool of sulfuric acid, creating a poisonous plume. Since death results from asphyxiation, the condemned person gasps and struggles for breath. The discomfort and anxiety level of witnesses to the execution is at least equal to that of witnesses to a death by electricity.

Debate again centered around whether the contortions of the dying person were painful to the victim or were reflexive movements of an unconscious person oblivious to discomfort.[61] The late Justice Thurgood Marshall of the United States Supreme Court in 1994 quoted with approval a description of death by lethal gas given by Dr. Richard Traystman in 1983:

> Very simply, cyanide gas blocks the utilization of the oxygen in the body's cells. Gradually, depending on the rate and volume of inspiration, and on the concentration of the cyanide that is inhaled, the person

exposed to cyanide gas will become anoxic. This is the condition defined by no oxygen. Death will follow through asphyxiation, when the heart and brain cease to receive oxygen. The hypoxic state can continue for several minutes after the cyanide gas is released in the execution chamber. The person exposed to this gas remains conscious for a period of time, in some cases for several minutes, again depending on the rate and volume of the gas that is inhaled. During this time, the person is unquestionably experiencing pain and extreme anxiety. The pain begins immediately, and is felt in the arms, shoulders, back and chest. The sensation is similar to the pain felt by a person during a heart attack, where essentially, the heart is being deprived of oxygen. The severity of the pain varies directly with the diminishing oxygen reaching the tissues.

The agitation and anxiety a person experiences in the hypoxic state will stimulate the autonomic nervous system. (The person) may begin to drool, urinate, defecate, or vomit. There will be a muscular contraction. These responses can occur both while the person is conscious, or when he becomes unconscious.

When the anoxia sets in, the brain remains alive for from two to five minutes. The heart will continue to beat for a period of time after that, perhaps five to seven minutes, or longer, though at a very low cardiac output. Death can occur ten to twelve minutes after the gas is released in the chamber.[62]

For crimes committed between July 1, 1935, and July 5, 1983, the gas chamber became the exclusive method of execution in North Carolina. During that period, death sentences from all states came under frequent scrutiny by the United States Supreme Court. The North Carolina practice that allowed a person charged with a capital offense to receive life imprisonment whenever he pleaded guilty with the consent of the prosecutor and the presiding judge was declared unconstitutional. Constitutional restrictions were placed on jury selection so that the state could no longer excuse for cause an unlimited number of people who stated generally that they did not believe in the death penalty.

The new test was whether the juror had a belief so strong that he or she could not consider the death penalty.[63] The decade from 1960 to 1970 saw critical decisions by the United States Supreme Court regarding the death penalty in particular and crime in general. The court placed new constitutional restrictions on the states in criminal cases. As the legal and ethical challenges to the death penalty mounted nationwide, the numbers of executions dwindled. North Carolina conducted executions in 1954 and 1961,[64] but then no prisoner was put to death until March 16, 1984.[65]

It appeared that the demise of the death penalty was itself imminent, and some newspapers proclaimed it so. North Carolina Governor Robert Scott and Attorney General Robert Morgan opposed the death penalty. Between 1967 and 1977, no execution occurred anywhere in the United States. The United States Supreme Court declared all death penalty statutes unconstitutional in 1972.[66] Later that year, the North Carolina Supreme Court reacted by declaring that the United States Supreme Court's pronouncement had the effect only of declaring the death penalty scheme unconstitutional where a jury was given unbridled discretion to avoid the death penalty by recommending mercy.[67] Thereafter, in North Carolina, all capital crimes would carry a mandatory death sentence. The North Carolina General Assembly passed a statute giving legislative effect to the ruling of the state's Supreme Court by making death the punishment for rape and first degree murder in all instances.

The United States Supreme Court struck down the North Carolina interpretation. North Carolina enacted its current death penalty provisions and continued its lethal gas method of executions.

On January 17, 1977, Utah executed Gary Gilmore by firing squad. Gilmore had opposed all attempts to delay his execution, and seemed almost to have a death wish. The question remained, however, whether a state would be able to execute a person who vigorously opposed his execution. On May 25, 1979, the State of Florida provided an answer. John Spenkelink used all available legal maneuvers to stave off his execution. Florida attorneys moved rapidly to fend off all legal challenges and when that state executed Spenkelink it was obvious that capital punishment had reappeared in America after a ten-year hiatus.

On July 5, 1983, the North Carolina Legislature authorized condemned persons to choose either lethal gas or lethal injection as the method of their executions. The introduction of lethal injection was based, as in the case of other methods of executions, on humanitarian reasons. It was important that neither the prisoner nor the witnesses experience discomfort during executions. Thereafter, as appeals ran out and the final dates for executions were set, nearly all condemned men and the only condemned woman during this time selected lethal injection because it was considered to be painless.

David Lawson was executed in the gas chamber in North Carolina on June 15, 1994. He selected the gas chamber as the method of his death instead of lethal injection. In doing so, he sought and obtained national publicity directed toward North Carolina's mode of executions. Television personality Phil Donahue, who opposed capital punishment, wanted to film the execution for national television.

While screaming the words, "I'm human! I'm human," for long minutes on end, Lawson then "convulsed. He gasped several times and was then still."[68] Lawson had murdered Wayne Shinn, and the victim's brother witnessed the execution: "I personally think lethal injection is too easy. I think they should have to suffer. He did have to suffer some."[69] On the previous day the United States Supreme Court rejected Lawson's appeal that the gas chamber was cruel and unusual punishment with only Justice Blackmun dissenting.[70]

Convicted murderer Ricky Lee Sanderson defaulted on his choice of execution method in 1998. Under existing law, default meant he would be given a lethal dose of gas. Except for those two cases, all others who have been executed under the statute that allowed the condemned persons to choose the method of execution have selected lethal injection.

North Carolina changed its law on October 30, 1998. From that time on, executions would be by lethal injection of an extremely short-acting barbiturate in combination with a chemical paralytic agent. The most commonly used drugs for the lethal injection death are sodium pentothal (puts the inmate to sleep); second, pancuronium bromide (stops respiration); and third, potassium chloride (stops the heart). North Carolina varies this protocol in that thiopental sodium is injected to put the inmate into a deep sleep. Persons who now are executed simply fall asleep. This is the preferred method of execution for prisoners who are sentenced to death by courts of the United States and other states.

America believed it had discovered a polite and painless method of execution, seemingly free of violence and mutilation. Witnesses were allowed more comfort in what they were viewing. The family and friends of victims, however, sometimes express that the prisoner has not suffered enough. Glitches in this system occurred; sometimes it was difficult to locate a vein to establish the intravenous connection and prisoners suffered violent reactions to the drugs. In some cases the straps were drawn so tight that they prevented the flow of drugs into the veins. In a few instances, the tube got clogged with the drugs and a different tube had to be used.

Reid Coffey was the first person ever convicted of first-degree murder in Avery County. Of North Carolina's one hundred counties, Avery, in 1911, was the last to be established. Some state legislators had long wanted an even 100 counties to make up the Tar Heel State. Avery was a small county, named after Revolutionary War hero and the first N.C. Attorney General Waightstill Avery. Avery's additional distinction was that he fought a duel with Andrew Jackson without resulting in a fatality. The county seat was named after William C. Newland, a Democrat from Lenoir, who was Lieutenant Governor when Avery County was established. As in the other remote northwestern parts of the state, life was hard in this part of the mountains. Avery County is unique by never having elected any Democrat to public office.

Judge Johnson Hayes in his autobiography wrote about the time when he first went to Avery County as the solicitor:

The county seat is in the Toe River valley and near the foot of the Grandfather Mountain. It is a cold place. When I went there to attend court in April, 1915, I had on new spring clothes, BVD underwear and a sailor straw hat. Snow was blowing in every direction and even the courtroom was cold. The room was heated with two pot bellied stoves stationed at the ends of the bar railing and beside the jury boxes. After the judge ordered the sheriff have the janitor punch up the fires which failed to heat his section of the courtroom, the judge made the sheriff hunt up a thermometer and told him if he did not keep the heat up to 72 degrees he would adjourn the court. He showed the sheriff where to hang it. The sheriff went to the store, the only store in town, but it just had a broken one where a little mercury stood at 72. So the sheriff got it, hung it on the wall and told the janitor to keep both stoves red hot. At times the judge got too hot and ordered the sheriff to check the thermometer, and he reported it stood at 72. The sheriff had the janitor slow down the stoves, then the judge would complain of the cold, order the sheriff to check the thermometer, and the sheriff always reported it standing at 72. The farce continued throughout the week without the judge knowing what happened. The lawyers advised the sheriff not to let the judge know about it, fearing he would put the sheriff in jail for contempt. After the court was adjourned and the court had no power to try him for contempt, Governor Newland told the judge what happened and he got a big kick out of the sheriff's trick.[71]

Avery County continues to use the only courthouse ever constructed in the county. The courthouse was made from locally-produced brick, styled like those in use in Watauga and Ashe counties. From the front door stretched a hallway that fully traversed the length of the building. Small offices lined the hall, and a hidden, narrow stairway led to the upstairs courtroom. On one occasion when Judge Frank Huskins was presiding over a trial, an assailant climbed this narrow stairway and punched Judge

Huskins. After that reported incident, a sign was placed at the stairway advising use was "for court personnel only."

Lockie Rominger was the first woman elected to public office in Avery County. She became a county commissioner in 1972, the year the county went from a three-person to a five-person board. She favored improving and expanding the courthouse. She persuaded the board to renovate the old courthouse by adding wings to both sides and reshaping the interior.. The narrow stairway in the rear was removed and a new elevator was installed.

During the Depression era of the 1930s, many Avery County residents were hard pressed to find work locally. Even now many hunt, fish and make do with seasonal work. Because of the small population base, the lack of an industrial base and a general conservative inclination of politicians, taxes have not been adequate to provide popular government services.

Linville was built by outside developers and became the area's first resort for the wealthy; it was incorporated as a town but citizens failed to run for office and the town government withered away. The resort flourished with expensive second homes, a lodge and a golf course. This area now supports several of the most exclusive country clubs in North Carolina. The wealth of the resort clashes with the poverty elsewhere in the county.

In the early 1970s only two stoplights existed in Avery County; one in Linville and the other in the resort area of Banner Elk. The stoplight in Linville was regularly riddled with bullets, and when a new glass bulb was placed in the traffic light, it would often be blasted again within days. This sequence was repeated several times, and eventually the State Highway Commission gave up the fight. No one ever got arrested for shooting the traffic light. For years thereafter a stop sign regulated the traffic where U. S. 221 intersects with N.C. 105 and N.C. 181. In 1990, true progress came when the state placed an electronic traffic light at this intersection and it remained thereafter.

Newland has a short street named Railroad Street. Similarly named streets in other towns mean that the street follows a railroad, or that a depot is located nearby. Avery and its adjacent county, Watauga, never had major railroads. A narrow gauge railroad ran from Johnson City, Tennessee, to Elk Park and Cranberry to Minneapolis, Newland and then to Boone in Watauga County. This narrow gauge railroad was known as the Eastern Tennessee and Western North Carolina (ET & WNC) Railroad. In the Town of Boone, Depot Street was named for the railroad depot that was located there. This railroad existed from the early part of the twentieth century until a giant flood in 1940 destroyed most of the track.

Mr. Phil Vance of Boone was the last to ride this railroad when, as a youth, he left Boone to visit relatives in Plumtree. Mr. Vance recalls that even after the flood, the railroad wanted to rebuild the track, but Appalachian State Teachers' College would not give a contract to haul coal. The railroad was originally built to accommodate the commerce generated by sawmilling timber from the surrounding area. After the railroad's demise, cowboy actor Gene Autry bought the train and used it in Hollywood for some of his movies. Mr. Grover Robbins eventually brought the train back to Watauga County and named it "Tweetsie Railroad," which is now a well-known tourist attraction.

The lack of a railroad shows the degree to which Avery County was isolated during the early decades of the twentieth century. In other mountain counties the railroads opened trade with the outside world. Since Avery always voted Republican, and road policy was set in the state capital, a Democratic stronghold, state government never favored this county.

Roads in Avery County usually are narrow winding slits in between a mountain on one side and a steep drop on the other. Whenever the terrain allows for a segment of level roadway, people call this a "straight."

Transportation was made even more difficult by the harshness of winters. Bob Grier, who lived in Beech Bottoms, knew when Toe River was one of the most accessible means of travel. When the river froze, wagons drawn by horses with special cleats in their shoes used the river as a road.

The redoubtable Jim Hughes knows almost everything that has ever happened in Linville. His father, Columbus H. Hughes, was a merchant who was active in Avery politics, and he knew most of the citizens of his time. Lum, as he was called, died an old man, and his son Jim continued his involvement in Avery County and state issues.

As a youth, Jim and some compatriots practiced mischief, some of which was directed toward the congregation of the Linville Holiness Church.

The church was located in an area somewhat north of the main Linville community, which in the 1930s did not have Highway 105 running through it. Hugh Morton did not develop Grandfather Mountain until the time of Governor William Umstead in the 1950s. United States Highway 221 did traverse the mountain terrain from Linville to Blowing Rock. Lum Hughes' store had a telephone, which was unusual in Avery County.

Young Jim Hughes and some of his friends sometimes crawled under the floor of the Holiness Church. Before the final floor was finished there was only a sub-floor which was made of sawed boards that had cracks in between. Jim took a weed and thrust it through the cracks in the floor and rubbed the weed over the exposed legs of women who sat overhead. The response was what one might expect.

Jim and his friend Elbert S. Watson got caught. As they were under the church, the two boys saw a rush of people toward the spot above them. Jim Hughes could see one was wearing a suit and that meant it had to be Preacher Townsend. The two boys fled. Elbert jumped a fence, but Jim did not fare as well. As he attempted to leap the fence, he sliced his left leg with a long barbed-wire seam. Punishment followed. First his father, Lum, administered corporal punishment. Elbert and Jim later went before the Justice of the Peace, Sherman Bowman. Jim Hughes says: "Mountain boys had to make their own entertainment." Of course, the boys were not actually charged with a crime, but they thought they were. Hughes remembers that his father approved as Justice Bowman gave the two boys a severe tongue-lashing.

The church building in which Jim Hughes played his pranks was constructed in approximately 1937. Prior to the construction of the church, the congregation worshipped in an old bunk building, part of the old sawmill located in "sawmill holler." This was where the Church was meeting during April, 1936. Paul Hughes, standing in his driveway off Hollerth Street can point to the location where both buildings stood. The first Holiness Church building where the events described here took place was destroyed long ago.

While meeting in the original building, one devout member on occasion would demonstrate his piousness by opening the door to the woodstove and putting his head inside. When he removed his head from the interior, all could see that the Lord had saved him harmless. Two local troublemakers, Reid Coffey (the subject of this chapter) and his friend Rhonard McCrae, sat on the front pew one night expecting that this demonstrative man would place his head in the stove. When the pious one put his head in the stove, he would take care to see that the embers were burning low. Coffey and McCrae brought pieces of an inner tube and surreptitiously placed them on the embers. On this night, when the gentleman stuck his head into the stove, he encountered an unexpected blast of heat that severely burned his head.[72]

On the night of Sunday, April 5, 1936, nineteen year-old Reid Coffey arrived late for church service at the Linville Holiness Church. Reid was wet and muddy "plum up to his shoulders"[73] on a day when the rain was heavy. While not a regular member, he had been attending this church recently. Before the church service ended that evening, Sheriff Wilburn H. Hughes arrested Ernest Reid Coffey for the murder of Hardy Coffey. Rhonard McCrae, frequently known as "Dutch", was arrested as a material witness. Dutch McCrae also was at the church but he arrived earlier than Reid did.

Reid Coffey lived all his life in Avery County and attended the school in Linville through the fifth grade. People who knew him then say that he was in good physical shape,[74] allowing the possibility that he could have run a distance of close to a mile from Hardy Coffey's residence and the Linville Holiness Church and be in attendance for the service. The time of the assassination of Hardy Coffey and the time of Reid's arrival at the church became a critical question that eventually required a response from the Governor of North Carolina.

Late this Sunday evening, Hardy Coffey's daughters screamed at Lum Hughes' service station that their father had been shot while he sat in his family room. The Coffey family had no telephone. A call was placed to the Sheriff's residence from the Lum Hughes' store, and shortly thereafter, Sheriff Wilburn Hughes formed the opinion that Reid Coffey was the murderer.

Footnotes

[60] This entry appears in the original records of the Supreme Court maintained in the old records building of the State of North Carolina. It is also in Avery County Court Minutes in the Clerk of Court in Newland, North Carolina. Use of the misspelled name "Reed" appears throughout the court history and the subsequent prison records as well as the Governor Commutation and parole. Coffey was generally known by his second name Reid. The misspelling probably occurred in the earliest court document at the coroner's inquest. No one ever bothered to correct the misspelling.

[61] Dr. Page Hudson was North Carolina's first Chief Medical Examiner. He gave expert opinions when North Carolina was considering lethal injection as a method of execution. He maintained that the victim suffered less discomfort than the persons who watched the execution.

[62] *Lawson vs. Dixon*, 512 U. S. 1215 (1994)

[63] *Witherspoon vs. Illinois*, 391 U. S. 510(1968)

[64] Theodore Boykin on October 27, 1961

[65] James W. Hutchins

[66] *Furman vs. Georgia*, 408 U. S. 238 (1972)

[67] *State vs. Waddell*, 282 N.C. 431 (1972)

[68] *New York Times*, June 16, 1994.

[69] *Ibid.*

[70] *Lawson vs. Dixon*, 512 U. S. 1215 (1994) Blackmun wrote in dissent: "I find petitioner's constitutional challenge to the gas chamber to be a serious one. Only four states, Arizona, California, Mississippi, and North Carolina, still use the gas chamber as a method of execution. Its cruelty has been attested to on more than one occasion."

[71] Hayes, *Autobiography, Ibid.*

[72] I once told this story in a newspaper story. It was not received well by a Holiness Church member. The ritual was not a part of the church liturgy, rather, it was the act of a single devout person. The anecdote was separately told by Jim Hughes, Paul Hughes, Doug Coffey and others. It is believed by me to be true.

[73] This was the assessment of Sheriff Wilburn Hughes in his testimony. Numerous references will be made to the Hughes testimony at trial. Usually this reference means the narrative transcript which is known to exist only in the Supreme Court original records. Narrative transcripts were required by rules of the appellate courts. Because the question and

answer format was eliminated, there usually exists subtle instances where a party has misstated the actual account. District attorneys were historically remiss in reading the narrative presented by defense attorneys for their consideration so that narrative transcripts are never fully accurate, but they are the only transcript available.

[74] This is the assessment of Jim and Paul Hughes. The *Descriptive Prison Index* in the North Carolina State Archives shows that when he was admitted to Central Prison, Reid Coffey was five feet nine and three-fourths inches tall and that he weighed one hundred ninety-five-and-one-half pounds. This would make him heavy for his stature. It is not unusual for one confined in jail to gain weight and perhaps Coffey did.

Chapter 2: A Bad Crime

Hardy Coffey lived to be 52 years old and was the father of seven children. Mr. Coffey lived with his wife, Lilly, his three youngest daughters, and a son in a frame house located to the west of U. S. Highway 221 near Linville. For historical and cultural interest, Lilly Coffey was never at any time, in the trial or any court documents or the documents later to be sent to North Carolina's Governor, referred to by any name but Mrs. Hardy Coffey. The Coffey house was located north of Lum Hughes' store and filling station. The house sat perhaps 150 feet from U. S. Highway 221, a paved road. A side room of the house had a fireplace, and on this rainy night, the family had a fire burning. In the front of the house stood the main entrance door and beside it was a window. A porch spanned the exterior front of the building. As one faced the old house on the right side one could see a porch going from front to back. In the evenings, Mr. Hardy Coffey would sit with his back to the window on the right side of the house in a family room, joined by his wife, and daughters Irene, Evelyn and Eva. Irene was twelve years old, Evelyn seven, and the youngest, Eva, was only five years old.

Hardy Coffey once worked as a caretaker for some of the owners of resort homes in Linville. In 1935, after Wilburn H. Hughes became sheriff, Hardy Coffey became a deputy sheriff of Avery County, and he was given general responsibility to look after homes in the Linville community.

Hardy Coffey's brother, John Wesley, also lived in Linville, in a house that no longer stands but was situated generally behind the little stone church in Linville. Jim Hughes recalls that John Wesley Coffey was active in Avery County politics and was a Justice of the Peace. Ernest Reid Coffey lived with his father, John Wesley Coffey. Reid was Hardy Coffey's nephew.

On the evening of April 5, 1936, Hardy Coffey sat in a chair in front of the window with his daughter, May Irene, to his right side. Mrs. Lilly Coffey sat to the side of the window near the fireplace, and the other two girls also were in the room.

Superior Court was due to begin in Avery County on the following day, April 6th. Reid Coffey and Dutch McCrae had cases on the criminal docket consisting of the accusations of breaking and entering into the Linville residence of a wealthy lady and a separate case involving larceny of possum skins. Hardy Coffey was expected to testify before the jury in those cases; his testimony would have incriminated Reid Coffey and Dutch McCrae.

As Hardy Coffey sat in his home with his little children close to him, singing with them, a shot came through the window. Coffey was hit in the back and the pellets, bunched together,[75] penetrated his heart. He died within minutes. May Irene's hand was burned by the powder and gases from the blast. Eva Jane Coffey Keller was so young that she remembers only glass blowing inside the house. Just moments earlier her father held her on his lap, then sat her down to help Irene with a music lesson. The family dog, a "biting dog," was tied outside and shortly before the shooting Irene and Eva remember the dog barking and their father saying, "I should have turned him loose."

Eva was also burned under her eye. She has few recollections of her father but her favorite is the times when he came home from the store. The girls would rush him, patting his overall pockets to see if he had brought hard candy for them. May Irene Coffey Pyatte recalls that after the shooting her father jumped up, went for the door and cried, "Oh my God, I've been shot." Mrs. Pyatte recalls that neighbors brought food and some men cleaned the blood from the room. People tried to offer condolences and be helpful. Their friend Mrs. Henley sat in a chair in their house that night and the chair tilted backward into a window. The sound of glass breaking and falling to the floor this night sent terror through the hearts of the three young girls.[76]

The small cemetery in the Montezuma Community sits on a knoll. Hardy Coffey is buried there, his homemade tombstone is of rock and cement. Its bronze plaque reads:

At Rest
J. H. Coffey
Jan. 19, 1884—Apr. 5, 1936

As the investigation into the murder proceeded, Mrs. Coffey's estimate of the time of the shooting became an issue troubling Governor Clyde Hoey. Since Reid Coffey's presence at the Holiness Church could be established by witnesses there, whatever time Mrs. Coffey estimated as being the time of the shooting could mean either that Reid Coffey had time to kill and flee, or that someone else altogether must have murdered Hardy Coffey.

The next day, in the Superior Court in Newland, the cases involving breaking and entering Mrs. Milton's residence and the larceny of possum hides were continued. Hardy Coffey was not there to testify. But Reid Coffey was arrested for murder. On the same day a coroner's inquest was held in Hampton's Store in Linville, with Coroner Finley P. Guinn presiding.[77] The jury found good and sufficient cause to hold Reid Coffey for murder.

Historically, coroners served two basic functions. First, in the event of a vacancy in the Office of Sheriff, the coroner became sheriff. Mr. Carl Osborne, during one of his terms as coroner, became sheriff when the incumbent vacated the office. Second, whenever there was a death of a person and there was a probability that the death was due to homicide or negligence, the coroner was charged with the responsibility to investigate the death and determine its cause. Both of these historic functions of the coroner have been diminished by statute.[78] Statutory law now provides that vacancies in the Office of Sheriff will be filled by the county commissioners. When the office of medical examiner was created, the historic function of coroner was assumed by the medical examiner who is always a physician. Because of these statutes, there is no further need for coroners even though the law providing for coroners has never been repealed. Most counties simply do not budget for coroners' salaries and no one ever bothers to seek the office. The Legislature has abolished the Office of Coroner in several counties, but in other counties the office still is provided for but usually vacant.

In 1936, Avery County's coroner was Dr. Finley P. Guinn.[79] The law required the coroner conduct an inquest in the presence of the dead body[80] whenever there was a murder victim.

Bill Allen Guinn beams with pride when he discusses his father, Dr. Finley Patterson Guinn. First, Dr. Guinn was a schoolteacher. He then studied medicine at the University of Tennessee. Bill Allen Guinn lives now in the same house his father occupied in Elk Park. During the early part of Dr. Guinn's medical practice, he rode horseback to visit his patients. In 1936, Dr. Guinn had a truck to travel in, but he did not have a telephone. Someone had to come and get him. He visited the Hardy Coffey residence on Sunday night April 5, 1936.

On Monday, Dr. Guinn conducted a coroner's inquest into the death of Hardy Coffey. Mrs. Lilly Coffey and her daughter, May Irene, were both called as witnesses before the coroner's jury, according to an affidavit that Dr. Guinn later filed for consideration by the governor. Irene Pyatte does not recall testifying before the coroner's inquest although she does remember vividly her testimony in Superior Court. To require the widow and small daughter of a deceased to appear formally before a coroner's inquest the day following their witnessing his bloody murder seemed insensitive, and did not contribute to reasoned testimony. Regardless, this move represented the normal process of the coroner's inquest which required the presence of witnesses to give testimony publicly under oath as soon as practicable after a homicide. A later chapter will deal with the fact that during Governor Hoey's consideration of commutation of Reid Coffey, Dr. Guinn gave an affidavit that Mrs. Coffey stated the time of the murder to be different from the one she later asserted during the trial. If this were true, then possibly the process itself was at fault since no widow is first going to consider the time when she witnessed a catastrophic event like the murder of her husband. At trial Mrs. Coffey testified that the fatal shot was fired well before 8:00 p.m., but Dr. Guinn's affidavit stated she testified at his inquest that the fatal shot was at 8:15 p.m.

Solicitor John R. Jones may have been an active participant in the coroner's inquest although it cannot be established with certainty. He was not in court on this Monday. The law envisioned a collaborative effort on the part of the solicitor and the coroner, and provided that "immediately" when information developed that a death may have been homicide, the coroner was obliged to notify the district solicitor. Further, the law provided that the coroner permit the solicitor to be present and participate in the inquest and to examine and cross examine witnesses.[81] John R. Jones lived in Wilkesboro, North Carolina. Jones was present in court on Tuesday and the days following.

If one deficiency of the system was to force recently bereaved widows to testify publicly, then another would be the lack of any requirement that the coroner be specially trained. There was no requirement that the coroner be a physician (although Dr. Guinn was), and many North Carolina coroners were not physicians nor were they required to have any knowledge of the law. Cause of death is generally a medical question. Even so, facts and circumstances surrounding one's death are useful in determining whether the victim died as a result of homicide. Current practice under the medical examiner system generally involves a trained law enforcement officer working with a pathologist together with a legal representative before charges of murder are brought. Under the coroner system the coroner's jury acting alone made this preliminary decision. The Coroner presided over the proceeding and was free to receive or decline legal advice from the solicitor.

A statute required the Coroner to put the testimony of all witnesses in writing and have the witness sign the report.[82] However, the fact the statute required the written report does not mean it was done. If Mrs. Coffey testified that her husband was shot at 8:15 p.m. and if the Coroner had prepared a report of her testimony and had Mrs. Coffey sign it, there would have been no need for the Coroner to give an affidavit reciting her testimony. If testimony was ever put in writing it was not discovered among any court documents.

The probable presence of Solicitor John R. Jones poses another difficulty. Jones would have known of Mrs. Coffey's testimony, and whether he was present or not, he would have made an effort to discover his case. If the testimony was in writing, Jones would have received the written statements. Later, when Governor Hoey considered commutation for Reid Coffey, he relied heavily on the affidavit of Coroner Guinn. The Governor did not seem to have any conflicting statement from the Solicitor, leaving the Coroner's statement unchallenged. Surely, Solicitor Jones would have taken issue with the Coroner had Jones known the affidavit to be incorrect. Of course, it is certainly possible the Governor did not consult with Solicitor Jones on this point although the Governor did note that the Solicitor opposed commutation.

In 1963, the United States Supreme Court held that suppression of material evidence by the prosecution so that a defendant would not know about it, whether in good or bad faith, constitutes a denial of due process of law.[83] Also, the North Carolina State Bar's Rules of Professional Conduct currently impose a special responsibility on the prosecutor to disclose to the defendant all evidence that might negate guilt. Prosecutors have been disciplined for non-compliance of this rule. Neither the constitutional ruling nor the state bar rule existed in 1936. John R. Jones may or may not have known of a statement by Mrs. Coffey that her husband was killed about 8:15 p.m., but in that era, he was not required to disclose this information to the defendant.

In recent years, considerable litigation took place, numerous cases were reversed, and many persons convicted were set free over the issue of prosecutor's failure to disclose evidence favorable to the defendant. This is one of the most prevalent issues in current practice.

The Coffey case poses considerable difficulties in assessing the Coroner's inquest. If Mrs. Coffey spoke incorrectly, this is certainly understandable considering the trauma of the whole proceeding so soon after the tragedy. Most coroners' inquests were relatively straightforward and benign. The rules contemplated that witness' statements would be available for corroboration or impeachment at trial. The inquest conducted by Dr. Guinn has unusual, if not historical, significance because it produced evidence that caused the Governor great concern even though it was not an issue during the trial.

The Coroner's jury finding was the equivalent of a preliminary hearing by a Justice of the Peace. Reid Coffey was ordered held without bond in custody of the Sheriff. North Carolina law permitted no bond when one was accused of a capital offense. In fact, the procedure that existed in the courtroom would identify the accused as "prisoner." In the jury's presence the accused would routinely be called prisoner, a stark contrast to current procedure where great pains are taken to prevent the jury from knowing that a person may be in custody.

In Solicitor Jones' absence from court on Monday, April 6, 1936, Avalon G. Hall was the prosecutor. Prisoner Reid Coffey was indicted by the Grand Jury on April 7, 1936, for the murder of Hardy Coffey, and Solicitor John R. Jones signed that indictment. In 1936, anyone found guilty of first-degree murder, arson, rape, or first degree burglary was automatically sentenced to death. Reid Coffey was taken by Sheriff Hughes to the Buncombe County Jail to await trial. During part of his incarceration, Coffey was confined at Central Prison in Raleigh.

A large crowd of spectators gathered for the trial, filling the courtroom and the balcony. The first trial for first-degree murder in Avery County had created quite a stir in the small, tight-knit community.

Although large numbers of people were present during the trial, the crowd never became threatening. The Avery County Jail was located in a building near the courthouse, necessitating that the sheriff bring the prisoner from the jail to the court building and return him two or three times a day. The prisoner would have passed people who were in the yard. Throughout the trial these trips were conducted without incident.

Reid Coffey's case began Tuesday July 7, 1936,[84] the same day he was indicted. Newland attorney Byron E. Williams was retained by John Wesley Coffey to represent his son. A panel of jurors is summoned in advance of every superior court week and individuals are selected for each trial during the week. The county commissioners, while in session, drew the names of jurors. Capital cases generally require more jurors because of the care given in the selection process. There were not enough jurors to try a capital case and Judge John H. Clement indicated that he would order Sheriff Wilburn Hughes to summon additional jurors. In an unusual motion, Lawyer Williams objected that the Sheriff be the one to summon jurors due to his interest in the case; Hardy Coffey had been acting deputy sheriff for two years. Judge Clement then appointed J. H. Von Cannon, who served Avery County as its first elected sheriff, to serve as a special commissioner to summon 50 additional jurors to report to the Courthouse on Wednesday, July 8, 1936. Commissioner Von Cannon complied with the court order and summoned the required 50 jurors. Practice at the time required that a child should draw trial jurors' names from the list of those who were summoned, and the child in this case was Phil Daniels, the son of Max Daniels.[85] The jurors who were seated for the trial of Reid Coffey were all men; women were not yet permitted by law to serve on juries.[86]

The arraignment of Reid Coffey followed the procedure of that time. Clerk Eller directed the prisoner to stand, holding up his right hand. The Clerk of Court read the indictment verbatim, after which the clerk inquired: "How say you, Reid Coffey, are you guilty of the felony of first degree murder whereof you stand indicted, or not guilty?" When the prisoner's lawyer answered, "Not guilty," the Clerk inquired, "How will you be tried?" At this time Attorney Williams answered, "By God and my country."[87]

Jury selection took three hours and in the early afternoon of July 8, 1936, Solicitor John R. Jones called the first witness for the State, Mrs. Lilly Coffey. Mrs. Coffey testified that she and her family were in the family room of their home on Sunday, April 5, 1936. Her husband, Hardy, was singing with his daughter from a hymnal when the dog barked. Suddenly, she heard a gun shot at *"it must have been something about twenty minutes till eight or a quarter of eight. It could not have been any later than a quarter of eight"* (Emphasis added). The shot entered the window in the second pane up from the bottom. She failed to see anyone, but she heard someone run. Her husband jumped up, attempted to open the door but fell to the floor. Hardy Coffey died in the corner of the room. No witness actually saw the killer.

Evidence in court consists of two types: the first is the direct evidence where there is a witness to the actual event, and the second category is the indirect circumstantial evidence. In the case of circumstantial evidence, the jury hears all the evidence and may draw inferences from the facts proved. In this case, Solicitor Jones contended that the jury should infer from the circumstances that Reid Coffey was the murderer.

The *Avery Advocate* was a weekly county newspaper, generally on the newsstands on Thursday evenings. To be out on

Thursday, it was at least partially printed on Wednesday. The July 9, 1936, *Avery Advocate* reported:

> Evidence in the case was circumstantial, but from the very beginning of the trial the prosecution headed by Solicitor John R. Jones, slowly started drawing the clouds of lethal gas about the head of the accused youth.

North Carolina's law required a greater burden of proof when circumstantial evidence was the means of proving guilt than if the proof was of direct evidence.[88] The jury in this case determined, even under this greater burden of proof, that Reid Coffey was guilty. The circumstantial evidence of the trial will be summarized below.

Although the witnesses did not all agree, there was evidence that Reid Coffey had an opportunity to kill Hardy Coffey. Mrs. Coffey testified the killing occurred about a quarter until eight. Lum Hughes' testimony was consistent. He allowed that he actually saw Reid Coffey at approximately 7:30 p.m. at his filling station, and that Reid left and "within 15 or 20 minutes." Lum heard children screaming from the Hardy Coffey residence that their father was shot. Lum Hughes further testified that he visited the Coffey residence briefly and then left to get a physician. Mr. Hughes told that he returned to the residence with Doctor Boyd McGuire at approximately 8:20 p.m.

This strong testimony was apparently not given much consideration by Governor Hoey when he considered an affidavit by Dr. F. P. Guinn. That affidavit charged that Mrs. Coffey testified at the Coroner's Inquest that the shooting occurred at 8:15 p.m. The Hardy Coffey residence was about 400 yards from the filling station, and less than a mile from the Holiness Church. Some of the witnesses testified that at approximately 8:00 p.m., Reid Coffey arrived at Walter Townsend's residence adjacent to the building used as the Holiness Church. The State contended that no credible witness saw Reid Coffey from the time he left Lum Hughes' filling station at 7:30 p.m. until approximately 8:00 p.m. when he arrived at the Townsend residence. A young man in good health could well have traveled the distance from the filling station to the Coffey residence and to the residence near the church within the time span.

Coffey, however, had no firearm when Lum Hughes saw him. Unless a gun were concealed nearby, Coffey would first have had to go to another place to get a gun. John Wesley Coffey's residence where Reid lived was perhaps a mile and a quarter generally south from the filling station. Testimony showed the murder weapon was owned by John Wesley Coffey and kept by him in his residence. If Reid Coffey had first gone to his residence, gotten the weapon, and then returned the same way to the Hardy Coffey residence, then to Walter Townsend's, he could not have arrived at Walter Townsend's by 8:00 p.m.

The State had an explanation. Solicitor Jones called twelve-year-old William Eugene Southerland. Southerland and Paul Hughes were shooting marbles in the Old Linville Hotel yard early in the afternoon on April 5, 1936, when Reid Coffey walked by. Southerland testified that Reid was wearing a blue coat and carried under his arm a single barrel shotgun. Southerland identified the single barrel 16 gauge shotgun belonging to John Wesley Coffey as the gun Reid Coffey carried.[89]

Evidence showed that Reid Coffey indeed had a plausible motive to kill Hardy Coffey, who was planning to testify in court the following day against Reid and Rhonard McCrae. Mrs. Hardy Coffey testified that she knew that her husband was a witness in a court case against Reid Coffey about possum hides. Moreover, according to Rhonard McCrae, Reid Coffey made incriminating statements about the murder. Rhonard McCrae testified that he and Reid Coffey were under indictment for larceny of possum hides from Hardy Coffey and also for a breaking and entering into a Linville home. Hardy Coffey was to be the witness against both men in court on Monday, April 6, 1936. McCrae testified that a couple weeks before the murder, Reid told Rhonard McCrae that if Reid were required to serve a prison term over getting those possum hides then Hardy Coffey "never would see another court."

On Sunday night, April 5, 1936, Reid Coffey arrived at the Holiness Church about 8:00 p.m. Witnesses' recollections about

Reid Coffey's arrival varied a great deal, but most persons placed his arrival at approximately 8:00 p.m. Rhonard McCrae was there for some time. When Reid arrived, Rhonard asked him if his Uncle Hardy was going to press that case against the two of them. Reid stated, "No, he won't be there."[90] If such a statement was actually made, it was before there was a general knowledge that Hardy Coffey was shot and killed. Later that night both young men were kept in the Avery County Jail. Bloodhounds were brought in by the sheriff's department to track the scent of the killer. During this time, Reid stated to Rhonard, according to Rhonard's testimony, "If they get them damned dogs over there, they will find the gun Hardy Coffey was killed with."[91]

The murder weapon was a 16-gauge shotgun missing without explanation from the John Wesley Coffey residence. Junior Forbes, who was assisting Sheriff Hughes and Rob Forbes in looking for the murder weapon, found the gun the next day. It was in a clump of rhododendron near the wooden bridge crossing the Linville River, off a trail often traveled near Hardy Coffey's residence toward the Holiness Church. Investigators also found by the gun a "rung" shotgun shell with the words "Peters 16 gauge Victor." Other shells by this manufacturer were found in John Wesley Coffey's residence. Reid Coffey was arrested the night before at the Holiness Church by Sheriff Hughes, Robert Forbes and Junior Forbes.

George Garrison was a deputy sheriff in Buncombe County who studied fingerprint comparison. He testified that he examined the shotgun and found Reid Coffey's right thumb print on top of the barrel back next to the breech.[92] He testified that he found three points of comparison. Lawyer Williams objected to Garrison's testimony based on the three points of comparison, but Williams never asserted this point in his appeal to the North Carolina Supreme Court, so it was not considered by the court.

When Reid Coffey was arrested at the Holiness Church, the blue coat he wore had mud on it "plum up to the shoulders" and Sheriff Hughes thought that indicated Coffey had been running.

Reid Coffey testified in his own defense.[93] The *Avery Advocate* wrote:

Coffey took the stand himself and in a defiant mood stood up under a severe cross-examination for several hours. He expressed his animosity toward his uncle, and this with the fact that the defense was unable to account for the actions of the youth between 7:30 and 8:00 p.m., the time of the shooting, is believed to have had much to do with his conviction.

Avery Advocate, July 9, 1936

Reid denied any knowledge of his uncle's killing, and denied carrying the shotgun earlier that Sunday. He testified that he fired the murder weapon at a rabbit some days earlier, and that this might account for his thumbprint being on the gun. He denied making the statements to Rhonard McCrae that McCrae had attributed to him. Defendant Coffey testified that he was indeed at Lum Hughes's filling station but he placed the time of his arrival there at 7:10 p.m. He said he stayed about five minutes; meaning that he left at approximately 7:15 p.m. This is fifteen minutes earlier than Lum Hughes' recollection of his departure from the filling station. Reid Coffey then asserted that he went directly to the Holiness Church:

> I don't know exactly the time when I first got there, but after I went in the church, after I had went in the church and set down I looked at my watch. It was then fifteen till eight. Services had begun. They was signing one song when I come up and they was singing the second one that I heard when I went in.[94]

The jury apparently did not accept Reid Coffey's statement that he was in church at a quarter until 8 p.m., which would have constituted an alibi. Moreover, other people appear to have given little credence to this statement. Notably, Governor Hoey, when he considered commutation, stated that the defendant could not account for his whereabouts between 7:00 p.m. and 8:00 p.m.

Reid Coffey said at one time that he walked fast because the rain was coming down hard after he left Lum Hughes' filling station. He thought he arrived at the church in fifteen minutes. If his estimated departure from the filling station was accurate, then he should have arrived at the church at 7:30 p.m. His testimony that he looked at his watch and he was clearly at the church at a quarter until eight is inconsistent with other testimony. If he arrived that early, he would have entered church before the services began, and yet he said that a hymn was being sung. Reid Coffey recalled that he saw Marvin Hartley, Andrew Yoder, and Jim Coffey (Hardy Coffey's son) when he was at Lum Hughes' filling station. Not one of those people was ever called as a witness either by the State or the defendant. This seems almost incongruous in that the time he left the filling station was of utmost importance in establishing an alibi.

As for the motive, it was alleged that Hardy Coffey was going to testify against the two men in court on the following day. Coffey's wife, Lilly, testified to this in court, as did Rhonard McCrae. That motive, however, was contradicted by Ira Coffey, Reid Coffey's brother, and two of Reid's sisters, Louise and Adell, all of whom testified that their Uncle Hardy Coffey had told them he did not plan to appear against Reid Coffey and Rhonard McCrae.

Reid Coffey and Rhonard McCrae were indicted by the Avery County Grand Jury in October, 1935, for breaking and entering into the residence of a lady in Linville. The larceny of possum hides owned by Hardy Coffey came later. Jake Hartley was the foreman of the grand jury that indicted the two young men for larceny. The defendant called Hartley as a witness and, in a strange move, asked Hartley about things that happened within the grand jury. All grand jury proceedings are kept secret. Grand jurors are forbidden ever to reveal what has transpired. This is so the jurors can deal with the issues before them without fear of reprisal. Although his statement should never have been allowed, Hartley testified that Hardy Coffey told him the larceny case was a family matter and that he did not want it to go further. Hartley said that the grand jury considered it to be their obligation to return a true bill of indictment.

The rules in regard to cross-examination were tightened since 1936. Reid Coffey was asked questions about things that he may have done before he was indicted. Judge Clement permitted extensive cross-examination and, from the contemporary accounts,

Reid Coffey may have actually damaged his case by choosing to testify. For instance, Coffey was asked about the larceny of possum hides from his Uncle Hardy. "I had not stolen hides from him. Some other fellows stole them and I 'stoled' them from them. I got them, but I didn't steal them from my uncle and when I found out they was his hides." Reid Coffey went on to testify that he and Rhonard asked his Uncle Hardy to take the hides back, but according to Reid's further testimony, Uncle Hardy wanted Reid and Rhonard to cut three cords of wood for the damage to the hides. Reid was asked about breaking into Mrs. Milton's house and he stated, "We went in it." He admitted to stealing rhubarb wine and vanilla extract, both of which he drank. Solicitor Jones asked Reid Coffey about having stolen a wheelbarrow from the State Highway Commission. Reid denied this but testified that he found the wheelbarrow near the highway with laurel bushes piled on it. He took it and sold it.

Neither lawyer seemed particularly prepared for this trial, and both seemed to want it concluded as soon as possible. In the modern era, the same issues would have involved far more evidentiary examination. The huge expense now associated with trials can be a burden on the system and participants, but it is also justifiable. The trial of Reid Coffey left much to be decided later.

Sheriff Hughes handed the shotgun over to the Buncombe County Sheriff when he delivered Reid Coffey there to be held in the Buncombe County jail. Attorneys never asked about how Sheriff Hughes kept the gun to prevent contamination of the evidence; that possibility existed and became a highly contentious issue in more recent criminal trials. Yet the issue never came up in Reid Coffey's trial.

The trial ended Thursday, July 9, 1936. Reid Coffey is the first person ever to be convicted of first-degree murder in Avery County and he is the first person ever to be sentenced to death in that county. Judge John H. Clement ordered the warden of Central Prison to cause Reid Coffey to inhale lethal gas of sufficient quantity to cause the death of Reid Coffey on September 11, 1936.

If the jurors did not already know each other, there was little time during the deliberation to get acquainted with each other. Their deliberations lasted 33 minutes.

Footnotes

[75] Testimony during the trial of Reid Coffey described the shotgun shell as having been "ringed" or "rung." To ring a shell one takes a knife and cuts around the circular shell. In 1936, shotgun shells were of a thin paper and ringing would be easy to do. The effect of ringing a shell is that the collective shot continues to cluster together as the shot travels after the blast. Eventually, as the paper shell falls, the shot begins to separate. The victim is likely to experience a high concentration of the shot instead of a large spread of shot. This would allow the shooter to focus most shot into one single body. This very act, although more lethal to the victim, could have spared others in the room from being more severely injured. A witness during the trial, R. J. Ollis, gave testimony that he, Ollis, examined a knife that Reid Coffey had in his pocket, shortly after Coffey's arrest. According to Ollis, the knife had on its blade a small piece of fabric that appeared the same as the fiber from the "rung" shotgun shell which was found by the sheriff the morning after the killing.

[76] The conversation with May Irene Pyatte and her sister Eva Jane Coffey Keller occurred in their residence in the early months of 2001.

[77] On the Coroner's jury were J.J. Hampton, Cecil Eller, Lum Hughes, L. C. Clark, and Ira Pritchard.

[78] Avery County has not had a coroner since Dr. A. P. Dickson served in the late 1960s although the office of coroner still exists in the General Statutes of North Carolina and it was never abolished in Avery County. On a county by county basis, the North Carolina Legislature abolished the coroner's office in several counties. Carl D. Osborne was the last person elected in Avery County as coroner, but when he left that office in 1968 to become Avery County's first magistrate under the reformed court system, Dr. Dickson was appointed to fill his term. Dr. Dickson became the first county medical examiner under the new system. The office of coroner has not been filled since that time.

[79] Dr. Guinn, a Republican, defeated Democrat Dr. Eustace Henry Sloop for this position in the election of November, 1934.

[80] To say that the inquest must be over or in the presence of the dead body did not mean that all witnesses were called and gave testimony while the body lay there. It was a practice that the coroner first visit the site where the body was discovered and begin his inquest. Usually the hearing was actually conducted elsewhere and outside the presence of the body.

[81] Judge Joe Freeman Britt of Lumberton, North Carolina, was also a former District Attorney. Robeson County, in his district, continued to have an active coroner's office later than most other counties. District Attorney Britt often participated in coroner's inquests. This was, according to him, the usual practice for other District Attorneys.

[82] Chapter 20, section 1020(10) North Carolina Code.

[83] *Brady vs. Maryland, 373 U.S. 83 (1963).*

[84] The term began on Monday July 6, 1936. The session first dealt with other matters. Jurd Hicks pleaded guilty to manslaughter of Charlie Winters. This was a 26 year old murder case, but Hicks was a fugitive living in Burke County and was only recently arrested.

[85] Deputy Sheriff Max Daniels later became a victim of homicide. Al Turner was convicted by a Watauga County jury for his murder. That case, too, made use of a special commissioner to summon jurors.

[86] Reid Coffey's peers who sat on the jury were Gardner Greer, G. W. Whitehead, Roosevelt Harmon, J. A. Sluder, John R. Greer, D. C. Laws, C. C. Burleson, Wallace Gentry, Cock Campbell, Jim Puckett, Harry Proffitt, and Roby Greer.

[87] This arraignment procedure was never formally abolished, but simply disappeared. The religious implications would surely evoke litigation in modern times. Cases determining how far a government can promote one religion over another are numerous. In North Carolina history, courts promoted religious concepts. During the nineteenth century, indictments were required to have the language to describe defendant's state of mind as "not having the fear of God before his eyes, but being moved and seduced by the instigations of the devil." Lawyers often recited the Bible, and judges often used Biblical phrases in court decisions. Cases such as *Shaw vs. Moore*, 49 N.C.25 (1856) prohibited persons from testifying as witnesses unless they had a fear of punishment by the law of God if the witness's statements were false. In recent times the courts have moved in the direction of forbidding religious law from the courtroom. A plaintiff challenged in Federal court whether the Ten Commandments could be carved on the marble walls of a Haywood County Courtroom. The case lasted several years and ended when the plaintiff died. Cases such as *State vs. Gell*, 351 N. C. 192(2001) held it improper to make Bible-based arguments to the jury. North Carolina enacted a new criminal procedure law which took effect in 1975 and this law provided that the district attorney, in arraigning defendants, could either read or fairly summarize the indictment to defendant. In 1977, the legislature went even further providing that defendants must be arraigned and have their plea recorded outside the presence of jurors. Moreover, this statute provided that the indictment cannot be read to the jurors. In enacting this statute, the General Assembly also enacted language of the Criminal Code Commission: "The Commission was aware that requiring arraignments to be held out of the presence of the prospective jurors may cause difficulties in some courthouses, but determined that the objective was desirable enough to be worth the trouble. The Commission thought that jurors hearing the stilted language of indictments and other pleadings and witnessing various motions upon arraignment are likely to get a distorted view of the case." When this legislation was passed, it was believed that some legislators had

particular concern abou the flair and flamboyance of Solicitor Marcellus Buchanan of Haywood County in arraigning defendants.

[88] Circumstantial evidence had to point unerringly toward guilt and disprove every reasonable hypothesis of innocence.

[89] Paul Hughes repeatedly said that he remembers this Sunday well, and that he remembers seeing Reid Coffey. He denies that Coffey had a gun. Yet Paul Hughes was never called as a witness by either side. Southerland, although only twelve, was a controversial witness during the trial and the credibility of his testimony became an issue after the trial. Lawyer Williams spent little time cross-examining Southerland, but instead called character witnesses to discredit the boy. The witnesses said collectively of Eugene Southerland: "He is a rowdy boy kindly uncontrollable; his general reputation is bad; he does mighty bad things; he is just a devilish boy in the community; his general character for truth and veracity is bad, I suppose; he might be a good boy if he were controlled; and he is worse than I was when I grew up." Doug Coffey, a nephew of Reid Coffey, said that the Coffey family was "amazed" by this statement. Some time after the Coffey trial the Southerland family moved away. Eugene Southerland has lived most of his life in Washington, D.C.

[90] Although the writer shows this as an exact quote, the narrative form of the transcript means that the questions of the attorneys and the answers of the witness are merged.

[91] Other circumstances were given by the witness, Mrs. C. C. Franklin, who testified that Reid and her daughter had dated. During the preceding summer she heard Reid Coffey make a statement in substance, "I don't like Avery's Uncle Hardy a bit. He is dirty. He is a dirty rascal. Some of these days he is going to go and nobody will know what became of him." Avery Coffey was Reid's younger brother and Mrs. Franklin's testimony indicated that Reid often refused to acknowledge that Hardy Coffey was his uncle, referring to him as "Avery's uncle." In addition, Lum Hughes and others gave testimony that they had observed footprints in front of the residence and going off to the right. Sheriff Hughes testified that he found tracks going down the bank behind the house and both men testified that the tracks appeared to have been left by rubbers, the type of footwear Reid Coffey was wearing when he was arrested. This evidence is at best ambiguous since many people were wearing rubbers on this rainy night. The trail indicated that the killer went toward the Holiness Church.

[92] Garrison went through the fingerprint school in Chicago, Illinois for eighteen months. He had about 10 years experience in fingerprint comparison since his graduation from that school. He was well trained and experienced for the time. In determining that Reid Coffey's right thumb made the latent print on top of the gun barrel near the breech, Garrison testified he found three points of comparison. Most modern finger-print comparison experts do not now express an opinion that the lifted print was left by a particular individual unless there are at least seven and sometimes eight points of com-

parison. Author Andre A. Moenssens was Associate Professor and Assistant Dean at Chicago-Kent College of Law of Illinois Institute of Technology. He was an expert in fingerprint history and research. He found that "it is impossible to find more than three identical characteristics situated in relative positions in two non-identical (different) fingerprints." Even so, Moenssens thought an expert could not identify a print unless he found eight points of comparison. There were appellate cases from some states contesting expert comparisons where the expert found as few as four comparison points. Generally the courts ruled the testimony admissible, but jurors could consider the weight of the testimony.

[93] In early history a party to a lawsuit or a defendant in a criminal case could not be a witness in the trial. It was reasoned that such a witness would have a compelling interest in the outcome of the case and therefore was not competent to testify at all. This rule has long been abolished in North Carolina. And since the nineteenth century, defendants in criminal cases may testify but they are subject to cross examination as would be any other witness. The North Carolina Supreme Court ruled in 1877 in *Gragg vs. Wagner,* 77 N.C. 246 (1877) that: "It is a privilege, but not the duty, of a party to an action to offer himself as a witness in his own behalf, and he is not the proper subject for unfriendly criticism because he declines to exercise a privilege conferred upon him for his own benefit merely. The fact is not the subject of comment at all." The United States Supreme Court ruled in *Rock vs. Arkansas,* 483 U. S. 44 (1987) that, "At this point in the development of our adversary system, it cannot be doubted that a defendant in a criminal case has the right to take the witness stand and to testify in his own defense." The American Bar Association *Standards for Criminal Justice* provides that the decision to testify in his or her own behalf is for the accused to make after full consultation with the lawyer. However, these standards did not exist in 1936. During that time and for some time thereafter, it was not unusual for attorneys to profess that this was a strategic decision to be made by the lawyer.

[94] North Carolina practice that required appealing defendants to put testimony in narrative form eliminates the question and answer format. An actual transcript does not exist. This quotation most likely consisted of more than one question and Coffey's responses.

Chapter 3: He is Guilty, But Maybe Not

Opponents of the death penalty invariably make the case that the possibility always exists for an innocent person to be condemned and put to death. The structure and procedure of criminal law continues to evolve as courts and legislatures seek to eliminate this possibility. The United States Supreme Court during the decades of the 1960s and 1970s began a trend of more intensely reviewing criminal cases in general, and death penalty sentences in particular. In doing so, the court used as a vehicle the Federal writ of *habeas corpus. Habeas corpus* provides a mechanism prompting the government to demonstrate that a person who had been found guilty was not denied due process of law and that the convicted person was afforded rights guaranteed by the Constitution.

As the courts used this process, Congress and the Justices themselves extended a deferential invitation to the various states. States were allowed to develop their own procedures that would allow convicted persons to challenge constitutional issues even after conviction.

Such deferential considerations generally required the persons seeking redress first to make use of, and then to exhaust state remedies before the federal courts will act. North Carolina now boasts a Motion for Appropriate Relief statute. Persons who are sentenced to death are granted an automatic appeal to the North Carolina Supreme Court. The review is limited to errors of law that may have been committed during the trial. The appellate attorney brings forth the errors that the attorney feels have merit based on the occurrences during trial. If the state supreme court affirms the conviction, then the United States Supreme Court may be asked to review the decision. This court takes cases that the justices deem appropriate, with a majority of cases declined for review.

If the United States Supreme Court declines review, then the decision of the state court becomes final. If the Supreme Court accepts review and affirms the ruling of the state court then that is the final decision.

After this first round involving an appeal and petition for discretionary review, round two begins. Usually a new lawyer appears for the defendant and, since most cases involve indigent defendants, the states pay this expense. The new lawyer reviews the original trial proceedings and often asserts, by way of a motion, that defendant's constitutional rights were violated. Most often the new lawyer contends that original counsel's work failed to represent the client properly and because of that ineffectiveness, the defendant was essentially denied the right to have counsel. Increasingly, the new lawyers are questioning whether the state made a full disclosure of information that might have been helpful to the defendant's case. Motions may relate to juror misconduct or the prejudice within the community that might have prevented the defendant from getting a fair trial. Motions are made in the trial courts of the state, and after the trial court rules, a new round of appeals and discretionary review begins. Once state court remedies are exhausted, a writ of *habeas corpus* is often filed in Federal Court and a new round of appeals and petitions for discretionary review begins. As a last resort, condemned persons may seek executive clemency from the chief executive of the state or the President of the United States.

Death penalty advocates stress, that after all of these safeguards, there is little likelihood that an innocent person will be put to death. Death penalty cases take many years and burden the states with heavy costs. The seemingly limitless reviews are a safeguard, but in addition to that safeguard, the state bears a heavy burden in initially proving one to be guilty. The burden of proof, which has always been beyond reasonable doubt, presents a heavy burden, and it, too, reduces the likelihood that an innocent person may be put to death since, presumably, innocent persons will not have been found to be guilty beyond reasonable doubt.

Scientific advances such as DNA testing also have been used to protect those who might be innocent. Significantly, convictions of a number of people were set aside when DNA testing showed that those convicted could not have committed the crime. North Carolina law now provides that DNA testing shall be made available to condemned persons whenever such evidence might have relevance in determining that person's guilt or innocence.

State legislatures and courts have sought to improve the competence of those who defend persons charged with capital crimes.[95] Acting to eliminate racism as a component of the criminal justice system, the United States Supreme Court has prohibited challenges of jurors that are based on race.[96]

Governor George H. Ryan of Illinois declared a moratorium for executions on May 4, 2000, after thirteen persons on death row had their sentences vacated. In doing so, Governor Ryan set up a commission to study capital punishment. Efforts thereafter followed in some states, including North Carolina, to have a similar moratorium. Shortly before leaving office in January 2003, Governor Ryan commuted death sentences of all one hundred sixty-seven death row inmates in Illinois to life imprisonment. In doing so, he said that the Illinois law was flawed. Death penalty issues will no doubt continue to be debated as long as there are state executions.

Reid Coffey appealed his conviction of murder and his sentence of death. The law did not provide for an automatic appeal. In 1936, the motions practice had not yet developed and neither had the inclination of the United States Supreme Court to become involved in review of state court convictions. Coffey was limited to one appeal to the North Carolina Supreme Court and, then, as a last resort, he might ask North Carolina's Governor for executive clemency. The murder of Hardy Coffey was bad, but the trial of Reid Coffey was unremarkable as a legal battle or landmark.

The remarkable story begins with the events that transpired after the trial. The trial was flawed at best. In at least two instances witnesses could have been called who would have either contradicted or impeached others' testimony. The appeal dealt only with issues raised at trial, and, since the attorney's failure to call certain witnesses was not made an issue, the appellate court could not provide a satisfactory conclusion.

Paul Hughes, referred to as "Lum Hughes' least boy" during the Reid Coffey trial by Attorney Byron, was a potential witness, but neither side called him. He did not even come to the courtroom during the trial. Paul Hughes remembers April 5, 1936, when he played marbles with Eugene Southerland and when Reid Coffey walked past the two boys. Reid Coffey, Paul Hughes said, was not carrying a gun. He was carrying phonograph records in a box, Hughes said.

After the trial, some of those who did not testify at trial were solicited to contradict some witnesses who did, and additional witnesses were sought who would add information not presented before the jury. When Governor Clyde Hoey later dealt with the commutation request of Reid Coffey, he was asked, essentially, to consider "new" facts that the jury was never told. Procedure now allows that judges can order new trials when that relief from new evidence can be shown to be appropriate. Although pardons or commutations granted by the chief executive are often controversial,[97] in 1936, executive clemency was the only avenue of appeal after review by the North Carolina State Supreme Court.

Dr. Finley P. Guinn was one witness at trial. Dr. Guinn signed an affidavit stating that Mrs. Hardy Coffey's trial testimony had contradicted her testimony at the coroner's inquest. During his trial testimony, Dr. Guinn was never asked about this discrepancy. Similarly, Lum Hughes, another witness at trial, and a coroner's juror who would have heard Mrs. Coffey's testimony at that inquest, was not asked about discrepancies in Mrs. Coffey's testimony.

Rather than end community speculation about Hardy Coffey's murder and murderer, the sketchy trial only fueled it further. Citizens continued to publicly debate the issue and to choose sides. Public opinion aside, of more immediate concern to Reid Coffey and his attorney was getting the case appealed to the North Carolina Supreme Court. The appeal process allows for a stay of execution until the appeal is heard.

Except for limited times when the United States Supreme Court held the North Carolina death penalty unconstitutional, that state has always had capital punishment, but the method of setting an execution date has changed. Early on, the condemned person had to be brought back before a Superior Court judge to have a date set. In some instances there was a wait of several months before the next term of court and, in those cases, the condemned waited in confinement. Later, authority was given the Governor to issue death warrants setting a time for the execution. But, in

1936, the statute provided for an automatic date. "In case of an appeal, should the Supreme Court find no error in the trial . . .," the condemned shall be executed "upon the third Friday after the filing of the opinion."[98] Such a law was feasible in 1936 because there was only one appeal provided. The United States Supreme Court had not yet begun its activist period where constitutional protections were applied to State court trials.

On October 14, 1936, the North Carolina Supreme Court held unanimously that Reid Coffey had received a fair trial:

> After giving the record that degree of care which a capital case imposes, it is not discovered wherein any error was committed on the trial. Apparently the prisoner has been tried in strict conformity to the established rules and sentenced as the law commands. Hence, the verdict and judgment will be upheld.

Under North Carolina's law which automatically sets an execution date, Reid Coffey's execution date was initially set for October 30, 1936. Coffey benefited from a reprieve of sorts because the execution chamber was being repaired and all executions for a time were put on hold.

John Wesley Coffey went to work for his son, and hired a new lawyer, J. V. Bowers. Only one person had the power to save Reid Coffey's life and that would be the Governor of North Carolina. John Wesley Coffey was a respected man and he used his position and influence as he visited homes and spoke with people. He talked with jurors and other people who were not called as witnesses. Jim Hughes recalls that many people signed affidavits out of respect for the man as well as the case. In 1936, most residents of Avery County knew each other. Witnesses have been known totally to change their testimony when visited by a relative of an accused person. People felt empathy for the grieving John Wesley Coffey. As he visited from house to house, Coffey accumulated affidavits and Lawyer Bowers was positioned to make a presentation to the North Carolina Governor.

Governor John C. B. Ehringhaus left office in January, 1937, and Clyde R. Hoey of Cleveland County became governor.

Hoey was a practicing Christian who was not reticent about his beliefs. He regularly taught Sunday school at his Methodist Church. On May 2, 1937, he did an extraordinary act in North Carolina. That day, the Governor of North Carolina went into Central Prison and taught the inmates a Sunday School lesson. Black inmates sat on one side of the auditorium and white inmates sat on the other side. The large congregation testified to the fact that the prisoners understood this man had the power to grant commutations, pardons, and paroles. Governor Hoey told the Biblical story of the divergent choices made by Abraham and Lot.

No governor before or since has entered into the state prison to deliver a religious service. Concerns for the safety of the top office holder in the state now would be enough to stop such an action; not to mention the perennial controversy surrounding the meaning of the separation of Church and State.

The gas chamber in North Carolina went out of service from late 1936 until mid-1937, creating a backlog of condemned persons awaiting execution. The Central Prison warden began scheduling executions after July, 1937. At one time six men were scheduled to die on August 6, 1937. Reid Coffey was one of the six. Twenty men had had been put to death by lethal gas since the North Carolina General Assembly substituted gas for electricity as the method of execution for crimes occurring after July 1, 1935. Twelve executions occurred in North Carolina in 1937, and all of them occurred between July 2 and December 22. Eleven of those were Black citizens and only one white person was executed.[99] Reid Coffey was not among them.

Following Governor Hoey's Sunday School lesson at the prison, Mrs. Harriette Gunn Robertson of Nashville, Tennessee, wrote a letter to the governor. The letter was dated May 11, 1937. It read in part:

> It was wonderful of you to go to the prison and hold service for the prisoners. Over 1100 of our partners around the world are so proud of you. It has been such a joy to be on my knees each morning in prayer for you, as also have been hundreds of consecrated men and women around the world. I know you have

experienced the spiritual power thus generated. The Holy Spirit urges me to ask you to reprieve Albert Plunkett. As you know he found Christ . . . Reid Caffey (sic) also has experienced God. Did you read his letter in the May partnership literature, where he is praying for the men who swore falsely and put him innocent in Death Row? He is a great soul, he is Christ-like to pray for his enemies. Please, oh, please reprieve him. I know that he will make good. I feel that he is innocent. It will be a blot upon the state of North Carolina to let an innocent man die.[100]

Governor Hoey gave a gracious response to Mrs. Robertson on May 13, 1937. It appears that Governor Hoey and Mrs. Robertson knew each other. Governor Hoey stated, "I shall give full consideration to these cases."[101]

Of the six men who were scheduled to die on Friday August 6, 1937, three got a stay by appealing their convictions. At the beginning of the week Governor Hoey (August 1, 1937) commuted the death sentence of William Jackson to life imprisonment. Nothing was said then of Reid Coffey and, for those interested in his fate, it must have seemed increasingly likely that he would die as scheduled. On August 4, 1938, the Governor commuted Reid Coffey's death sentence. On Friday, August 6, 1937, only George Exum, a Black man from Wayne County, was put to death. On October 26, 1937, Governor Hoey commuted the death sentence of Albert Plunkett, the second man mentioned in the letter from Mrs. Harriette Robertson.

While on death row in Central Prison, Reid Coffey wrote his aunt, Mrs. Lilly Coffey. Irene Pyatte remembers her mother was shocked when she got the letter. Reid Coffey believed that he would soon be executed. He wrote that he did not murder Hardy Coffey and asked for an opportunity to see his aunt. Mrs. Coffey sought counsel from a neighbor who advised her not to respond to the letter. Eventually the letter was burned.[102]

Throughout the rest of his life Reid Coffey maintained his innocence.[103] It is not uncommon that convicted persons deny their guilt.[104] Prior to the governor's commutation, any admission of guilt by Reid Coffey would have proven to be a bad strategy because the admission could have dissuaded the governor from commuting the sentence. It cannot be overlooked, of course, that Reid Coffey may have been innocent.

Persons serving a sentence of life imprisonment in the 1930s and 1940s in North Carolina could get their sentences shortened in two ways. They could prevail upon the Governor to commute the sentence to a definite period of years, or they could prevail upon the Governor to parole them. Paroles now are handled by a board, but the North Carolina Constitution at that time gave the Governor control over paroles. In late 1937, John Wesley Coffey must have been grateful that his son's life was spared but he could then look forward to the possibility that his son would die in prison unless Governor Hoey intervened again.

The North Carolina Constitution in 1937 provided that the Governor could grant reprieves, commutations, pardons, and parole after conviction for all offenses upon such terms as he thought proper. The Constitution has since been amended to eliminate parole from this delegation of power. Current procedure allows for a new trial based on newly-discovered evidence when such evidence could not have been reasonably discovered prior to the original trial but, in 1937, granting relief after a trial was generally beyond the power of a judge and was left exclusively to the Governor. When Governor Hoey granted a commutation to Reid Coffey he prepared a lengthy explanation which he entitled "Statement Concerning Reed Coffey (white) commutation."[105]

The Governor recited that he had received documents of three types: (1) several affidavits, (2) a petition by the men who sat as jurors, and (3) a petition signed by "a large number of good citizens of Avery County." Although the governor's statement exists, at least on microfilm, the documents upon which the statement was based appear not to have been preserved. Even so, the Governor's explanation of these documents is extensive. The affidavits made two points. The first point was that Mrs. Lilly Coffey misspoke when she testified at trial that the killing occurred no later than a quarter of eight. The second point made by the affidavits was that the witness, Eugene Southerland's testimony was not factual. It was mentioned that the Coroner, Dr. Finley P. Guinn, gave an affidavit that Mrs. Coffey testified before the Coroner's inquest that the killing occurred about 8:15 p.m. Two of Hardy Coffey's sisters, Mrs. W.W. Collins and Mrs. Viola Young, gave affidavits swearing that Mrs. Hardy Coffey had told them the killing had occurred shortly after eight o'clock. Governor Hoey wrote: "Had the widow and daughter of the deceased testified at the trial in the same manner in which they testified at the Coroner's Inquest, it is entirely possible that the Jury might have acquitted Reed Coffey, for while there was other evidence, much of it was consistent with the innocence of the prisoner." Obviously, the Governor accepted Coroner Guinn's affidavit as true even though, to do so, meant that the testimony of Lum Hughes and others at trial must be disregarded. It seems equally plausible that the Coroner may have been mistaken. The second group of affidavits were given by Loris Lambert, C.H. Hughes (Lum), Will Townsend, Gleason Cook, Fred Swift, Arlie Greene and Myrtle Greene. "The sum and substance of these affidavits is that the prisoner was not wearing an overcoat and was not carrying a gun at the time mentioned by the witness, Southerland." Actually none of those witnesses saw Reid Coffey at the same time that Southerland had seen him. Only young Paul Hughes was with Southerland when Reid Coffey walked by, and Paul Hughes was never a witness for either side.

Nearly all the persons who gave affidavits were witnesses at trial but none was specifically questioned about the subject of their later affidavits. If it troubled the Governor that he was now considering evidence that could have been explored at trial but was not, he gave no indication to that effect. The jurors made this recommendation to the Governor:

> We respectfully request that Your Excellency commute the death sentence imposed on the defendant to that of life imprisonment. We make this request for the reason that since the trial many things have arisen and other circumstances have come to light as to make us believe that there is a possibility that this defendant did not commit the murder. . . .We seriously doubt that the

defendant would be convicted if it was possible for the trial to be had again. For this reason we respectfully urge that you commute the sentence of death to life imprisonment, assuring you that such a step would meet with the most hearty approval of practically every citizen of this county.

Governor Hoey noted in his statement, "I must confess that I am deeply moved by the solemn recommendation of these twelve men. Their recommendation . . . cannot be ignored." There is an incongruity in an argument that one who is believed to be not guilty should nevertheless be sentenced to life.

Finally, the petition which was said to be signed "by a large number of good citizens of Avery County" reads in part:

> While the crime committed was a most brutal one, we also know that others living in our community had far greater reasons to commit the crime than the motive shown by the state in the trial of the cause on the part of Reed Coffey . . . we have grave doubts as to whether Reed Coffey actually committed the crime or had anything to do with it.

This petition went on to virtually repeat the language made in the jury recommendation. The fact that the petitioners said they had grave doubts that Reid Coffey committed murder on one hand, and on the other, recommended that he be sentenced to life imprisonment seems not to have troubled the Governor. Governor Hoey noted that, "Additional prestige is given this petition when we know that at least a dozen of the signatures are those of close relatives of the deceased." This ignores the fact that they were also close relatives of John Wesley Coffey and his son, Reid. By this time there was a strong incentive to band together behind the living. It is doubtful that these citizens would have favored a total release of Reid Coffey, but they appeared content that he serve life in prison.

Governor Hoey wrote, "We cannot be too careful in matters of life and death. I shall continue an investigation in this case in order that we may learn with more certainty the true facts.

If I become hereafter convinced of the prisoner's innocence, I shall extend a full pardon. Meanwhile, this case is surrounded with so much doubt that I believe it will be unwise and dangerous to exact the extreme penalty. I have decided to commute the sentence of death imposed on Reed Coffey to one of life imprisonment."

The trial judge, the trial solicitor, and the Avery County Sheriff did not concur in this action. Then, as was the usual practice, there was no mention of having asked the victim's family what they thought.

Lawyers representing commutation requests before the Governor essentially act as lobbyists. Rules of evidence apply only insofar as the Governor requires. J. V. Bowers had achieved much for his client—Coffey was spared the death penalty. Doug Coffey remembers Mr. Bowers meeting with John Wesley Coffey several times. John Wesley Coffey owned a gold watch which Lawyer Bowers thought had considerable worth. After one session, it was agreed that Lawyer Bowers would take the watch and have it appraised. The value of the watch was applied to Lawyer Bowers' fee.

Ernest Reid Coffey, then a resident of Raleigh, North Carolina, died of a heart attack on March 16, 1981. Mr. Coffey was a widower, and had worked for years in the printing department at North Carolina State University. He was 65 years old. Mr. Coffey's obituary was given scant attention both in Raleigh and in Avery County. Reid Coffey's sister, Mrs. Dick Cooke, called Irene Pyatte and told her of her cousin Reid's death. He had not lived in Avery since 1936, yet played a historic role in his home county. Superior Court Judge John H. Clement, who sentenced Reid Coffey to die in the gas chamber, died October 20, 1956. Solicitor John R. Jones was killed in Arkansas when he was run over by a car in 1958. Former County Coroner Finley P. Guinn died in 1956, and Sheriff Wilburn H. Hughes died August 5, 1960. The man who was condemned to die outlived all those officials who were part of his trial. How then did Reid Coffey get from a condemned man to a free citizen?

After Governor Hoey commuted Reid Coffey's sentence to life imprisonment, lawyer J. V. Bowers continued to work for John Wesley Coffey. Governors could not be elected to two terms consecutively. In the election of November 5, 1940, John Melville

Broughton of Wake County was elected Governor, and his inauguration was set for January 9, 1941. As a lame duck Governor in 1940, Clyde R. Hoey commuted Reid Coffey's life sentence to not less than twenty nor more than thirty years in prison. However, Governor Hoey never granted the full and free pardon that he promised in the original commutation if he were ever to become convinced of Coffey's innocence. In commuting Reid Coffey's sentence on November 20, 1940, Governor Hoey said, "The Prison Division informs me that this prisoner has now served, with gained time, more than four years, and his conduct has been good." Clyde R. Hoey was elected United States Senator and died in office in 1954. Governors and Presidents tend to grant more pardons and commutations shortly before they leave office than they do during their terms.

Hardy Coffey's daughter, Lala, married a relative of Lawyer James E. Holshouser of Boone. To assist Mrs. Lilly Coffey in fighting commutation, Holshouser's relative Gene Holshouser, and a neighbor of Mrs. Coffey, drafted letters that Mrs. Coffey signed. Mrs. Coffey wrote the Governor February 27, 1937, December 16, 1938, and November 4, 1940. She wrote the Commissioner of Paroles on March 11, 1944. In her letter addressed to Governor Hoey dated December 16, 1938, she referenced a notice that had appeared in the *Avery Advocate* announcing that a petition was now before the Governor for the pardon or parole of Reid Coffey:

> Information has come to me that the petition placed before you contains approximately four hundred names, I know that some of the more respectable citizens of this county were not requested to sign this petition and further I believe that the validity of some of the signers to represent the opinion and sentiment of the citizens of Avery County would bear very close investigation. The crime left me with three minor children to provide for in the necessities of life and at my age without special preparation for earning a living for the children and myself. I have suffered vastly more than the convicted man possibly can by imprisonment for his criminal act. To liberate him would be an act of injustice to the community and those directly afflicted. Wherefore I

sincerely beg that Your Excellency disapprove of any further clemency to Reid Coffey.[106]

On January 12, 1948, Governor Robert Gregg Cherry granted parole to: "Reed Coffey—(white)". Governor Cherry noted:

> The Prison Department informs me that this prisoner is now making an excellent record in prison, and with gained time he has completed approximately fourteen and one-half years on his sentence. The trial Judge, Honorable J. H. Clement, and the trial Solicitor, Honorable John R. Jones, have advised that they have no objection to parole. Parole in the case is recommended by the Sheriff of Avery County, the Chief Deputy Sheriff of Avery County and other officials.

In that era, families of victims were granted almost no legal rights before, during, or after trials, and no one apparently asked for their input. Reid Coffey's first full day of confinement was April 6, 1936, and from that day until January 12, 1948, his actual term of confinement had been eleven years and 281 days; he had been given "gain" time totaling two years and 266 days.

Reid Coffey learned the printing trade while in prison and he found work at North Carolina State College. While under parole supervision, he was restricted from going to Avery County.

John Wesley Coffey was buried at the Tate Cemetery, formerly known as the Love Cemetery, in Linville Land Harbor. Reid Coffey is buried at the Restlawn Memorial Garden in Raleigh. Hardy Coffey's resting place is on a hillside that affords a view of a considerable part of the Montezuma area.

The passage of time has dimmed the memories of those who lived through the murder of Hardy Coffey and trial of Reid Coffey. It is difficult to look back and truly sense how this murder gripped the people in the close-knit Avery County community. The North Carolina Supreme Court deals with legal issues and generally does not reveal what it believes to be the facts of a case, but in this case the court provided a revealing statement concerning Reid Coffey's appeal and guilt. The court was responding to an event during trial: Sheriff Wilburn Hughes testified that during the investigation he asked Reid Coffey, in the presence of Arcus Benfield, "What kind of gun does your daddy have?" Sheriff Hughes testified that Reid responded that his daddy did not have any gun that he knew of. Commenting on this exchange, the unanimous Supreme Court Justices said, "The defendant was seen with a gun on the afternoon before the murder. After the defendant's arrest, the sheriff asked him, 'Reed, what did you do with that shotgun?' His reply was, 'I don't know anything about any shotgun.' Question: 'What kind of shotgun did your daddy have?' Answer: 'He ain't got no shotgun that I know of.' The gun used by the assailant was readily accessible to the accused and he knew all about it. To feign ignorance when candor would serve better is to reveal a troubled mind."

It also is revealing that, in his commutation statement in 1937, Governor Hoey said: "According to the trial judge, sentiment was strong against the prisoner, as the census (sic) of opinion was that he was guilty of brutally killing his uncle." Ordinarily, trial judges do not gauge the sentiment of the community but rather confine their role to presiding over the trial. Such a statement contrasts with statements in the petition to the Governor that community sentiment held that Coffey was not guilty.

The cruel manner of Hardy Coffey's death, in front of his family, alone makes the crime a telling one. The murder created extraordinary suffering for Coffey's daughters, the little girls singing a hymn with their father just before the ambush. Nor should it be forgotten that a widow was forced to take heroic measures to support her little children after their father was killed. Mrs. Lilly Coffey worked as a cook and housekeeper for the Kirkpatrick and Crawford families, and at Crossnore School. May Irene Coffey Pyatte recalls that after her father's murder, she and her sisters would become so frightened that her mother had to walk around the house to make sure that no one was there. At times she still cries and lies sleepless, and to this day she has not forgotten. Closure is today's word for describing the end of a grieving period after the loss of a loved one; there was none for the women who were little girls back in 1936.

Footnotes

[95] North Carolina now has the "Indigent Defense Services Act," which sets forth, among other things, requirements that lawyers defending those charged with capital offenses demonstrate basic skills and experience.

[96] *Batson vs. Kentucky,* 476 U. S. 79 (1986)

[97] On January 13, 1992, North Carolina Governor James Martin commuted the death sentence of Anson Maynard to life imprisonment. In doing so, Governor Martin expressed personal reservations about the guilt of Maynard. This was a controversial decision. If the governor doubted the guilt of the condemned man, life imprisonment would seem not to be a good choice. If he is innocent, then a full pardon might be more appropriate than life imprisonment.

[98] Article 17 North Carolina Code of 1935, section 4663.

[99] *Addresses and Papers of Governor Clyde Roark Hoey 1937-1941,* Presses of Observer House, Inc., Charlotte, N.C., David Lee Corbitt, Chief Library Assistant State Dept of Archives and History, editor, 1944. These statistics were probably typical throughout the south and in other states as well. In 1972, when the United States Supreme Court ruled capital punishment unconstitutional throughout the nation, statistics showing that death sentences were imposed with disproportionate frequency upon Blacks were considered by some of the justices. Since that decision, efforts were made to convince the court that racial discrimination still exists. In *McClesky vs. Kemp,* 481 U. S. 279 (1987), the United States Supreme court was again asked to declare a state death penalty scheme unconstitutional based on a statistics-based challenge. A Georgia study showed that the death penalty was likely to be imposed when a victim was white and the defendant was Black. The majority of the justices rejected this type of analysis and held that the unconstitutionality of the Georgia system could only be shown in an individual case. Current death sentences and those who are actually executed do not reveal this disproportionality.

[100] Governor Hoey's loose papers, North Carolina Archives.

[101] *Ibid.*

[102] Conversation with author, May Irene Coffey Pyatte and Eva Coffey Keller during 2001.

[103] In several conversations, Doug Coffey of Morganton, N.C., said his uncle, Reid Coffey always maintained his innocence. Doug Coffey knew his uncle well. Boyd Coffey, another nephew, stated the same. Several of the Coffey collateral descendants, without exception, said Reid Coffey was innocent. Boyd Coffey once asked his Uncle Reid directly about the murder of Hardy Coffey, and Reid's response was that he did not murder Hardy Coffey, but someday, Reid would tell his nephew all about the crime. Boyd Coffey was with his uncle when Reid Coffey died. Immediate family members of Reid Coffey are all dead, but the current generation of Coffeys

maintains that Reid Coffey did not commit the murder, but rather another member of the immediate family did. This other male person was allegedly motivated by an altogether different reason to murder Hardy Coffey. There is no way to prove or disprove this theory.

[104] Bruno Richard Hauptmann was electrocuted in New Jersey in 1935, after the "trial of the twentieth century." He was convicted of the murder of the infant Charles A. Lindbergh, Jr., and a number of people believed that Hauptmann was innocent. The Governor of New Jersey secretly visited Hauptmann in prison and promised to commute Hauptmann's death sentence to life imprisonment if Hauptmann would confess and name others who were involved in the kidnapping and murder. Even after having been given this opportunity, Hauptmann continued to maintain his innocence. Similarly, in the case of Julius and Ethel Rosenberg who were electrocuted on June 19, 1953 in New York's Sing Sing Prison for espionage, there was considerable public debate about their guilt. The Attorney General of the United States offered the condemned couple an opportunity to have their sentences of death commuted to life imprisonment if they would confess and name other participants. The fact that the Rosenbergs continued to maintain their innocence caused frequent studies of the trial and verdict of guilt.

[105] Reed Coffey microfilm records, North Carolina Department of Correction, Management Information and Research, 831 West Morgan Street, Raleigh, N.C.

[106] Private family archives, Eva Coffey Keller.

CASE III

THE TROUBLE WITH HANGING

Chapter 1: Mysticism, Rehabilitation, History and Exaggeration

Death penalty opponents say that execution doesn't prevent crime. Proponents counter that returning to public hanging of capital offenders in the town square would present an effective deterrent. North Carolina acted early to prohibit public executions. On August 15, 1868, the North Carolina legislature ratified a bill entitled "An Act to Regulate Capital Executions." That act provided "the ends of justice, public morals, and the preservation of order, demand that the execution of all capital offenders should be made private and invested with the solemnity appropriate to the final act of penal law." This law allowed the sheriff to admit by ticket only a required guard, two physicians and necessary assistants, not more than thirty-six nor less than eighteen respectable citizens to witness for the State, the due observance of the law.

This was the law until March 13, 1879, when the legislature ratified Chapter 221 of the Public and Private Laws of North Carolina of 1879. This new amendment added this proviso to the earlier act, "*Provided, however* (emphasis added) for reasons which they may deem good and sufficient, the county commissioners may otherwise order."

The matter of public executions was finally resolved effective February 20, 1901, when the Legislature repealed the authority given to county commissioners to order public executions. Thereafter, the sheriff was without exception required to "provide for the execution within the jailyard enclosure, and as much removed from public view as the means within his control will allow." Even after February 1901, in many instances condemned persons were exhibited in public view, allowed to have dialogue with the audience, then were executed out of public view.

Public hangings were the norm in England and throughout Europe. The settlers brought this practice to the new country in Colonial times and through early statehood. With a small population and less crime, fewer hangings were conducted in the rural mountain counties of North Carolina than in the more urban areas of the state and country, but some of those hangings became a staple of the history of the mountain region. Many long time residents of Mitchell and Yancey Counties in North Carolina claim their ancestors were present at the hanging of Frankie Silver. Thanks to songs and stories written about it, this particular hanging has reverberated as a defining event for more than a century.

County sheriffs were made into executioners, a job many did not want. Sheriffs from surrounding counties came to a county seat when executions took place; the sheriffs formed very different views of such public spectacles. On the practical level, building a scaffold was an expense to a county government, and the scaffold owned by Buncombe County— the most populated in the region— was often transported by train from one county seat to another. The Sheriff of Iredell County, North Carolina, invited the Buncombe County Sheriff to attend the hanging of Wilford Roseboro and to bring his scaffold. That hanging occurred in Statesville on September 10, 1903. The same scaffold was used in the hanging of Peter Smith in Madison.

The name "Mayland" appears on no roadmaps and has no zip code. Nevertheless, as one travels the area of Spruce Pine or Burnsville, one sees signs and businesses using the name. The use of this word, and the word "Tri-County" shows that Mitchell, Avery and Yancey (MAY) counties share a common history. Mayland Community College serves all three counties. There are joint government efforts such as a library system. Yancey County, created by the General Assembly in 1833, formerly included what is now Mitchell County and part of Avery County. Settlers who lived in what is now Yancey County petitioned the General Assembly to form a new county. The petitioners said that travel from where they lived to Morganton and Asheville, the two county seats that governed their district, was too long.

Yancey County boasts Mount Mitchell, the highest mountain peak east of the Rocky Mountains. Its residents depend on income from raising burley tobacco, the main cash crop for generations in the area. Yancey County votes Democratic for the most part, but Republicans can and do win some elections.

Yancey County's low crime rate may account for the most famous case in the region still being talked about over one hundred and seventy years after the fact. Frances ("Frankie") Stuart Silver was hanged for the murder of her husband, Charles Silver, in Morganton, in Burke County on July 12, 1833, the same year that Yancey County was formed by the North Carolina General Assembly.

The place where Charles Silver is said to have been murdered was then in Burke, later in Yancey and now in Mitchell County. Some said that Frances Silver was the first woman to be hanged in North Carolina. This may not be true.[107] Death may have come quickly to Charles Silver, but the state's case was that Frankie chopped his body into small pieces and cremated the remains in the fireplace of their house.[108] Witnesses found a cabin that was scrubbed clean. Traces of blood were found in cracks of the floors and fragments of bone were found. This evidence, together with the fact that Charles was never seen again, gave his family and neighbors sufficient proof of his murder.

Frances Silver was tried at a time when defendants were not allowed to testify in their own defense. The judicial system used the term "lack of competence." Modern studies have postulated that, had she been permitted, she would have presented a testimony of self-defense based on her husband's abuse.After she was convicted and sentenced to death, Frankie escaped from jail and disguised herself as a man, part of what made the case first sensational and then legendary.

Contrary to the legend, Frances Silver may have been hanged privately.[109] A large number of people attended the spectacle and observed as much of the event as was permitted. One of the surviving legends says that on the gallows Frankie Silver recited a lengthy poem portraying the details of killing her husband. The poem is still quoted as fact, passed on by some who say they learned it from their relatives who were present. Other historians say the poem was written by another person who was condemned to die.[110] In any event, Frankie Silver could not have read a poem that refers to "murder in the first degree." North Carolina did not divide the common law crime of murder into two degrees— First and Second —until February 11, 1893, some sixty years after Frankie Silver was said to have used the phrase. In legend, the more spectacular the crime and punishment, the more exaggeration and fabrication.

Burgess S. Gaither from Burke County, a 39 year-old solicitor for Yancey County, prosecuted the Frances Silver trial. Solicitors then were elected by the General Assembly, but Gaither was destined to become a popularly-elected Congressman from North Carolina in the Confederate Congress. David B. Caldwell was presiding judge of the Superior Court and James Carter was the Sheriff of Yancey County. Superior Court met twice yearly.

No lawyers lived in Yancey County and the lawyers in the judicial district usually rode circuit with the court like a roving troupe of actors who went from place to place to perform.

In October, 1846, Daniel Angel, Jr. and John Angel, sons of the first sheriff of Yancey County, both accused of murder, were sitting in the jail without legal counsel. On Wednesday, October 21, 1846, Solicitor Gaither submitted a bill of indictment that charged the two brothers with the murder of Robert B. Roberts on June 6, 1846, and the grand jury returned that bill as a true bill of indictment. John Baxter of Hendersonville, North Carolina, was hired to represent the two brothers. He made no effort to get the case continued. The judge determined that the Sheriff had a connection with the defendants and therefore should not be allowed to summon jurors. The coroner also had a connection with the defendants, and the judge appointed two citizens, Thomas Gardner and Thomas Baker, as special commissioners to summon 115 jurors for the trial. Thomas Baker was a half-brother to Charles Baker who later served as Sheriff of Yancey County.[111]

Members of the Angel family later expressed their concern that Daniel Angel, Jr. did not receive a fair trial because the defendant did not have an attorney before court began, and he was not able to have his witnesses in court. This concern was expressed in a letter delivered to the Governor.

In 1846, there was no provision for public funding of a lawyer for the accused who could not afford legal representation. Court records from Yancey County show that both brothers did have an attorney at the time of trial, but they had no attorney for the weeks preceding.[112] In 1846, the Motion to Continue, a standard procedure in modern trials, was almost never brought to bear and was totally at the discretion of the trial judge. Cases simply did not get continued, and the lawyer in the Angel case never expressed his inability to try the case on short notice. The lengthening of time given an attorney to prepare his case is a recent reform because the courts recognized that due process requires a lawyer who is fully prepared.[113] This lengthening of time has come at a cost. Cases back up on the dockets, and public expenses associated with trials have soared.

Angel's case involved a spontaneous quarrel where Daniel Angel stabbed the victim with a knife. Several witnesses saw the fight. On Saturday, October 24, 1846, the jury rendered its verdict that Daniel Angel, Jr. was guilty of murder and John Angel was guilty of manslaughter. Daniel Angel was sentenced to be hanged on December 4, 1846. It was ordered that he be confined in the Buncombe County Jail in Asheville until his hanging.

Daniel Angel's appeal to the North Carolina Supreme Court hardly enlightened the proceedings. Lawyer John Baxter neglected to contend that the court erred by not continuing the case. The North Carolina Supreme Court validated the trial and sentencing of Daniel Angel, and Daniel Angel, Jr. was hanged in Burnsville on May 7, 1847.

No contemporary account of the hanging exists, but it likely was public. Daniel Angel was said to have told the crowd that whoever kicked the block from under him would die in three months. Of course, that curse was said to have come true.

What we now call urban legends surround many hangings. There is a tale passed down about Hol English, who was lynched near Bakersville. The local newspaper reported that an observer saw the deceased's spirit rising like an unfolded newspaper. His spirit is still said to haunt his gravesite.

When George Cunningham was hanged in Madison County on May 28, 1875, the hanging was private as mandated by statute, but hundreds of people had assembled anyway to observe it. That private hanging spawned the persistent rumor that the Sheriff hurriedly cut Cunningham down and revived him a short distance from the scene. Cunningham, given a new lease on life, supposedly left the area and prospered for the rest of his life.

Rumors also swirl around the case of Peter Smith. Smith was buried in secret at night, where it is said he haunts his gravesite even now. Of all execution rituals, hanging seems to have grabbed hold of the public's imagination.

The public often turned out in the thousands to witness hangings taking place in remote rural mountain county seats. Madison County had a railroad, and when Peter Smith was hanged in Marshall on October 2, 1905, some bought tickets and rode by train. Some rode horseback and others traveled with families by wagon.

When James Byers was hanged in tiny Wilkesboro, North Carolina, on July 13, 1888, it was estimated that 6,000 to 8,000 people were in attendance. Peter Smith's hanging in Marshall attracted a crowd estimated to be 1,200 to 1,500. When George Cunningham was executed on May 28, 1875, in Marshall, an estimated 1,500 people attended.[114]

The lynching of Nease Gillespie, John Gillespie, and Jack Dillingham in Salisbury in 1906 was sufficiently advertised so that 5,000 people observed it.[115] John Wilson's hanging in Burnsville on February 7, 1890, reportedly drew thousands of bystanders.[116]

To attend a hanging in these tiny towns then would have required at least an all-day excursion and considerable discomfort because there were no public facilities for such large crowds. The crowd of 1,500 people in Marshall could well have been the largest gathering to observe one event in the history of Madison County. People drank, fought, and vandalized at these spectacles.

Before he was privately hanged, George Cunningham captured his audience with his seeming contriteness when he acknowledged that he should have spent more time reading the Bible than playing cards.

A newspaper reported that John Wilson "knelt and prayed fervently for himself, his enemies, his family, and the widow and children of the man he had murdered."[117] Wilson was drunk when he shot and killed Thomas Edge at a turkey shoot on September 22, 1888.[118] Wilson lost 30 pounds during his confinement awaiting execution. He attracted some fame for letters he wrote lamenting the choices he made in life. He appeared to repent, but

Governor Daniel G. Fowle refused to commute his sentence to life imprisonment.

In Buncombe County on February 26, 1902, one of North Carolina's more garish hangings took place. Ben Foster and Frank Johnson were hanged while a large crowd of onlookers gathered outside the prison wall. Before the prisoners were taken inside for the private hanging, one of the condemned men performed as if he was in a stage production. Known as the Emma Burglars,[119] Foster and Johnson were the only two who were hanged of the original gang of four men convicted of first-degree burglary. Governor Charles B. Aycock commuted to life imprisonment the death sentences of the other two condemned. First-degree burglary is no longer a capital crime.[120]

Prior to the hanging, the two men were given a chance to speak to the throngs of people who had gathered outside the prison. Speaking from one of the jailhouse windows, Foster used his time to exhort the congregation to get religion.

> I know that I have faced on earth my last congregation of people, but I have a hope that I will face a greater congregation of today. I want to meet everyone on the other shore and I leave the peace of God with everybody.

According to the *Asheville Citizen* dated the following day:

> Foster then produced a hymn book. 'I want to ask everbody that will,' he said, 'to help me sing *Pass me not O Gentle Savior.*' Foster waited a few minutes for some one to start the hymn with him, though there was no response. "There is no one here that can sing," came a voice in the crowd: "sing it yourself." Foster then commenced to sing amid a profound stillness. The condemned man sang the first verse and had started to sing the second stanza of the hymn when he suddenly stopped his song and darted back into the jail cell. The deputy sheriff who stood beside him yelled to the crowd, that Foster did not want his picture taken. Foster had apparently spotted an eager cameraman in the audience.

After these two men were executed, souvenir hunters asked for pieces of the ropes. The ropes were cut into small lengths and distributed to the crowd. The Sheriff from Rowan County observed the hangings. He had several hangings scheduled in Rowan County and perhaps felt he needed the experience. Sheriffs frequently attended hangings in other counties, and it was not unusual for newspaper reporters to ask their opinions about how the hanging had proceeded. The Rowan County Sheriff said: "It was one of the most complete hangings I ever witnessed."

During the period when executions occurred in the county seats, lynchings of people who were never convicted of crime became commonplace as well. This manuscript deals with efforts by North Carolina's governors in preventing these illegal acts.[121] Lynchings, like hangings, often attracted a large crowd. Lynchings did not end with the statute that provided for electrocutions in the state capital. In the years after 1889, when the North Carolina Attorney General started keeping criminal statistics, more lynchings were recorded in North Carolina than legal executions. Whether the fact that legal executions were relegated to county officials in the county seat resulted in more frequent lynchings cannot be known, but both activities had a local component. When North Carolina began treating executions as a state matter and set the place of execution at the state capital, the state government, led by Governor Glenn, acted with greater vigor to suppress the lynchings that appeared to have replaced executions at the local level.

Governors sometimes commuted death sentences to life imprisonment.[122] Sometimes new trials were granted. On average, only one hanging was carried out in North Carolina each year. The *Asheville Citizen* editorialized: "One of the attorney generals, some years ago, declared that the laws were 'too bloody,' but the number of executions does not prove this, the average being only one hanging a year."[123]

Condemned men in rural mountainous Western North Carolina added a footnote to the era of hangings in the county seat. A good many have avoided the death penalty altogether by escaping from jail. In its history, Yancey County has sentenced five men to be hanged, but only two were actually hanged. The two who were executed were confined in the Buncombe County Jail. The other three, detained in the Yancey County Jail, escaped.

The first of the three men to avoid the gallows in Yancey County by escaping jail was William Haney, convicted of murder.[124]

In 1878, Thomas Boone[125] killed Samuel Butler, and was indicted for murder. Boone fled North Carolina and was found in Tennessee. On September 10th of that year, North Carolina Governor Zebulon B. Vance requested his Tennessee counterpart to deliver Boone to North Carolina authorities. Boone complained he could not get a fair trial in Yancey County and a judge ordered his trial to be held in Madison County. There, Thomas Boone was convicted of murder in 1879. Boone was sentenced to death, and appealed to the North Carolina Supreme Court. While his case was on appeal, Boone was confined in Yancey County's jail. In January 1880, by the time the North Carolina Supreme Court affirmed his murder conviction, Thomas Boone had already escaped.

In the same year that Boone murdered Samuel Butler, another man also named Thomas Boone was indicted for killing John S. Woodfin in Yancey County. The second Thomas Boone was tried for and convicted of murder in Yancey County.[126] Like his namesake, he was also held in the Yancey County jail under a sentence of death, and like his namesake, he escaped. The two Thomas Boones escaped at the same time.

On October 28, 1879, North Carolina Governor, Thomas J. Jarvis, offered a reward of one hundred dollars for the apprehension and delivery of Thomas Boone who "stands charged with the murder of John Woodfin," and, on the same date, offered a reward of one hundred dollars for the apprehension and delivery of Thomas Boone who "stands charged with the murder of Samuel Butler."[127] Neither reward was ever collected.

Superior Court Judge David Schenck presided over the trial of the younger Thomas Boone. His diary reveals the dilemma of a judge presiding over a murder trial when there was no division of murder into first and second degree and when punishment was automatic for those found guilty of murder. The following is from volume 8 of the *David Schenck Diaries:*[128]

Yancey County, Burnsville, Oct. 12, 1879, Sabbath: I
have nearly closed my Court here; will finish tomorrow
and have some days for recreation and pleasure.

Sentence of Thomas Boon

It was painful duty to pronounce the judgment of the
law upon Thomas Boon who was convicted twelve
months ago, at this Court, for the murder of John
Woodfin, a resident of this place. . . . Boon is quite a
young man, not more than 22 years of age, light hair
and blue eyes and his complexion now very pale and
delicate from long imprisonment. He greatly excited
my commiseration by his youthful appearance. When I
asked him what he had to say, why sentence of death
should not be pronounced upon him, he replied in a
firm voice, 'I am not guilty of the crime for which I am
convicted.'

I said but few words to him and extended all the mercy
I could by postponing his execution to the 5th day of
December, that his counsel might have time to intercede
for mercy with the Governor for the state. It was
conceded he did not fire the fatal shot but the jury found
he was present aiding and abetting. He was convicted
on his idle boasting while under the influence of liquor.

Thomas Boone, who murdered Samuel Butler, was married
and had a child in Yancey County. Mrs. Nola Edge Westall of
Burnsville is a descendant of this Thomas Boone. She recalled
that when she was 16 years old, a lawyer from Oregon came to
Burnsville. Her ancestor died in Oregon and left an inheritance to
Mrs. Westall's mother. Thomas Boone married a schoolteacher
there and had a family in Oregon. His relatives did not know his
whereabouts after his escape until this lawyer appeared. Boone
had changed his name, prospered as a farmer, and led a respectable
life in Oregon. He kept a Wanted Poster from North Carolina in
a trunk, the only reminder of his dark past.[129] Solicitor Joseph S.
Adams sought to indict Sheriff N. W. Wilson for allowing a prisoner
to escape after the two Boones fled, but the Yancey County Grand
Jury did not return a true bill of indictment.

Waightstill Avery Anderson, who awaited execution after his conviction of murder in Mitchell County, also avoided the death penalty by escaping jail on July 13, 1885. He escaped from the Buncombe County Jail, considered the most secure facility in the mountains. With outside help, Anderson and his brother-in-law, Edward W. Ray took control of the jail and overcame the Buncombe County Sheriff and a deputy.[130]

None of the four escaped murderers, Anderson, Haney, and the two Boones, was ever captured. One of the Boones is known to have prospered and led a respectable life and that may have been true for others as well. These men were all convicted under a law that did not divide murder into two degrees.[131] It made the death penalty mandatory for anyone guilty of murder. Had there been an offense of second-degree murder at the time, where the death penalty was not applied, some of these men might have escaped the death sentence. By today's standards, the trials of Frances Silver, Daniel Angel, John Wilson, George Cunningham, and the above four escapees failed to demonstrate premeditation and deliberation.

The history of the death penalty involves a continued and unmistakable trend on the part of legislatures, judges, and prosecutors to exempt certain categories of cases and defendants from the sentence of the death penalty. The division of murder into two degrees with first-degree murder punishable by death and second-degree murder, punishable by a lesser sentence, represents an early example of this historic trend.

Society continues to wrestle with death sentences, and standards and moral attitudes are evolving with the times. The states set minimum age limits for those who can be executed and the United States Supreme Court has exempted the mentally retarded from the death penalty.

Hangings sometimes produced unanticipated results. When the victim was not hanged properly, two undesirable things could happen. There were cases where the victim's head was jerked off his body, resulting in death by decapitation. In other instances, as in the case of John Wilson, the victim slowly asphyxiated. Wilson writhed and wiggled for fifteen minutes or longer. It was reported: "Hundreds turned their backs upon the awful scene while thousands gazed intently at the victim suspended motionless at the rope's end."[132]

After some experience with hangings, a free fall of at least six feet was determined to be generally sufficient to bring about instantaneous death. In such instances, there was enough injury to the spinal cord or to the brain stem to cause immediate unconsciousness and death. Such a fall usually separates the second and third or the third and fourth cervical vertebrae which then causes the upper cervical cord to be stretched or torn. This type of result was most preferred, and the visiting sheriffs congratulated each other when the victim did not show conscious signs of suffering. Hangings that did not cause this type of neck injury could produce death by constriction of the neck, but such deaths took longer and the victim appeared pitiful as he struggled before the witnesses. In these instances, death occurred either by obstruction of the arteries of the neck or by obstruction of the airway. Spectators found such deaths grotesque as the victim dangled.

Hangings in the county seat produced crowds that were hazards in themselves. One little girl who witnessed the events surrounding the hanging of John Wilson said: "When John Wilson was to be hanged, people and their children began to arrive in town at daylight to see it. Mother pulled down the blinds in our house and refused to let the children look out."[133]

Footnotes

[107] Young, Perry Deane, The Untold Story of Frankie Silver, Down Home Press, Asheboro, N.C.,1998.
[108] Many people studied and wrote about the case of Frankie and Charlie, including the late former United States Senator, Sam J. Ervin, Jr., former Superior Court Judge Ronald Howell, the late Attorney Robert Byrd, Perry Deane Young, and others.
[109] Young, Perry Deane.
[110] Young, Ibid.
[111] When Charles Baker was sheriff, according to Judge James L. Baker, Jr., he is said to have stolen public money and absconded. Other Baker relatives sold their property to pay the loss and thereafter, in shame, left

the area. It is to the credit of the Baker family that towns on both sides of the United States were named after them—Bakersville, North Carolina and Bakersfield, California.

[112] Thomas Wilson was retained earlier as lawyer. This lawyer also represented Frances Silver. He left the area before the matter was scheduled for trial. In Governor William A. Graham's loose papers in North Carolina Archives there is a letter written by Angel family members to North Carolina State Senator Michael Francis, an attorney from Waynesville, North Carolina and, at the time, state senator for Yancey County: "Sur, I want you to attend to Daniel Angel's case known State against him, whar in he has been. . . found guilty. . .and has taken an appeal to the supreme court. In his case, whar the said Angel his atterny he first imployed in this case he has haponed to some missfortons and has left the contry and has left said D. Angel with out any counsil, and being in prison was left with (out) chance of getting any atterny or any witnesses until the day of trial and the said Angel was oblige to come on trial without his witnesses or any atterny, on the a count of said Wilson removing. And we worsh you thar fore to make intersession with the court and gove said Angel a fair trial on this case whar he was convicted, as not having any opertunity of having his witnesses present at trial."

[113] In between the Angel case where the lawyer did not even ask for a continuance and modern procedure is the case of Frank Henderson of Madison County. In September, 1920, Henderson was sentenced to death by a Madison County Judge for the murder of his wife. One of Henderson's attorneys was Mark W. Brown who later in this manuscript will be discussed at length. Brown wanted the case continued and asked for a continuance during trial on the ground that he did not have time to prepare for trial. The murder happened on August 24, 1920. Henderson was tried during the week of September 27, 1920. The judge refused the continuance and the defendant appealed to the North Carolina Supreme Court on this and other grounds. Unanimously, the justices of the North Carolina Supreme Court ruled that the judge did not commit error in denying the continuance. Henderson was electrocuted on October 10, 1921, after proclaiming that his sentence was "unjust" because he was drinking at the time of the murder. A modern case illustrates the change in attitudes. As a young assistant district attorney, I arraigned Defendant Steven Louis Moore, before Judge Ronald Howell in the Watauga County Superior Court. Moore's attorney moved the court for a continuance on the ground that he had insufficient time to prepare and on the further ground that he had not had time to secure the presence of witnesses. The attorney contended that to force him to trial at that time deprived the defendant of a constitutional right—that is, the right to have effective counsel. Writing an opinion for the North Carolina Court of Appeals after the defendant was convicted of several felonies, Judge Harry C. Martin wrote: "While the prompt trial of criminal cases is to be encouraged, we must not allow

justice to fall into Charybdis in seeking to avoid Scylla. In preventing delays, courts should not try cases with such speed as to raise a suspicion that 'wretches hang that jurymen may dine'."

[114] *Asheville Citizen, May 29, 1875.*

[115] *The Salisbury Post, July 14, 1974.*

[116] *Asheville Democrat, February 13, 1890.*

[117]*Ibid*

[118] Wilson's case before the North Carolina Supreme Court is significant. Wilson sought to use his intoxication to show that he was insane. This was rejected by the Supreme Court. Later when murder was divided into two degrees, the courts developed the law that intoxication may be relevant to the issue of whether one had the ability to form the specific intent to kill, an element of premeditation. Intoxication would not be a defense to second degree murder, but could reduce the case from first degree to second degree.

[119] The condemned men believed that their death sentences were excessive. In their minds, they committed only a store breaking. First degree burglary is breaking and entering into a dwelling during the nighttime while it is occupied with intent to commit a felony. The store building had a section which was used as a residence. The North Carolina Supreme Court seemed to have extended the law when the Justices affirmed the conviction of the Emma Burglars.

[120] First Degree Burglary was a capital offense in North Carolina in 1972 when the United States Supreme Court invalidated the death sentence throughout the United States. Although North Carolina's Constitution still provides that the Legislature may impose the death sentence for this crime, the Legislature, when it brought back back capital punishment, did not make First Degree Burglary a capital offense.

[121] Governor Robert B. Glenn in his message to the General Assembly of 1907, continued to press for criminal justice issues. In regard to lynchings, he said: "Mob rule is to be deeply regretted, and if possible should be stopped at all hazards." He proposed that when a mob assembles, the sheriff or other peace officer "be required to order them to disperse, and if they refuse to go, let all remaining be declared an unlawful assembly and liable to arrest. Make such officer after making the proclamation, also take names of all refusing to go and give them to the Solicitor for indictment. Such precautions will in many instances save all trouble. Authorize, also, any peace officer, in cases where it is absolutely necessary, to call out the military and take every needed step to disperse the disorderly crowd, for mob law is a blot on society and injures most seriously the entire State."

[122] (1) John Rinehart was sentenced to death in 1876 in Madison County. After the Supreme Court affirmed the conviction, the Superior Court Judge set his execution date for December 8, 1896. Governor Curtis Brodgen commuted this sentence to life imprisonment. Rinehart died in Central Prison in 1903. (2) Abraham Hensley was sentenced to be executed in

Madison County on October 2, 1885. He did not appeal. Governor Alfred M. Scales commuted this sentence to life imprisonment on September 28, 1885. Hensley died in prison in July 1899. (3) David Bell was sentenced to death in Madison County in 1888. Governor Daniel G. Fowle commuted the sentence to life imprisonment on August 7, 1889, and later, Governor Fowle gave a pardon to Bell. (4) Charlie Stines was sentenced to death in Madison County in February, 1905. Governor Robert B. Glenn issued a warrant for execution to take place on August 7, 1905, but on July 31, 1905, Governor Glenn commuted the sentence to life imprisonment. (5) William Whitson and (6) Thomas Whitson were sentenced to death in Mitchell County in 1892. Governor Elias Carr commuted the sentences of both to a term of years reasoning that the new law creating second degree murder, although was not in effect at the time of the crime, created an offense which would have covered the particular murder. On December 21, 1896, William Whitson was granted a pardon. (7) Riley Pate was sentenced to death in a Yancey County case tried in Mitchell County. In affirming his conviction, Justice Montgomery, who wrote the opinion for the Supreme Court, wrote: "The youth who was murdered was only fifteen years old and his slayer only about eighteen, addicted to the drink habit and drinking at the time he committed the murder. The boy criminal is by judgment of human law condemned to give his life as the penalty of his crime, but the great Spirit alone can know how much of that sin is chargeable to him and how much to those who have influenced his life and how much to those who, wherever they live, might have used agencies to make that life one of a higher order." Governor Daniel L. Russell commuted the sentence to life imprisonment and on March 7, 1899, granted a full pardon for the crime.

[123] *Asheville Citizen*, November 13, 1901.

[124] Haney was convicted of the murder of his kinsman, James Haney in 1872. Both men fought in the Confederate Army, but during the war each switched sides and fought for the Union Army. A dispute between the two men ended on October 30, 1871, when William fired a fatal bullet into James' body. At his trial and on appeal, William Haney contended that North Carolina's Amnesty Act, an act that was passed after the war to end prosecutions of criminal acts which may have occurred during the war, applied and that he could not be prosecuted under its provisions. Prosecutions, even those involving crimes while the offender may have been in uniform and in service during the Civil War, were generally left to the States of the Confederacy. The Supreme Court rejected Haney's argument on appeal, and the case was remanded for the Superior Court to set an execution date. In 1872, the case was calendared on the docket in Superior Court, but when the case was called Haney had escaped from jail and was missing. Superior Court met twice a year in Yancey County. Twice a year William Haney was noted to be absent from court and a *capias* or *alias capias* was issued for him. This apparent search for Haney continued until

April 28, 1890, when the court minutes show the single word "off" reflecting an apparent opinion that further efforts to locate Haney for hanging would not be productive or that there was some sense that he died. Coy Haynie was a prominent citizen of Madison County. Current citizens in Madison and Yancey Counties spell their names both ways. Coy Haynie took an interest in this case once it was mentioned to him, but was never able to determine whatever had happened to William Haney.

[125] Both of the Thomas Boones mentioned in this section had their names spelled "Boon" in court documents and in the Supreme Court file. These men were stated to be descendants of Daniel Boone. All current Yancey County Boones spell their name with an "e" at the end.

[126] Originally three men were indicted for this murder—Thomas Boone, Edward Boone, and a man whose last name was McAllister. McAllister and Edward Boone left the county after the death of John Woodfin. In the decision of the Supreme Court, the justices noted that Thomas Boone acted as an aider and abettor to the actions of Edward Boone. An aider and abettor is equally guilty as the principal. In time, Yancey's prosecutor elected not to prosecute McAllister. Edward Boone was apprehended in South Carolina, and in 1884, stood trial for murder. He was acquitted by the jury. Thomas Boone, the aider and abettor, was the only one ever convicted of this murder.

[127] The governor's proclamation described Thomas Boone, the murderer of John Woodfin as "about 23 years old, about 5 feet 9 inches high, sandy hair, blue eyes, fair complexion, thick lips and long upper teeth., He weighs about 175 pounds." Thomas Boone, the murderer of Samuel Butler was described as: "He has large round light blue eyes; light hair; fair complexion. He is inclined to be stoop shouldered. His left arm is stiff in the elbow and slightly crooked."

[128] Southern Historical Collection, University of North Carolina , Chapel Hill. The author expresses his gratitude to Professor Lloyd Bailey of Duke University Divinity School for his help in locating this document.

[129] Professor Lloyd Bailey contributed to this history of Thomas Boone.

[130] Anderson and his brother-in-law, Edward W. Ray, married daughters of J. W. Bowman, a prominent and wealthy citizen of Bakersville. Ray claimed an entry to mine mica at the Flat Rock Mine which was producing large amounts of mica by men operating under a competing claim. In an effort to dispossess the men working under the competing claim, Ray and Anderson provoked a confrontation where three men were killed. Ray was charged with the murder of John C. Miller and Anderson was charged with the murder of Edward Horton. The separate trials were conducted in Caldwell County and Ray was convicted of manslaughter and Anderson was convicted of murder. The Caldwell County judge found the Caldwell County jail unsafe, that there was a danger the prisoners would escape, and ordered that they be confined in the Buncombe County Jail. Ray appealed his conviction, but withdrew the appeal, and he was serving a sentence.

Anderson's appeal was affirmed and he was awaiting execution. The two men escaped together. Dick Anderson of Bakersville is the grandson of W.A. Anderson. According to Dick Anderson, in a conversation on October 9, 2002, his grandmother, Nora Anderson, was granted conjugal visits with her husband while he was confined in the Buncombe County Jail. Such privileges were not granted to ordinary prisoners, but W. A. Anderson was a man of status. Dick Anderson's father was conceived in the Buncombe County Jail. After the escape, W. A. Anderson fled North Carolina, changed his name to Charles R. Hood and settled in Nogales, Arizona. When Nora Anderson died, her papers consisted of a limited amount of correspondence showing that in 1913, she employed Bakersville attorney Charles E. Greene, and with Greene's help, inquired of the Southern Pacific Railroad Company of Mexico if her husband had an estate, and asked the details of his death. A scant version of the death of W. A. Anderson *alias* Charles R. Hood was provided by an assistant general superintendent of the Southern Pacific Railroad Company of Mexico. Hood entered "the Empalme Club House (Empalme, Mexico) late in the night of the 7th (ostensibly March 7, 1913) very much under the influence of liquor, displaying his gun and threatening to shoot the night clerk. The night clerk considered him sufficiently in earnest to induce him to grab a gun and do a little shooting himself. The result was that he killed Hood instantly, the supposition is. The night clerk was an American and after the killing escaped to the United States gun boat "Colorado" then in the harbor at Guaymas." (The correspondent) stated further that "the sympathies of the community in general were with the night clerk who did the killing." Governor Alfred M. Scales offered a reward of $400.00 for the apprehension of each of these men. The Buncombe County Grand Jury rendered a report that there was a previous effort on the part of the prisoners to make an escape and that the Sheriff was warned that an attempt to escape was imminent and that an effort to bribe a jailer was being made. The *Wilmington Star* reported that there was no mystery in the escape and said it was fully explained by the fact that the prisoners were rich. The *Salisbury Watchman* reported that the officers may have been paid to offer a weak resistance.

[131] Anderson was tried after the enactment of the law dividing murder into degrees, but the applicable law in his case was the older law. While the date of the offense is not made certain in the Supreme Court reports or the original file of the Supreme Court, it appears to have been committed in 1893. Anderson was a fugitive for some time, and that prevented his trial from being held earlier.

[132] *Asheville Democrat*, February 13, 1890.

[133] This interview was conducted by Professor Lloyd Bailey with Mrs. Gladys Ray Coletta on June 18, 1986. Mrs. Coletta lived in downtown Burnsville. The hanging, based on newspaper accounts, was public in all respects. Under the law this was possible at the time if the County Com-

missioners ordered the execution to be public. Interestingly, the volume of commissioners' minutes that would have covered meetings in 1890 is missing from the Yancey County Register of Deeds. The unexplained absence of this volume appears historic. This writer sought to find from the minutes the justification for a public hanging.

Chapter 2: Benefit of Clergy

The same jury that found Daniel Angel guilty of murder also determined that his brother John was guilty of manslaughter. John Angel was given Benefit of Clergy and it was ordered that he be branded on the brawn of his left thumb with the letter "M." He was then discharged. Had the judge not allowed Benefit of Clergy, John Angel would have been sentenced to death even though his conviction was for manslaughter. Benefit of Clergy is an historic relic, but this device represents the first effort to exempt a large category of people from the death sentence. As it developed, Benefit of Clergy exempted literate men, usually first-time offenders, from the death penalty. Even though most states abolished Benefit of Clergy or simply refused to apply it after the Revolutionary War, North Carolina and South Carolina continued its use until the Civil War era.

Benefit of Clergy derived from England during the twelfth century, when religious officials claimed that they should be exempt from secular courts and accountable only to God. All felonies then were punishable by death. The conflict between church and state was resolved when secular courts relinquished the right to put an offending cleric to death. The term "clergy" embodied not only priests but also clerks. By qualifying for Benefit of Clergy, felony offenders were effectively pardoned from civil law authority. The Benefit of Clergy became a means of reducing the number of those sentenced to death. As the law developed along class lines, all men who could read were deemed part of the *clericus* and were entitled to Benefit of Clergy. This concept made sense because most of the population was illiterate, therefore, a literate male must be a part of the *clericus*. As the number of people who were entitled to Benefit of Clergy was increased to include non-clergy, the idea of branding on the brawn of the left thumb began so that offenders could claim the benefit only once. The worst of crimes, such as murder, were not clergiable, but with those exceptions, all felons could seek Benefit of Clergy. If they were branded, they were not entitled to the benefit a second time, and if guilty of a second felony, they were hanged.

In the absence of death penalty for those given the Benefit of Clergy, branding, whipping and fines became appropriate punishments. One who was found guilty of a felony had to demonstrate his entitlement to the Benefit of Clergy by showing that he could read. An illiterate man or a woman could not be a part of the *clericus*. Trial judges had the discretion to determine whether the defendant could read. Most of the time, the judges instructed the defendant to read the same Biblical passage. This allowed the defendant and his lawyer, to fake the ability to read. This was sometimes granted tacit approval of the court since the court favored in certain instances a punishment less severe than death. According to the *Encyclopaedia Britannica* of 1911, the verse ordinarily used by judges to establish qualification for Benefit of Clergy was the first verse of Psalms 11: "In the Lord put I my trust: how say ye to my soul, Flee as a bird to your mountain." This Biblical verse became known as the "neck verse" because it had the effect of saving one from being hanged. Whenever the judge felt that it was appropriate, he could change the verse and the defendant might not qualify for Benefit of Clergy. Throughout history, whenever large numbers of people were being sentenced to death, counter measures were instituted to reduce the numbers of condemned persons.

As another means of controlling the sentences of offenders, the development of the lesser charge of manslaughter would become far more important in modern litigation than the Benefit of Clergy. Those killings acted out in passion, instead of pre-arranged malice, were defined as manslaughter. The North Carolina Supreme Court in 1820 described manslaughter in the following terms:

> Even the highest grade of which the law regards as the effect of human frailty; and it certainly has been, and may be again, committed by men whom neither cupidity nor revenge could prompt to the commission of a base or dishonorable action. The best of men may be overcome by momentary anger, and incited by strong provocation to an act of violence before the judgment has time to parley with itself.[134]

Manslaughter thus became a *clergiable* offense meaning that one who qualified as clergy was branded with an "M" on the brawn of his left thumb, whipped at the post or made to pay a fine. If, however, he had been branded previously then he was not entitled to Benefit of Clergy and was sentenced to be hanged. Moreover, if he failed to qualify by demonstrating that he could read, he was likewise condemned. This was the status of the law at the time of the settlement of the thirteen colonies. The colonies, which were subject to English rule, continued the law as it related to manslaughter and Benefit of Clergy.

North Carolina, while a colony, had at least one occasion to deal with one guilty of larceny where the Benefit of Clergy was allowed.[135] Elijah Stanton was convicted of larceny of less than forty shillings, a clergiable offense under English law. Stanton prayed for the Benefit of Clergy, and it was determined that he was entitled to this benefit. He was ordered to be branded with a "T" (showing conviction of a felony other than manslaughter) and was discharged upon payment of fees. Branding effected a pardon of conduct, and the offender was restored to his normal rights.

After the Revolution, several states ceased recognizing the Benefit of Clergy, but North Carolina continued its use. In 1805, females were determined by the N.C. Conference of Judges to be entitled to Benefit of Clergy. The Conference of Judges was a precursor to the North Carolina Supreme Court. This may well represent the first instance in the state where women were granted a position of equality with men under the law.

In 1816, the North Carolina legislature passed "An Act to Provide a Suitable Punishment for Persons Convicted of Felonies Within Clergy." This law provided that whenever any person is guilty of a felony and is allowed Benefit of Clergy, then instead of burning the convict's hand, the condemned would be punished by one or more public whippings or payment of a moderate pecuniary fine. Public whippings consisted of 39 lashes to the bare back. Courts later ruled that the judge could not require both a public whipping and a fine. The North Carolina Supreme Court expressed its agreement with the statute in 1820:[136]

The former punishment was burning in the hand, a relic of ancient barbarism, of little effect in the way of reforming the culprit or of example to the spectators. It seemed very absurd, too, that a person convicted of petit larceny should suffer whipping on the bare back, when, if the property stolen was over the value of a shilling, the convict could only be burnt in the hand.

The North Carolina court clearly felt that whipping was the more serious punishment, and made it clear that public whipping was too serious a punishment for manslaughter. In 1837, the legislature changed its mind and enacted a statute providing:

> Where any person shall, upon conviction of any felony, be allowed his benefit of clergy, he shall, if it be manslaughter, be marked with an M upon the brawn of the left thumb, and if any other felony, with a T on the same place of the thumb—these marks to be made by the sheriff openly in the court before the judge, before such person be discharged; or it shall be in the power of the court, before which such conviction was had, instead of burning the hand of such convict, to order and adjudge him or her to receive one or more public whippings, or to pay a moderate pecuniary fine, in the discretion of said court under all of the circumstances of the case, the entry of which judgment shall have the same legal effects and consequences, to all intents and purposes, as if the person so convicted had been burned in the hand in presence of the court.

This law was in effect when the aforementioned John Angel was found guilty of manslaughter.

There is an appellate decision from South Carolina interpreting Benefit of Clergy as late as 1850.[137] In 1844, the North Carolina Supreme Court called on it in the case of *State vs. Hardy Carroll*. Carroll, who was convicted of grand larceny, was previously granted Benefit of Clergy. Since he was already granted Benefit of Clergy, he was sentenced to be hanged.

Benefit of Clergy, once an important part of the law, has faded into historic oblivion.

Footnotes

[134] Contemporary law does not regard voluntary manslaughter this lightly. It is punishable as a serious offense involving imprisonment. Voluntary manslaughter occurs in either of two instances. If the killing is during the heat of passion when the passion is aroused based on sufficient provocation, this is manslaughter. If the slayer has a legitimate right of self defense, but acts excessively and takes a life when less violence was a reasonable option, this is manslaughter.

[135] *Colonial Records of North Carolina*, William L. Saunders, editor, Volume Two 1722, Edenton, North Carolina.

[136] *State vs Kearney*, 8N.C.53 (1820)

[137] *State vs. Sutcliffe*, 4 Stroh. 372(S.C.1850)

Chapter 3: Rape

In modern times, the crime of rape is exempted from the list of capital crimes. After North Carolina executed its condemned persons in the state capital, seventy persons were put to death for this offense. Two more persons were executed for rape in combination with another capital crime.[138]

When executions took place in the county seats, lists of those executed were not maintained. Nearly nineteen percent of those executed in North Carolina from 1910 until 1996 were executed for the crime of rape.

In 1972, while Richard Nixon was president, the United States Supreme Court ruled that the death penalty was unconstitutional as it existed in all the states and under the laws of the Congress of the United States.[139] Nixon favored the death penalty, and in a news conference the very night of the Supreme Court ruling he addressed the nation:

> I believe that capital punishment is a good, necessary deterrent for capital crimes of that type as far as the Federal jurisdiction is concerned. Kidnapping and hijacking.[140]

Nixon was among those who were convinced that capital punishment deterred crime. He noted there were fewer cases of kidnapping since kidnapping in some instances carried the death sentence. During the 1930s, killers such as Baby Face Nelson turned from bank robbery to kidnapping as a crime with high dividends and low risks. Kidnapping was a misdemeanor but was made a felony after the Lindbergh baby kidnapping. Congress passed the Lindbergh Law imposing the death penalty when a victim was kidnapped across state lines and held for extortion. President Nixon used this Lindbergh Law as proof that the death penalty deters crime.[141] He pointed out the erstwhile popularity of kidnapping among criminals, and demonstrated how the numbers of kidnapping dwindled after the enactment of this law:

I recall the situation at the time of the Lindbergh kidnapping. I recall that kidnappings were sort of par for the course, then any wealthy family was a possible subject for kidnapping. Kidnapping has been substantially reduced (after the death penalty).[142]

Soon after the Supreme Court invalidated capital punishment laws, states began revising the death penalty laws. North Carolina sought to overcome the constitutional problem that the justices found.

The North Carolina Supreme Court decided that the United States Supreme Court had done no more than to rule the North Carolina procedure invalid. The North Carolina procedure allowed the jury, in its complete discretion, to recommend mercy in a capital trial. Such a recommendation automatically carried imprisonment for life. The North Carolina Supreme Court reinstated the death penalty as it was historically practiced. That is, every person found to be guilty of first-degree murder and rape would be sentenced to death.

The Legislature, acting on this cue, quickly passed legislation reinstituting the death penalty for these two crimes. North Carolina's death row population soared. The Legislature divided rape into two degrees, and exempted those rapes that were determined to be second degree. The United States Supreme Court struck down the North Carolina death penalty law, but validated the law from Georgia. North Carolina then reacted by making only first-degree murder punishable by death, and for the first time in its history, exempted all rapes from capital punishment.

Although rape, theoretically, continued to be a capital crime in North Carolina until the United States Supreme Court ruling in 1972, no one was executed for this crime after 1961. After 1961, the number of people sentenced to death for any crime diminished and jurors regularly recommended mercy. In 1977, the United States Supreme Court ruled that imposing the death penalty for any rape of an adult woman was cruel and unusual punishment and therefore unconstitutional.[143]

People living in the nineteenth and early twentieth century, displaying more prudish attitudes, seldom used the word "rape."

Newspapers used the word "assaulted" when referring to the rape of Alice Thomas. The North Carolina Governor referred to Alice Thomas as the woman who was assaulted. Even the words "sexually assaulted" seldom appeared in public accounts.

Eva Suttles was the victim of Peter Smith and this story will occupy the remaining chapters of this part of the book. A 1905 photograph of Eva Suttles appeared in the newspaper, above the caption, "Eva Suttles, the girl whom Peter Smith was hanged with assaulting."

Because society treated rape as an unspeakable crime, the North Carolina Legislature regarded rape with more seriousness than even murder. In 1909, when the North Carolina Legislature enacted the law providing for electrocution as a method of execution, it further provided that persons who were found guilty of rape should be conveyed forthwith, upon adjournment of the court, to the state prison. Persons guilty of other capital crimes were ordinarily retained in the local jail pending their appeal.[144] This continued as law for years thereafter. The distinction between the place of confinement for those guilty of rape and those guilty of other capital offenses signifies a legislative belief that rapists posed a greater security risk than other capital offenders.

While walking around Marshall, North Carolina when criminal trials are being held, one can commonly hear residents discuss those trials. Lawyers often hear their performance critiqued by citizens sitting on park benches outside the courthouse. Madison County citizens were among the most devout in attending and following criminal proceedings.[145] "Court watching" has been a part of the past in other small towns in North Carolina, but the citizens of Madison County probably have been at the forefront in sheer numbers of people who have attended trials and who then dissect and rework trials during and after the fact.

Madison County was named after the fourth president of the United States. The little town of Marshall is squeezed into a small area in between the French Broad River and a steep mountain. The road into Marshall is so twisting that the mountain has come to be known as "Corkscrew." A small stream passes under the current courthouse, which replaced the original structure back in

1905. Nearby Asheville, the largest town in Western North Carolina, provides some of the lawyers who practice in Marshall. Newcomers to the area are sometimes told that a chain holds a gigantic rock formation from falling from the cliff onto the courthouse. Over the years, a good many people believed this story. Stories are abundant about prior court events, but the most famous story from Madison County is the story of the hanging of Peter Smith. Large numbers of people watched that trial; after the passage of nearly 100 years, people still talk about it.

The Town of Hot Springs was built around a natural wonder, and once thrived as a first-class resort town. Two leading families, Safford and Rambough, owned the springs where other well-to-do persons came to heal themselves in the mineral water gushing from underground at a constant temperature of 100 degrees. Old Daniel Bigelow Safford had worked for Chase Manhattan Bank, and lived many years in Paris. President Andrew Johnson had a daughter-in-law who married into this elite family. They played croquet on plush grassy lawns at a resort hotel named Mountain Park Hotel. The president of Southern Railroad traveled the area in his private car when he came to Hot Springs for vacation. The resort's contemporary marketing literature quotes Governor Daniel G. Fowle:

> In 1860, I was a visitor at this delightful spot. Again it has been my good fortune to rest within the circle of these beautiful mountains, and I can conscientiously declare that nowhere in America have I found a sweeter or more restful spot than these Springs. In location and beauty it is the gem of the mountains; in air, walk, and water it has no superior.

One of the first golf courses in the state was laid out in Hot Springs, and the hotel could boast one of the biggest ballrooms in America. Hot Springs had its golden era during the late nineteenth and early twentieth centuries. It was difficult to reach by road. Its importance dwindled as the automobile became more popular and fewer people traveled the railroad. In the 1970s thieves broke into the Safford and Rambough mausoleum to steal the gold in Daniel Bigelow Safford's false teeth and a few other trinkets of gold; skulls were tossed around the cemetery. Since that low point, Hot Springs has rebounded as a destination for outdoors enthusiasts.

Even in its heyday, many residents of the Hot Springs area lived in abject poverty. Farmers tried growing tomatoes but this did not prove profitable. Tobacco was the only means of earning a living for many people. Madison County offers little relief from the steep mountain slopes, and few good roads. Farming in rural mountain counties in Western North Carolina generally means working a few acres between or on the steep hills.

On November 8, 1904, Theodore Roosevelt won a popular vote majority for president of the United States, while Robert B. Glenn was elected governor of North Carolina. Republican Roosevelt easily won in heavily Republican Madison County, while Democrat Glenn lost the county. On election night Eva Suttles, with a packed suitcase, was found assaulted in the woods. She told her rescuers that Peter Smith raped her and tried to kill her.

Since 1868, North Carolina's Constitution provided that: "The object of punishments being not only to satisfy justice, but also to reform the offender and thus prevent crime, murder, arson, burglary, and rape, and these only, may be punishable with death, if the General Assembly shall so enact."

Rape was an offense that was punishable by death in 1904. In 1905, two people were hanged in North Carolina—one being Peter Smith. Smith was the second person hanged in Madison County and his execution resembled a raucous revival meeting with much singing, preaching, and praying.

Peter Smith's statements were conciliatory, humble, and accusatory. Smith exhibited great passion when he publicly denied his guilt only minutes before being executed. While denying his guilt, he relished the singing of hymns whose wording portrays how an unrepentant sinner is prevented from entering Heaven. At the same time, he pointed his finger at men who were never under suspicion of an unsolved murder. His trial and death made its mark on Governor Glenn, who spoke unfavorably about North Carolina's method of executing criminals.

In November 1904, Eva Suttles was fifteen, and Peter Smith was sixty-two. Eva's father, Alexander, one of twenty-six children, worked hard all his life but had little to show for it. He often left home in search of employment, leaving his brother Garfield,[146] who was only a few years older than Eva, at the house. The family lived in a one-room log cabin on Dogget Mountain in the Spring Creek area. Eva and a younger sister, Ida, who was thirteen, slept in the same bed, and father, Alexander, and son, James, twelve, slept in a second bed.

According to Alexander Suttles' testimony during the trial, the young son of Mason Early stayed with the family on the night of November 8, 1904, and slept with Alexander and James. Eva had few clothes and no closet space; she kept her best Sunday clothing in a satchel on the floor under the head of her bed. There were no neighbors close by. Among the neighboring families was Peter Smith who lived with his wife and a ten-year old son. Smith had lived in this neighborhood for about three years. He was impoverished and lived in a tiny, dirty rented log cabin.

On November 8, 1904, Mayo Reeves and Lyda Wells were hunting in the forests near Sugar Camp Fork of Spring Creek.[147] At around midnight, their dogs began barking and running on the mountain above Jesse Seigle's land, and the two men sat down, waiting for the dogs to return. Reeves testified later that he heard a noise which he thought sounded like a woman hollering, and within two or three minutes, Eva Suttles came running in his direction. Eva said, "Peter Smith is up there trying to kill me!" She wanted the two men to take her home. Since it was too far away, he and Wells took Eva Suttles to Jesse Seigle's home where they all spent the night. The next morning, Reeves followed the road going back to his home. He found a place where people had scuffled and a "heap of blood along the road. It was scattered along up the road from about where the girl come to us back to the ford of the branch."

Eva Suttles testified that earlier that night everyone in her house went to bed, but she felt sick and got out of bed to go outside. As she was returning to her home, Peter Smith grabbed her:

He had his gun in his hand and my Sunday clothes in the satchel and my shoes when he grabbed me. He said he was going to take me to Garfield Suttles. I told him I would die and sink before I would go. I told him I was going to call my father for help. He put his hand over my mouth so I could not speak. He put his arm around my waist and his hand over my mouth and took me to the top of the hill at Sol Gentry's field which was about 200 yards from our house. I carried the satchel with my clothes in it after he put it on my arm and made me carry it. He took me to the top of the hill before he would let me put my clothes on. I was undressed. He said he was going to take me to South Carolina and make a wife out of me for himself. I told him I would not go. At the top of the hill, I put my clothes on. On the way up he put his hand over my mouth all the time except when he knew I was out of hearing from anyone.

Suttles said Peter Smith raped her four times. She described his blows and said he put a knife on her throat telling that he was going to kill her, with the back of the knife blade passing over her skin. Her ordeal lasted for several hours over miles of rough terrain through the laurel. On some of the hills, they could barely walk up the steep slope. Impenetrable thickets of rhododendron choked the hillsides. In 1904, only a wagon trail opened up the outside world to Spring Creek; all other access was by primitive walking trails. Eva Suttles could not have felt more alone with the armed man attacking her in the wilderness.

Dr. T. J. Frisbee examined Eva Suttles on Sunday morning after the Tuesday tragedy. Beginning at her head, Dr. Frisbee found a "right smart sized knot on the left side of her head. It was blue. On her left shoulder blade there was a bruise about the size of a dollar. There was a knot there covering the bruise but not so much as on the head." On Eva's genitalia, Dr. Frisbee found a piece of skin about as big as a grain of corn had been torn off:

> Her external genital organs were wonderfully swollen and inflamed. I found a high state of inflammation in the vulvae. Her hymen was torn and there was a little

abrasion or tear in the lower part where the external labia meet. There were some bruises on the vulva or spots that indicated bruises. I then introduced a speculum and examined the vaginal cavity from the vulva to the womb. There were some little points that kinder showed pus formation or sufforation or something of that kind. The vaginal cavity or tract did not have the resistance that virgins usually have in introducing instruments.

Examining Eva's clothes, Dr. Frisbee found splotches of blood and dried spots that indicated dried semen or seminal discharge. He noted that Eva's genitalia was not only swollen but also covered with blood. Her hair was matted.

Her condition indicated to me that some violence had been done to her. With her own free will and consent she could have had sexual intercourse with a man without being injured much. I am sure the injuries were very painful. She appeared to suffer a great deal of pain on account of her swollen genitals. I am sure she suffered an immense amount of pain.

Further, Dr. Frisbee noticed a red mark three or three-and-one-half inches long around her neck. It was scarlet red but there was no abrasion. "She told me the prisoner had tried to cut her throat but had the back of the knife turned to the throat." Statements by Dr. Frisbee were compelling.

During his trial, Peter Smith testified that on the night of November 8, 1904, he was at his home in bed. His wife was absent that evening to give assistance to another family. Smith's son, a ten-year old boy, was also at home in bed asleep. Smith heard someone holler and step onto his porch. Smith got up and lit the lamp and opened the door to find a strange man there. He was young, thin and wore stripped [*sic*] clothes. The man said he lived in Haywood County, but Smith never learned his name. He did not answer when Smith asked who he was, but kept talking. He wanted Smith to go over the top of the mountain to Sandy Mush with him. Old man Smith told him he would not go. But the younger man begged. He said Smith could make $3.00 in less than a night's work. He kept begging Smith to go. At last Smith agreed and, first locking his son inside his home, he showed the man the way. They found Eva Suttles, he said, sitting on a log near the road. Smith reported that since there were two of them they could hunt the way themselves, but Eva and this strange man kept begging for his assistance. At last Smith agreed and the company went down the road to the main Spring Creek road and then up that road to Seigle's mill and then turned to the left. They went above Jesse Seigle's and Smith could not see and got hurt. He then demanded one half his pay, but the young stranger started cursing him and called Smith a God damned old son of a bitch. The young man said Smith could not get paid until Smith had gone as far as he had agreed, and he cursed Smith again. Smith, holding Eva's satchel in his right hand, struck the young man with the gun held in his left hand. Eva and the strange man ran off down the road.

      C. L. Brittain took a photograph of Eva Suttles during her testimony in the courtroom.[149] This same photographer took a photograph of the Peter Smith hanging. Both photographs appeared in the *Madison County Record* of October 13, 1905. The caption for the hanging photograph said: "Peter Smith who was hanged here October 2, making his last statement to the world." The Brittain negative of the Peter Smith hanging is now a part of the Ewart Ball Photograph Collection at the University of North Carolina at Asheville. The location of the negative of Eva Suttles is unknown and is assumed long lost. Eva's picture shows her wearing a hat. Women wore hats whenever they were dressed well. During her travails with Peter Smith, she had all her best clothes except for her hat, which was left in her little cabin. A young woman freely planning to elope with a man surely would have included her hat.

Footnotes

[138] North Carolina Department of Correction, lists of persons executed in North Carolina.
[139] *Furman vs. Georgia*, 408 U. S. 238 (1972)

[140] *New York Times*, June 16, 1994.

[141] Other factors such as improved investigative and surveillance techniques made it difficult for kidnappers to receive the ransom money. If they did receive it, it was difficult to spend it without detection. These factors, too, probably helped reduce the popularity of kidnapping. President Nixon's thoughts were not dissimilar to words of the North Carolina Legislature which in 1867, thought that capital punishment would deter horse stealing: "*An Act for the Better Suppression of the Crime of Stealing Horses and Mules.* Whereas, the crime of stealing horses and mules hath of late, notwithstanding the punishment provided by law, become much more common than formerly, to the great loss of many persons, and the injury of public morals; for remedy whereof, *it is enacted* That every person who shall steal any horse or mule, and shall be thereof convicted according to due course of law, shall suffer death." Laws 1867 Chapter LXII.

[142] *New York Times, Ibid.*

[143] The United States Supreme Court opinion which ended capital punishment was composed of various separate opinions and in the end a majority was reached when two concurring justices determined that the infrequency with which the death penalty was imposed was the critical factor. In a dissent, Chief Justice Burger wrote "This factor (infrequency of use of death penalty) is taken not as evidence of society's abhorrence of capital punishment . . . but as the earmark of a deteriorated system of sentencing."

[143] *Coker vs. Georgia*, 433 U. S. 584 (1977)

[144] Public Laws of North Carolina, Session 1909, Chapter 443.

[145] In 1982, Guilford County Superior Court Judge Douglas Albright was assigned to hold court in Madison County. During an extended recess of court, Judge Albright took great pleasure in sitting on one of the benches on the main street in front of the courthouse. He visited with some of the regulars who frequently sat there. Aware of the mystique which Madison County held in North Carolina, Judge Albright vowed he would not forget this experience.

[146] Garfield Suttles was Eva's uncle although he was only a few years older than Eva. Garfield will be mentioned throughout this chapter.

[147] Statements about the event are taken from the case on appeal which is a part of the Supreme Court's original files in the State Archives. As previously discussed, appealing attorneys prepared a narrative of the evidence. This narrative was then presented to the Solicitor for approval. The narrative is the only form of the testimony in existence. In that it eliminates the question and answer format, it does not always accurately reflect the actual proceedings of the trial.

[148] This narrative is from the testimony of Eva Suttles in the narrative case on appeal.

[149] That the photograph is a courtroom scene cannot be proved, but the author thinks this is the the the most likely site.

Chapter 4: She Said—He Said

In the late 1970s, the author, then Assistant District Attorney for Madison County[150] asked Sheriff E.Y. Ponder to help him locate the grave of Peter Smith. We rode in the old cruiser, dinged and dented from years of rough work. Riding with Ponder ranged from memorable to unforgettable. He ranged across the road, slow down, speed up, waving to everyone, pointing out crime scenes.

The Sheriff took me to the little cemetery behind the Spring Creek Fire Department. Despite the possibility that Smith was buried anonymously or in an unmarked grave, I nevertheless took my camera. Smith was buried in isolation at the extreme boundary of the cemetery near a fence, his grave blazoned with a well-marked and sculpted stone and plastic flowers. Neither Smith nor the Suttles family had much money; they both lived in rental property. Yet, both sides retained an attorney during the trial. Lawyers sometimes work high profile cases for recognition. In contrast, Alexander Suttles was buried years later in a church cemetery with no headstone. Standing over the grave of Peter Smith, I realized that more than seventy years had passed since Smith was hanged, yet the recent floral display showed someone still remembered.

Peter Smith was once accused of raping Mary Carver. This case never resulted in an indictment by the grand jury. Smith was presented by the Madison County Grand Jury with murder. A presentment is an initiative by the grand jury itself and is not a formal legal accusation since the District Attorney did not sign the indictment. In Smith's case, after the grand jury presented him for murder, District Attorney J. M. Gudger submitted a bill of indictment but it was not returned a true bill. Smith was indicted for and convicted of the misdemeanor offense of carrying a concealed weapon while off his own premises. Ultimately, he was hanged for rape.

Proving rape is always difficult. It requires presenting embarrassing and painful details, and the victim is often further victimized. When Eva Suttles testified, only men served as jurors, judges, law enforcement officers or attorneys. Men made up most of the courtroom audience. During her testimony, Eva Suttles was asked point blank whether she and her uncle Garfield slept together. She said no. Garfield was a young man in his early 20s and was hired by Eva's father, Alexander, to stay with the family when Alexander went to work. Eva was asked whether she had had a bastard child. She said no again.[151] As a final indignity, Eva Suttles' photograph appeared in the local newspaper when the trial was over.

Courtroom attorneys attempt to make the victim look culpable for the crime, a crime generally committed in secrecy where only the victim and accused person knew what happened. With this strategy in mind, Smith's defense lawyer attacked Eva Suttles.

The law itself set forth an exaggerated rule. Appellate court decisions of that period were often written about the victim's *failure to make outcry.* Cases sometimes were decided based on how strenuously victims resisted, and the courts expected the victims to fight for their purity. Failure to do so gave the defense even more cause to hammer at the credibility of the victim.

During her testimony, Eva Suttles said Peter Smith always displayed his gun during the commission of the crime. At various times he said he was going to kill her. He told her that he and another man raped and murdered his stepdaughter. He told Eva that even after he killed her, he was going to return to her body and continue to use her body until it rotted. According to Eva, Smith said that he was going to take her younger sister after he killed Eva and that he was going to rape and kill her as well. Peter Smith never let her forget she was in the utmost danger.[152]

Eva's credibility was an issue from the beginning, especially when she said that Smith was waiting outside her cabin with her satchel and forced her to accompany him thereafter. For him to have possession of that satchel, he would have had to enter into her little one-room house while others slept there. The testimony at the trial showed that he had been inside the Suttles' house and would have known where Eva kept her Sunday clothes. But the night was dark with little moon. It would have been risky for Peter Smith to enter and search in darkness for a satchel under the bed. Beyond this fact, it is difficult to understand that Peter Smith would have known that Eva was going to leave the house that night. It seems a strange coincidence that she felt sick and had to go outside. If she had not gone outside, would Peter Smith have been so bold as to enter the cabin and force her to accompany him while her father and siblings were sleeping nearby?

Eva's story was difficult to believe in its entirety, and some case could be made that Eva initially accompanied Peter Smith by previous arrangement. Some witnesses at the trial described Smith as having a reputation for his involvement with women, and the undercurrent of some of the testimony indicates that there were jokes among Garfield Suttles and others about Peter and Eva going to South Carolina.

Smith testified that he "fastened" his ten-year-old son alone in his log cabin when he made the decision to accompany the stranger to the top of the mountain. One has to wonder about the propriety of doing this and what manner of man would do so.

This question becomes more perplexing when one realizes that on the night Hannah Plemmons (Smith's stepdaughter) was first missing, Peter Smith's wife was not at home, and Smith, on that night, locked his little son in the home.

Early in the morning on November 9, 1904, Alexander Suttles woke up before dawn. His youngest daughter Ida was upset because her sister Eva was gone. Alexander Suttles discovered Eva's Sunday clothes and shoes were missing (but not her hat) and went looking for her. Later that morning, he found Eva at the Seigles' residence, and after hearing her version of the events of the preceding night, he looked for her satchel. Later, he found the satchel where Peter Smith discarded it. Immediately, Alexander Suttles took his daughter to Justice of the Peace H.S. Davis, but Justice Davis had no blank warrant forms and the man and daughter then went to Justice of the Peace, J. F. Askew, who had Eva Suttles sworn to tell the truth. Justice Askew then issued a warrant charging Peter Smith with rape. Alexander Suttles and his daughter wasted no time in their efforts to have Peter Smith brought to justice. The warrant was placed in the hands of Deputy Sheriff James Baker for service. The warrant was served by Constable J. H. Price, who was the officer in charge of the five-man posse.

Even though Peter Smith had "fastened" his ten-year-old son alone in his cabin, Smith did not return home that night or the next morning. Smith testified that after his confrontation with Eva Suttle's traveling companion, he discarded her satchel. Since his feet were sore, instead of returning home, he went looking for corn for his milling operation. In any event, the posse looking for Peter Smith found him on Saturday, November 12, 1904, and arrested him. Smith was found with J. P. Plemmons, who later testified that Peter Smith had sent for him. Smith went to the house of Plemmons' father, and after the younger Plemmons arrived, Smith inquired about what the posse was doing to catch him. During the afternoon, as the two men talked, the posse arrived. Plemmons described the gun that Smith carried as a "little short rifle gun." Peter Smith had hidden in the woods from Tuesday night until that Saturday afternoon.

One of the five posse members, L. S. Plemmons, helped arrest Peter Smith, and stayed with him until he was delivered to the Madison County jail. When Smith was arrested, he was carrying both a gun and a knife. Plemmons heard Smith say:

> If I ever get out of this here scrape, I never allow to be
> guilty of being back in jail again. When I left the jail
> before I never aimed to be back in jail again, and if I
> ever get out of this scrape I never intend to be back in
> jail again. I was in jail about three years ago accused
> of killing that girl and when I left jail I never aimed to
> be back there any more.[153]

Plemmons testified to this conversation during the trial and the judge allowed the jury to hear it over defense objection. The jury that convicted Peter Smith of rape also knew of the death of Hannah Plemmons. They heard, through Eva Suttles, that Smith confessed about murdering a girl and they heard through the witness L. S. Plemmons that he was jailed for her murder. Later, the North Carolina Supreme Court ruled this evidence to be admissible. After his conviction for rape, it was contended that the jury really convicted Peter Smith because they believed that he murdered Hannah Plemmons.

After his arrest, the posse delivered Smith to the Friezland School for a hearing before the Justice of the Peace. The hearing was hastily convened for 1:00 p.m. on Sunday, November 13, 1904. A large crowd gathered as word spread through the community that he was arrested. Witnesses, including L. S. Plemmons and Jasper Ebbs later testified that there was talk of lynching Peter Smith. Madison County had no history of lynching, and on this occasion Jasper Ebbs appears to have been instrumental in dissuading the group not to start now. Ebbs testified, "Men come to me and said I would lose friends if I took the prisoner's part. Some young men said they would like to shoot or lynch the prisoner. I called them off and told them to be quiet and there was nothing more of it. There was no attempt made to harm the prisoner."

Jasper Ebbs was prominent in the Democratic Party and served on the school board. Sheriff E.Y. Ponder said that "Jasper Ebbs was the father of modern education in Madison County." Ebbs rode circuit throughout Madison County organizing new schools. Ebbs' son, Plato, later became Mayor of Hot Springs. Jasper Ebbs' brother was I. N. Ebbs, a Republican lawyer from Hot Springs. During Peter Smith's trial, I. N. Ebbs called Jasper Ebbs as a witness for defendant to testify about the events at Friezland School.

At the probable cause hearing at Friezland School, Jasper Ebbs made himself available and agreed to represent Peter Smith. He was not paid.[154] When Lawyer I.N. Ebbs called his brother, Jasper, as a witness, he wanted to hear about the restive nature of the crowd. After Jasper's statement, the prosecutor cross-examined and established damaging evidence against Peter Smith.

During cross-examination, Solicitor Mark W. Brown asked Jasper Ebbs what Peter Smith had said to him during his representation of the defendant. I. N. Ebbs objected, asserting that what Smith said was in the nature of a client speaking to his attorney and in such a case, the attorney must keep it confidential. The judge heard from the witness Jasper Ebbs at length as to the circumstances of the statement. Jasper Ebbs testified that he managed the case for Peter Smith to make sure that the trial was conducted properly. As an inducement for Peter Smith to speak, Ebbs told Smith that he could not properly manage the case or propound questions to the witnesses if he did not know what the defendant's version was. For a while the judge left his ruling open, but later required Jasper Ebbs to answer the question. Thereafter, the witness who made himself available to help the defendant helped the state.

Ebbs testified, "The prisoner told me that a man come to his house that night. He did not state what time of night it was. He said he asked him to take this girl to Chestnut Gap somewhere between Spring Creek and Sandy Mush and agreed to pay him $1.00 for it. He said he consented to the contract and went over somewhere toward Suttles' house or near his house and there met the girl and she had her satchel and everything ready and he carried her on his back till he got to John's Branch. He said the man was sitting there by the road." At this point, according to Ebbs, Peter Smith wanted to be paid and he and this strange man quarreled. Smith left their company after a violent altercation. Ebbs' testimony differs from Peter Smith's own testimony in that Smith testified that he and this strange man went together to meet Eva Suttles. The law allows prior inconsistent statements made by witnesses because it tends to reflect on the credibility of the witness.

Lawyer Ebbs raised an issue on appeal to the North Carolina Supreme Court about his brother being required to divulge a confidential communication at trial. The Supreme Court noted that Jasper Ebbs was not a lawyer and the defendant could not assert that his communication was privileged.

J.F. Askew's record of the probable cause hearing states the following:

> State of North Carolina and Eva Suttles against Peter Smith. The defendant was produced in Court and the following proceedings had the case was called up and the Defendant plead not guilty and after examining five witnesses for the State[155] the Counsel for the State rested and then the counsel for the defendant rested and it was adjudged that the Defendant was guilty and that he be bound over to the next term of the Superior Court for Madison County.[156]

Madison County had a two-week term of Superior Court beginning February 27, 1905. Peter Smith was indicted for rape and the Judge, Fred Moore, ordered jurors to report on Saturday March 4, 1905. The court excused twenty-five jurors for cause, a large number indicating a prejudice against the defendant. Citizens may be excused for cause whenever they cannot apply the law fairly to the facts of the case. At that time in the development of our law, a juror could be excused simply by asserting that the juror did not believe in capital punishment. Considering what some witnesses said about the defendant's reputation and considering the notoriety of the case, most people who were excused for the case likely had already formed a negative opinion of the defendant. In addition to those excused for cause, the defendant exercised preemptory challenges to fourteen other jurors. Selection of the jury was completed on that Saturday, but even by modern standards a large number of jurors had been excused.

The trial began Monday March 6, 1905. By the following Wednesday, the jury found defendant Peter Smith guilty of rape.

Later, when the Governor was considering a commutation, a prominent Madison County citizen wrote the governor a letter reflecting the feelings of a good many people at that time. Thomas N. James was a banker at the Madison County Bank in Marshall and a member of the Democrat Party State Executive Committee. On August 24, 1905, he wrote Governor Glenn:

> I am prompted by purely a human failing to address you on a subject which in connection with similar appeals from over the state doubtless are a source of considerable worry to you and I wish we had a pardoning board to relieve you of this worry and responsibility. Old man Peter Smith of this county was tried and convicted here some time ago of the crime of rape and as you are aware now sentenced to be hanged Sept. 14. I dislike to put myself in the attitude of defending the perpetrator of such a crime but there are some mitigating circumstances. He is a man now I believe 65 years old and his stooping position and tottering walk as well as his wrinkled face makes him

look fully that or more. My investigation of him through the best citizens of his community reveals the fact that his abnormal passions has been practically his one fault in life. Good citizens tell me that he is regarded as truthful, honest and always ready to accommodate any neighbor.

Of course his proportion of intelligence would not permit to his amounting to anything of account in life. I heard practically all the evidence in his case and held the lamp by which his sentence was pronounced and looked him in the eye at the time and I believe he is guilty of going further than the girl desired, but I don't believe that there is a person who heard all the evidence but what believes that the girl left her home with him voluntarily and had he been more gentle, the crime of which they were both guilty would never have been revealed. His roughness and injuries to her made it necessary for her to expose herself to a physician, then her humiliation sought revenge.

The greatest trouble Peter was up against all the time was that people suspected him of having assaulted (and then killed) a girl once before. This crime was committed without an eye witness and as Peter had a bad reputation for women he was the one charged however he was released by the Grand Jury because there was not a scintilla of evidence to convict him, yet in his last trial and since the feeling has existed that he was perhaps guilty of the first crime and escaped punishment. Now he may not be as guilty of the last crime as charged but let him suffer anyhow.

In other words, he was without friends and without money.

Now nature teaches us that Old Peter Smith would have to suffer the pangs of death soon by the same divine hand that gave him life. That if you could see yourself justified in doing so, that he might be confined in the state penitentiary at hard labor for the remainder of his life, that society would be rid of his obnoxiousness, our county's reputation would not be besmudged by his hanging, the ends of justice would be fully met and he would have the remaining few years of his life in which to prepare his soul to meet its creator in peace. Would be glad to hear from you and if you will entertain it, I think I can get strong petition in his behalf now signed by jury and perhaps court officers.[157]

In 1904, a North Carolina statute made it illegal for a man to abduct a girl under fourteen years of age. Even if a girl under 14 consented to leaving with the abductor, her age would make the consent immaterial and the male would be committing a crime. This continued to be North Carolina's law until 1996. Since Eva was fifteen, this law gave no protection.

Presently, North Carolina law prohibits the abduction or inducement to leave home of a child who is at least four years younger than the abductor. The statute itself does not define 'child' but in conjunction with other laws suggests protection of any child up to the age of 18. Moreover, North Carolina's current statutory rape statutes prohibit intercourse with any child who is 15 even when the child may have consented. Modern attitudes require a longer period for the protection of children. Eva Suttles choosing to go with Peter Smith that day does not preclude the possibility of rape.

Footnotes

[150] The writer.

[151] The history of rape trials is that questions of this type were regularly asked. Many generations later, states, including North Carolina, passed statutes called "Rape Shield Statutes" which prohibit questions about the victim's past sexual conduct that are not relevant to the particular charge.

[152] This writer recalls from his experience as a prosecutor the case of Daniel Brian Lee who kidnapped a female victim in Boone on September 24, 1989. He raped the victim and forced her into sex acts against her will. Lee told the victim that he earlier kidnapped, raped and murdered another woman, and described where he left the dead woman's body. This resourceful woman found an opportunity to escape, and led law enforcement to the earlier victim's destroyed and abused body.

[153] The narrative form of the transcript sometimes creates repetitions reflecting that the attorney asked the same question more than once.

[154] The sixth amendment to the United States Constitution gives accused persons the right to be represented by an attorney at all critical stages of the trial process. In 1904, courts had not yet defined this proposition, and there was no legal concern whether Smith was represented by an attorney at a probable cause hearing.

[155] The witnesses who testified for the State at the probable cause hearing were Eva Suttles, Dr. T. J. Frisbee, Mayo Reeves, Lyda Wells, and Alexander Suttles.

[156] Criminal actions are brought in the name of the sovereign against the individual. It was erroneous to name Eva Suttles in the caption of the case since her status is that of a witness and not a party. Prosecutors have historically encountered witnesses who are victims who sometimes assert that they are the real party and that the prosecutor serves as the attorney representing that party. The prosecutor's true role is that of representing the sovereign. The justice's finding that the defendant was guilty was also erroneous in that a justice of the peace had no jurisdiction to try a felony. His finding was actually a finding that probable cause existed.

[157] Loose papers, Governor Robert Glenn, N.C. Archives

Chapter 5: Reason For Doubt

The jury that found Peter Smith guilty of rape expressly stated that it did not find that Smith had "carried" Eva Suttles from her residence. The court minutes show: "The jury through their foreman say that they find that the prisoner did not *carry* the prosecuting witness Eva Suttles away from her home by force and that they therefore recommend the prisoner to the mercy of the court." They simply didn't believe that Smith could have carried Suttles for two miles. Decades later, North Carolina law would permit the jury to recommend mercy, and if the jury did so, the convicted person would be sentenced to life imprisonment instead of death. In Peter Smith's trial such a recommendation meant nothing.

Bill Moore hailed from Joe, North Carolina, a tiny community that lost its post office. Moore became chairman of the Democrat Party in Madison County and was fond of saying that Madison County ought to build a monument to Peter Smith for having hanged an innocent man. Moore told his good friend E. Y. Ponder that he did not believe in the death penalty because he knew that at least one innocent man, Peter Smith, was wrongfully executed. On occasion, Bill Moore implored the author to investigate the circumstances of the Peter Smith hanging and find a means of clearing his name. Like the jury, Moore also insisted that Peter Smith could not have "carried" Eva Suttles for the distance of over two miles.

Charles B. Mashburn, Jr. was a prominent attorney who lived and practiced law in Marshall, North Carolina. Mashburn's father, who died when Junior was a small child, appeared in the Peter Smith trial as private prosecutor. North Carolina recognized private prosecutors. These are attorneys who were hired privately and who appear with the State's attorney as prosecutor. The extent to which they participate is left to the discretion of the District Attorney. In Peter Smith's trial, this lawyer was allowed by District Attorney Mark Brown to take an active role. Lawyer Mashburn's final argument to the jury lasted one hour and one minute. In May, 1991, the Madison County District Attorney asked Mashburn about his father's involvement in Smith's case. Mashburn said that his mother told him that his father always doubted Peter Smith's guilt. Mr. Mashburn thought there was a great conflict between Peter Smith's and Eva Suttles' statements. Mashburn did not think Peter Smith could have "carried" this victim for over two miles in that terrain.

Rachael Gillespie was elderly by the time the author knew her. Mrs. Gillespie lived her entire life in the Spring Creek area. Many mountain people can trace their ancestry back generations, and often they continue to live on the same small piece of ground that their forebears did. They are familiar with events from long ago because they have heard the stories when they were young and they have passed those stories on as they have grown older. She did not think it possible that Peter Smith could have "carried" the victim for over two miles.

Even if he did not win the case, Smith's defense lawyer was able to convince many people in the community of Smith's innocence; their belief, in turn, swayed others. So, why was the jury not convinced?

During her testimony, Eva Suttles said Peter Smith "carried me in some way from the home towards the field."[158] She later testified she went with Peter Smith for some distance, and only one time used this phrase. Passing along the trail, there were three houses that Smith and Eva Suttles would have passed—first Peter Smith's house, then the McCrays' and finally the residence of the Fleming family. Past these houses, the two would have traveled in the fields near the Seigle house. Suttles said that after they passed the Fleming house that Smith "carried in some way." On other occasions when Eva Suttles testified, she used the words, "he took me," "he dragged me," and "we went." She made it clear that Smith had a gun and that she feared him.

Asked if he was familiar with the terrain where the event occurred, Dr. Frisbee said he was; that a trail went from Eva's house to the Gentry house. To the next question, "Do you think that a man could have carried Eva that distance?" Dr. Frisbee answered, "I don't think a man could take a woman that route against her will unless she went through fear." Frisbee, however, seemed assured that Suttles' injuries were consistent with rape.

During his testimony, Jasper Ebbs testified that Peter Smith admitted that he had gone toward the Suttles' house, met Eva Suttles, and *carried* her on his back till he got to John's Branch.

C. L. Brittain photographed the hanging of Peter Smith, showing clearly, among others, Jesse James Bailey. Bailey became legendary in the area by serving both as Sheriff of Madison County and then as Sheriff of Buncombe County. Bailey told the author that "lots of people in Madison County did not think that Peter Smith was guilty." All, perhaps, but the jury.

Shortly before Peter Smith was executed, his lawyer, I. N. Ebbs, wrote the Governor of North Carolina. The action was in response to an unusual procedure which was requested by the Governor to determine whether Eva Suttles still insisted on her version of the events. The Governor had requested that Eva Suttles be questioned by the Judge, Solicitor and Defense Attorney. Lawyer Ebbs wrote that the Solicitor had "carried" Eva Suttles to Asheville, and the meeting had already occurred in his absence. It is ironic that the lawyer would use this word since it was used so often to argue against the notion that Peter Smith was guilty. Of course, Peter Smith could not have carried this teenager over that terrain for as long a distance as two miles. The word "carry" was used in the legal definition of kidnapping. One could be found guilty of kidnapping if one carried another without consent from one place to another, but the law does not require that one literally pick up the body of the other person. This definition, perhaps not emphasized at the trial, lies at the heart of many citizens' doubts about Smith's ability to "carry" his victim.

Many supporters thought the jury convicted Peter Smith of raping Eva Suttles because they thought he murdered Hannah Plemmons. The death of Hannah Plemmons is worthy of discussion here.

North Carolina Highway 207 travels south from Hot Springs through Spring Creek toward Trust. One traveling south will encounter the Meadowfork Road turning right or to the west. Some distance along this road on the left is an old but stately two-story frame house that stands out among the smaller and more humble homes dotting this countryside. Here lived Isaac Newton Ebbs. Prior to being admitted to the practice of law in 1896, I.N.

Ebbs was a surveyor and often took his fees in land. Ebbs was able to put together a 1,000 acre tract of land, much of it rich and valuable bottomland. Ebbs' granddaughter lives now in the old house. Ebbs was Peter Smith's attorney during Smith's rape trial.

Past the Ebbs' residence, and through the Joe community, one reaches a dilapidated old log cabin. In June of 1991, Tony Plemmons had lived there 55 of his 87 years. Plemmons lived all his life in this remote, isolated and rural section of Madison County. His father once left Madison County and lived in Arkansas but, as with many people who move away from Madison and other mountain counties, he returned home.

Standing in a field east of his old cabin in June 1991, Tony Plemmons points to a grassy area amongst trees on a hill across the road, near the point where Peter Smith lived ninety years earlier. Henry Frisbee owned the land and lived in that area as well. Hannah Plemmons was a teenager with a bad reputation. According to Tony Plemmons, she was pregnant when she died. Any investigation into a homicide of a pregnant young teenager will concentrate on the pregnancy as a possible motive. Men often killed to spare their reputation and the drain on their financial security when illegitimate children are expected. In Hannah's case, her head was cut off, making the murder an especially passionate and vengeful act. Only her head was found.

Strangers rarely passed through this neighborhood in 1901, and if one did so, the people of the community would have noticed the stranger. Hannah, it can fairly be said, was killed by someone who knew her and who lived in the community. Medical science in that year would not have progressed to the point where cause of death could be determined when only the head was found and not the rest of the body.

Peter Smith was then 58 years old. Court records do not show the exact date of Hannah's death. Solicitor James M. Gudger, Jr., who served Madison County in 1902, submitted a bill of indictment for the grand jury to consider on February 24, 1902. Solicitor Gudger, in his indictment, charged that the murder took place on February 24, 1902, which was the date of the grand jury session. This is a clear error and the researcher must look elsewhere for the date of death of Hannah Plemmons. Tony Plemmons states that she was missing for a period without explanation when her head was discovered by Josiah Suttles. The *Asheville Gazette News*, quoting Peter Smith, reported that Hannah had been missing a full month when her head was found. Justice of the Peace James D. Balding issued a warrant for the arrest of Peter Smith on November 8, 1901. At the Eva Suttles rape trial, Peter Smith testified that he was arrested for the murder on November 14, 1901.

Feelings were running high against Peter Smith in Meadowfork in the fall of 1901, and he was probably arrested for murder soon after the warrant was issued on November 8. T.M. Keener was selected by the Justice of the Peace to make the arrest, but his return of the process does not show the date of arrest. The date of discovery of Hannah's head would probably coincide with the date of the warrant being issued—November 8—and the date of Peter Smith's arrest could have been any day between November 8 and November 14.

If Hannah was missing for 30 days prior to the discovery of her head, and if her head was discovered on November 8, 1901, then she would have been missing since October 7, 1901. This is precisely the date that James Allison used in procuring the warrant for arrest. James Allison—whom Peter Smith later labeled as a witness, who could testify that Henry and Columbus Frisbee murdered Hannah Plemmons—produced the affidavit securing the warrant for the arrest of Peter Smith. His affidavit is as a follows:

> State of North Carolina, County of Madison. James Allison personally appeared before me a Justice of the Peace of Madison County and after being duly sworn deposes and says that on or about the 7 day of October, 1901, one Peter Smith did to the best of said plaintiff's belief willfully and maliciously murder and kill and conceal Hannah Plemmons contrary to law in such cases and against the peace and dignity of the State.

This affidavit was signed by James Allison and Justice of the Peace James D. Balding. The head of Hannah Plemmons was found between Peter Smith's residence and the place where he was cutting wood during that time. Her body and her clothes were not discovered. Peter Smith disputed the allegation. On the date

On her way to Raleigh.
—(Citizen Photo).

Thomas Family

Left—Major E. P. Robinson, of North Wilkesboro; center—General Metts; below—Col. D. W. Adams, City Engineer of Spruce Pine, with Capt. C. E. Earle, Jr., of Morganton; Right—Capt. Kenneth Caldwell, of Company E, 120th Infantry, Concord.
—(Citizen Photo).

Second Bunch Of Negro Laborers Return

Negroes arriving in Spruce Pine over C. C. & O., Tuesday afternoon.
—(Citizen Photo).

Mr. and Mrs. Mack Thomas, and three sons, with Hubert Holloway, of The Citizen, on the left, and Robin King, of The Associated Press, on the right.
—(Citizen Photo)

No. 1—In the trenches overlooking the town. No. 2—Cavalry guarding approach to the depot as negroes arrive on C. C. & O. Railroad. No. 3—Concord Company making Camp. No. 4—Asheville boys give The Citizen the "once over."
—(Citizen Photo).

On 143rd Anniversary   **Reading The Citizen**

On The Nature Of Politics

By CALVIN COOLIDGE,

President of the United States

Politics is not an end, but a means. It is not a product, but a process. It is the art of government. Like other values it has its counterfeits. So much emphasis has been put upon the false that the significance of the true has been obscured and politics has come to convey the meaning of crafty and cunning selfishness, instead of candid and sincere service. The Greek derivation shows the nobler purpose. Politics means city-rearing, statecraft. And when we remember that city also means civilization, the spurious present ment, mean and sordid, drops away from the real figure of the politician, dignified and honorable, a minister to civilization, author and finisher of government, is revealed in its true and dignified proportions.

There is always something about genius that is indefinable, mysterious, perhaps to its possessor most of all. It has been the product of rude surroundings no less than of the most cultured environment.

here held in reprehensive scorn and professional office seeking in contempt. Every native born American, however, is potentially a President, and it must always be remembered that the obligation to serve the State is forever binding upon all, although office is the gift of the people.

**Political Life
Does Not Pay**

Of course these considerations relate not to appointive places like the Judiciary, Commissionerships, clerical positions and like places, but to the more important elective offices. Another reason why political life of this nature is not chosen as a career is that it does not pay. Nearly all offices of this class are held at a financial sacrifice, not merely that the holder could earn more at some other occupation, but that the salary of the office does not maintain the holder of the office. It is but recently that Parliament has paid a salary to its members. In years

In The 'Chow Line'

Ready for a scrap with the Mess Sergeant's offerings.

Tablet commemorating the visit made by Revolutionary soldiers to Spruce Pine, on September 28, 1780, on their way to Kings Mountain. Asheville and Morganton troops arrived in the town on September 28, 1923. Just 143 years after and at about the same hour in the evening.

Concord boys get the news from The Citizen, of course. "It gets there first."

Page 3 of the *Asheville Citizen* of October 5, 1923 entitled "People and Places in Spruce Pine."

Mitchell County. {Grassy Creek} Township.

STATE OF NORTH CAROLINA,

Before

Frank A. Carr,

Justice of the Peace.

Stokes McKinney _against_ Pete Biddix & Jap Green &
Fogett Ward, Dot Buchanan, John Pittman,
Logan Ward, P. E. Boelton, Mott McNeel,
C. H. S. Taffore Motter Buchanan, Andrew Green
Lane Buchanan, Roby Buchanan

On the 9ᵗ day of _October_ 1922, upon the oath of
L. H. Wright, setting forth that _the above named defendant_
did on or about the 26ᵗ day of _October_ 19.23
Commit crime as shown in the certified copy of warrant attached

contrary to the form of the Statute in such cases made and provided, und against the peace and dignity of the State.

A Warrant of arrest was issued by _J. J. Bennett, J. P._ an acting Justice of the Peace of _Grassy Creek_ Township, State and County aforesaid, against said defendant..and delivered on the _9ᵗ_ day of _October_ 1923.., to _R. B. Forbes_ _Sheriff_ a constable to be served _____ warrant returned the _12ᵗ_ day of _October_ 1923..

The following witnesses were sworn and examined on behalf of the State:
and the evidence adduced was in substance as follows:

Tᵗ Buchanan and Stokes McKinney remanded to jail

To be held to the special Oct. 22, 1923 term of court at Bakersville N.C.

whereupon the said defendant _____ held to bail in the sum of
_____ Dollars, to appear at the next term of the Criminal
Court for said County, to be held on the _____ Monday _____ 19..

Justice of the Peace Frank A. Carr's handwritten record of the probable cause hearing in which Stokes McKinney and Dot Buchanan were remanded to jail and other defendants were released on bail. _Mitchell County Clerk of Superior Court Office._

This 1920s photograph of a funeral shows the cozy relationship that sometimes existed between law enforcement and the Ku Klux Klan. W. R. Messer, Asheville Chief of Police, is second from the left. Governor Morrison instructed Adjutant General Metts, "Don't fool with Ku Klux. None of our business." *Courtesy of Ewart M. Ball Collection, University of North Carolina, Asheville.*

Superior Court Judge Thomas Brown Finley. He was critical of the Ku Klux Klan during the *State vs. Goss* Grand Jury instruction. Source: *The Old North State and the New, Vol. IV. Courtesy of North Carolina Archives.*

Governor Cameron Morrison.
Courtesy of North Carolina State Archives.

THE STATE'S PRISON
Raleigh, North Carolina

To ...., Clerk of the Superior Court

of *Mitchel* .... County:

We do hereby certify that *John Goss* was

duly electrocuted on *Friday* the *7* day of *December* 192 *3*

in accordance with law and in execution of the judgment pronounced against him at the

Special 192 *3* term of the Superior Court of *Mitchell* County,

which judgment, on appeal, was affirmed by the Supreme Court, and which date was

fixed for the electrocution by the Governor in accordance with law.

Witness our hands this the *7* day of *December* 192 *3*

S J Busbee
Warden of State's Prison

J H Norman m. d
Physician of State's Prison

The following persons were present and acted as witnesses:

S V Mougon   *G W Kidd*
Paul C High   *J F Swain*
Rudolph Mahieu   *F H Batson*
B R Evans   *H Treadway*
R C McCall   *Jacob F Litaker*
D D Honeycutt   *Lou Powers*
     Robinson

State Prison Warden's certificate showing that John Goss was electrocuted in accordance with law.
Mitchell County Clerk of Court records.

The lynching of Nease Gillespie, John Gillespie, and Jack Dillingham in Salisbury, North Carolina on August 6, 1906. It was reported that 5,000 people observed this illegal execution. North Carolina Governor Robert Glenn testified at the trial of George Hall, "I wanted to stop this lynching in North Carolina." *Photograph courtesy of Dave Graham, Jr. of Salisbury, N.C.*

Hardy Coffey. *Photograph Courtesy of Mrs. Irene Coffey Pyatte.*

Reid Coffey on the left and his brother, Ira. After his parole, Reid Coffey was apparently law abiding and productive. He always denied that he was guilty of Hardy Coffey's murder. *Photo courtesy of Doug Coffey.*

Mrs. Lilly Coffey. For a long time, neither victims nor their survivors had any legal rights in the matter of granting parole to convicts. Mrs. Coffey was the lone voice against an organized group of people who appealed to the governor to grant parole or early release to Reid Coffey. *Photograph courtesy of Irene Coffey Pyatte.*

The residence of Hardy Coffey. The murderer was positioned on the right side. *Photograph courtesy of Mrs. Irene Coffey Pyatte.*

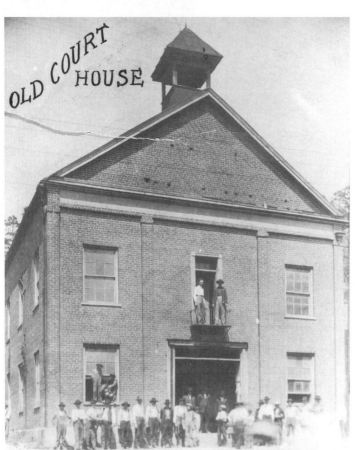

Madison County
Courthouse as it appeare
in 1905. Peter Smith was
sentenced to be hanged
this building. *Courtesy of
Leo White Collection,
Mars Hill University.*

Yancey County's original
Courtesy of Jody Higgins

OLD JAIL

Madison County's Jail in 1905. *Courtesy of Leo White Collection, Mars Hill University.*

The Watauga County Courthouse can be seen in the background of this 1917 photograph. Clarence Potter was sentenced to be hanged in this courthouse. E.S. Coffey's law office is in the foreground. The debris shown in the photograph was from the flood. This photograph, heavily damaged by humidity, appeared in the centennial edition of the *Watauga Democrat*. It was attributed to Mrs. Christina Critcher.

Attorney Mark W. Brown. Solicitor/District Attorney for Madison County. He later became president of the North Carolina Bar Association.
Courtesy of Attorney Bruce Brown.

C. L. Brittain's photograph of Eva Suttles which appeared in the *Madison County Record*, October 13, 1905. This photograph may have been taken during Suttle's testimony at the Peter Smith trial.
Photograph artistically enhanced by John Lee of Boone, NC.

The February 13, 1896 hanging in Newton, North Carolina of Thomas Covington (wearing hood). At the moment of exposure, Sheriff T. L. Bandy is striking an axe to a rope which would set the trap free. The Catawba County Commissioners had voted that the execution be private, but the large number of spectators shows a breach of this edict. *Courtesy of Sheriff David Huffman, Catawba County, N.C.*

$300 REWARD.

The Governor of North Carolina has issued two several proclamations, offering one hundred dollars reward each, for the apprehension and delivery of Thomas Boon Sr, who stands convicted of the murder of S. T. Butner, and Thomas Boon Jr, who stands convicted of the murder John S. Woodfin, to the Sheriff of Yancey county, N. C. And I hereby offer a reward of one hundred dollars for the apprehension and delivery to me at Burnsville in the County of Yancey, N. C., of the above Boons, or fifty dollars for either of them. The said Boons made their escape from the jail of Yancey County, on the night of Oct., 22, 1879.

N. M. WILSON,
Sheriff of Yancey County.

DESCRIPTION:

Thomas Boon Sr. is about 25 years of age, about 5 feet, 7 inches high, weighs about 175 pounds, eyes light blue, large and round, complexion fair. Has a down look, left arm stiff in the elbow and slightly crooked, rather chony shouldered.

Thomas Boon Jr. is about 22 years old, about 5 feet 2 inches high, weighs about 150 pounds, eyes blue, hair randy, complexion fair, lips thick, teeth long and lapped.

Sheriff N. M. Wilson's proclamation of reward for the capture of the two Thomas Boones. *Courtesy of Lloyd Bailey.*

C. L. Brittain's photograph of the hanging of Peter Smith, Marshall, N.C., October 2, 1905. This photograph appeared in the Madison County Record, October 13, 1905, and was sold locally. The actual execution took place in private behind the screen which is attached to the old jail. Robert D. Gilmer, Attorney General of North Carolina, wanted executions to take place in the State Capital in part to "check the mock heroism which attends so many executions." *Courtesy of Ewart M. Ball Collection, University of North Carolina, Asheville.*

Tombstone of Peter Smith.
Photograph by the author.

Clarence Potter lived 62 years 4 months and 13 days after he was sentenced to be hanged by the neck until dead. Those who knew him say that he committed other killings and acts of violence.
Photograph contributed by James Marvin Potter.

"Lucky Joe" Wilson. *Contributed by Forrest Wilson.*

Amos Wellington Howell from a tintype photograph. Wellie Howell was the first law enforcement officer to be killed in Watauga County in the performance of an official duty. However, during the second trial of Clarence Potter, the judge's charge to the jury allowed the jury to question the legitimacy of Howell's law enforcement status and issue the "not guilty" verdict. *Photo courtesy of Mrs. Lizzie Howell Fairchild.*

State of North Carolina

MAY 20th 1775

ESSE QUAM VIDERI

Executive Department

To His Excellency, the Governor of _Wyoming_

The Annexed Papers, *duly authenticated in accordance with law, show that by*

Affidavit and indictment ...., *in the County of* _Watauga_

State of North Carolina,

Boone Potter

stands charged with _murder_

....................*which is a crime against the*

laws of this State, and it appearing that the said _Boone Potter_

has fled from justice and has taken refuge in the State of _Wyoming_ ;

Therefore, *In pursuance of justice, and by authority of the Constitution and Laws of the United States,*

I. _Charles B. Aycock_, *Governor of the State of North Carolina, do hereby require that the*

said _Boone Potter_

be apprehended and delivered to _James S. Squires_

who is hereby authorized and commissioned as the Agent of this State to receive said fugitive and convey him to the

County of _Watauga_ , *in the State of North Carolina, to be dealt with according to law.*

In Witness Whereof, *I have hereunto set my hand and*

caused to be affixed the Great Seal of State.

Done at our City of Raleigh, this _14th_ *day of*

August , *in the year of our Lord one*

thousand eight hundred and ninety _three_ , *and*

in the one hundred and _twenty eighth_ *year of our*

American Independence.

Charles B. Aycock

By the Governor

P. M. Pearsall

Private Secretary.

Governor Charles B. Aycock's request for rendition of Boone Potter from Wyoming. The letterhead sho
the then existing Great Seal of North Carolina together with artistic rendering showing the variety of No
Carolina's geography and culture.
Courtesy of Wyoming State Archives, Museums and Historical Department, Cheyenne, Wyoming.

when Hannah was discovered missing, Tony Plemmons heard that Peter Smith "fastened his boy in his house," took his axe and went out to cut wood. When Smith returned he had no wood; leading to the belief that he took off Hannah's head with his axe. According to Plemmons, Smith killed a dog and left its carcass in the same area where Hannah's head was found, so that anyone smelling decaying flesh would think that it was the dog. It is instructive to hear Tony Plemmons recite that Smith fastened his boy in his house. This part of Plemmons' recollections sounds similar to Smith's own testimony during the rape trial. For Smith to have fastened the boy in the house suggests that Peter Smith's wife was not at home. Is it only an historical coincidence that the wife was absent from the household on both occasions when Peter Smith was alleged to have committed violent crimes?

After Hannah's head was found, dogs belonging to citizens in this area began bringing home strange, human-looking bones. A local doctor identified one bone undeniably as a human pelvis. This bone was discovered after a heavy rain in the area where Hannah's head was found.

Obviously, the severing of one's head would cause death, but Hannah could have been dead when her head was removed. She may have died nude or clothed. Her body may have revealed evidence of sexual abuse had it been recovered.

Dr. T.J. Frisbee, Henry Frisbee's brother, testified at the Grand Jury investigation that considered indicting Peter Smith. As a medical expert, he could have spoken about any visible head wound and if such a wound existed, then whether it might have caused Hannah's death. Peter Smith did offer up a rather startling version of Hannah's death just before he was hanged, describing a serious head wound which would have caused death.

Tony Plemmons said that Peter Smith was arrested and the trial was conducted by Justice of the Peace Vance Ledford. Although Plemmons referred to this as a trial, with a Justice of the Peace presiding, it could have been only a probable cause hearing. One popular version of events pronounced that Peter Smith's wife carried her dead daughter's head to the trial in a flour sack "poke." This gruesome story suggests that Mrs. Peter Smith may have had some interest in giving evidence against her husband; contradicting the statement made by Peter Smith at his trial that his wife did not accuse him.

The Grand Jury returned a presentment accusing Smith of the murder of Hannah Plemmons, but a presentment must be followed by an indictment for there to be a criminal charge. Solicitor Gudger submitted a bill of indictment but it was not returned as a true bill, so Peter Smith was never formally accused of the murder. No evidence beyond Smith's proximity to the crime was presented at the grand jury investigation. Witnesses at the later rape trial reported that Smith's reputation was already bad.

Tony Plemmons repeated the most common local belief about what happened to Hannah's body. Hogs were not confined in those days; people generally fenced their gardens and homes to keep hogs and livestock out. So the belief is that the hogs ate her.

During the rape trial, Eva Suttles testified that Smith told her he raped and killed Hannah. Such statements made by a defendant about the crime are considered probative and are generally held as admissible. Eva's credibility is a jury question, but sufficient evidence would now have justified a murder charge.

During the trial, Smith's lawyer asked witnesses if Eva Suttles had reported Peter Smith's statement to them. The witnesses did not recall her saying this before—an important point in deciding whether to believe Eva Suttles. But it is also important to understand that legally this circumstance does not in itself destroy her credibility. Traumatized rape victims will often not recall all the details in their initial accounts. In many instances, a rape victim will remember some small detail for the first time at trial. Guilt, terror, and humiliation can play havoc with memory, and most of Eva Suttles' questioners would have been men.

Moreover, many questions simply were not asked, for example, whether she told Solicitor Brown, private prosecutor Mashburn, Sheriff Cole or any other authority about Smith's prior statement. One can only speculate how the jury dealt with this evidence, but there was a basis for its being satisfied that Peter Smith was Hannah's murderer.

The second version of Hannah's death was Smith's accusation just before he was hanged. The Sheriff allowed Peter Smith to meet privately with newspaper reporters before he was taken to the gallows. According to the newspapers, on the morning of his execution, Peter Smith named Henry and Columbus Frisbee as responsible for Hannah's death. Although the accusation was carried in varying degrees in the *Madison County Record*, the *Asheville Citizen*, and the *Asheville Gazette News*, only the *Gazette News* gave a detailed account:

> In the course of the statement Smith declares that his stepdaughter Hannah who was murdered and himself were the objects of much persecution; that one night several men went to his home and stoned the house, fired shots into the door and tried to scare Smith and his daughter into leaving the country. It is alleged that the conduct of Smith and his stepdaughter was such that the people of the neighborhood were incensed and Smith declared that both he and Hannah had been threatened with death. Smith says that the last time he saw his stepdaughter was at his house; that she left one evening and a month afterwards her head was found. The body was never found. He said that Henry and Columbus Frisbee carried the girl into the woods and cut her throat. He did not state how he knew this. He did say, however, that Jim and Ben Allison would swear that Henry and Columbus Frisbee cut the girl's throat.
>
> The night of the murder the woods in the neighborhood were set on fire, and it is presumed that the body of the girl was cremated, the head having been thrown in a hollow some distance from where the murder is alleged to have occurred. Sheriff Reed said this morning that he believed the statement to be 'false.'

The reporter concluded,

> Smith was arrested, charged with the crime and although there was not sufficient evidence to convict, it is the general belief the he was the guilty person.

Elsewhere in his article, the reporter told that, "those most familiar with the circumstances believe that it was given out by Smith for the purpose of aiding him to secure a commutation of the death sentence."

The Asheville Citizen reported that Smith named two persons without repeating the persons' names. *The Madison County Record* reported Smith's accusations and named Henry and Columbus Frisbee.[159]

Smith's statements given on the morning of his execution should be evaluated with care. Officers love confessions; so does the public. Any investigation involving the death of a young girl under mysterious circumstances would have produced several efforts to interrogate Peter Smith during the investigation itself. Interrogations have been such a standardized part of criminal investigation that Supreme Court Justices in the 1960s set up guidelines to safeguard defendants' rights. If Peter Smith ever said anything at all during his numerous interrogations by law enforcement, it appears not to have been recorded or noted prior to the morning of his hanging. Despite the numerous opportunities Smith had to report this version to law enforcement prior to October 2, 1905, there simply is no indication that he did so. Smith's version was reported in the media as being a new revelation at the time of his execution.

Smith must have known at least a day or two before he died that the Governor was no longer going to intervene. The Governor refused his application for commutation on September 8, 1905.[160] The newspapers reported on October 1 that the Governor would not intervene. The Sheriff received the death warrant two days earlier. On September 29, 1905, the Governor wrote the Sheriff:

> Mr. George M. Cole, Sheriff; Dear Sir: I respited Peter Smith until Monday-October 2, 1905, and when the respite expires and you have no further orders you can carry out the sentence of the court by executing the prisoner on that day. In order, however, that there may be no mistake about it, I hereby direct and command you as Sheriff of Madison County to execute Peter Smith October 2, 1905, between the hours and in the

manner ordered by the trial judge when sentence was passed.

Affixed to this letter was the great seal of North Carolina.

One does not walk nonchalantly to one's execution, especially after applying for a commutation of the death penalty. If Peter Smith suddenly began to think what new devices by which he might try to avoid death, then it could be said that anybody in his right mind would try to do the same.[161]

What he said about Hannah's death could be a sincere and honest statement from one newly-converted Christian, or it could be a devious statement calculated to persuade the Governor to grant relief. Would law enforcement have tried to intervene to prevent his hanging had they believed him? Not likely. The Sheriff for one did not believe him. Smith's execution in 1905 provides a good reason why condemned people are given only limited time to say their last words and why their access to the news media is limited.

When the Grand Jury did not indict Peter Smith, based on the evidence they had in February 1902, the jury spared the Solicitor the embarrassment of having to prosecute a man for murder without any evidence. Of the two versions of Hannah's murder, Peter Smith would be a necessary witness to the one where he said the Frisbees committed the crime and Eva Suttles would be a necessary witness to the other version—that involving Peter Smith as culprit. Although a finding of "not a true bill" does not prevent subsequent bills being submitted for the same charge involving the same defendant, no further effort was ever made to charge anyone with the murder of Hannah Plemmons.

When the Grand Jury returned no true bill of indictment, Peter Smith was discharged from custody. He moved his family from the Meadowfork section to a cabin on the Dogget Mountain area where he lived during November 1904. This is a rugged territory and at least 10 miles separate the two residences.

Tony Plemmons expressed the prevalent opinion that, "It is not possible for Peter Smith to have carried a rifle gun, Eva Suttles' satchel, and held his hand over her mouth for over two miles in this rugged terrain." Like many others, he did not think Peter Smith should have been found guilty of rape.

In 1905, the word "serial" was not used to describe multiple crimes committed by the same person. Now we have all heard of serial killers and serial rapists. A young lady's head is discovered severed from her body. A few years later another young girl maintains that she was raped, and that her rapist moved a knife across her throat stating that he was going to kill her and further, that he killed the other young lady. A serial killer is defined as one who repeats similar acts after some lapse of time.

Originally, three acts were required before one could be labeled a serial criminal. But sociologists now say that one can be defined as a serial criminal after the commission of two acts. What would have been the conclusion of events on November 8, 1904, if Mayo Reeves and Lyda Wells had not been in the area? Eva Suttles testified that she was able to escape Peter Smith and ran toward Reeves and Wells. Their presence could have saved her life. Those who are not convinced of Peter Smith's guilt maintain that Reeves and Wells accidentally came upon a young woman who voluntarily left her residence and then claimed rape simply to cover for herself.

Eva Suttles' testimony gave evidence for the first time that Peter Smith killed Hannah Plemmons. She testified that Peter Smith confessed the murder in an attempt to frighten her into submission. If Peter Smith did confess to Eva Suttles that he murdered Hannah Plemmons, then he may have been Madison County's first serial rapist and murderer. A serial rapist/murderer may have been thwarted early in his career.

The statement that James Allison would be a witness favorable to Peter Smith is incongruous. James Allison was a witness before the Grand Jury when Solicitor J.M. Gudger, Jr. sought to indict Peter Smith for murder. Allison originally testified before James D. Baldwin, Justice of the Peace, to issue a warrant against Peter Smith for the murder of Hannah Plemmons. Proceedings before the Grand Jury are secret; one can never know what James Allison said, but clearly the Solicitor and the Justice of the Peace viewed his evidence unfavorable to Peter Smith and that it would mitigate against the guilt of Henry and Columbus Frisbee. Columbus Frisbee was also a witness before the Grand Jury in the furtive effort to indict Peter Smith for murder as was his uncle, Dr. T.J. Frisbee. Moreover, Henry Frisbee was subpoenaed as a witness although he did not testify. James D. Balding, Justice of the Peace, issued the warrant for murder.

Footnotes

[158] Since the only record of the trial is the narrative prepared by the attorneys, it cannot be known whether Eva Suttles used this word or whether the attorney used the word in a question and called simply for a specific answer.

[159] In 1905 newspapers were not widely distributed in the Spring Creek area and damage to persons' reputations probably was minimal. Bill Hart, a feature writer for the *Asheville Citizen*, May 14, 1970, published an article in the *Marshall News Record* which received wide circulation and did great hurt to descendants of the Frisbees still living in this area. The article by Bill Hart, coupled with a large reproduction of the C. L. Brittain picture of the hanging of Peter Smith, occupied a large space on page 6 of that paper. In his article, Hart reported a variant of Smith's version as it appeared in the *Gazette News*. Columbus and Henry Frisbee (erroneously stated to be brothers) were both sexually interested in Hannah. In a quarrel between the two, one threw a rock at the other and missed. The rock struck Hannah in the head, and as she lay bleeding the two men decided to kill her. They forcibly confiscated an axe from Peter Smith, who was nearby cutting wood, and used it to remove Hannah's head. In an effort to destroy evidence, the two men then set fire to Hannah's body but inadvertently allowed the head to roll to the place where it was later found. Hart's article said that "the Frisbee brothers reportedly left the country and were not heard from again." Ed Frisbee, who lives in Upper Shutin in Madison County, tells this writer that Columbus Frisbee was the son, not the brother of Henry Frisbee. The last surviving sibling of Columbus Frisbee, Willie Frisbee, grew indignant at Peter Smith's accusation reported in Bill Hart's article, reading it first in 1970. He maintained that it was false and denied that the Frisbees fled the country. He stated they remained in Madison County at all times. Columbus Frisbee's daughter, who lived in the Meadowfork section of Madison County, was incensed over the accusations in the Hart article and maintained there was no truth in them. Mr. Bill Moore's version coincides generally with the Hart article. The origin of Moore's version is not certain; but it appears not to have been in vogue prior to the Smith hanging, and is probably a facsimile of Peter Smith's statements. Under Moore's version, Smith would be a necessary witness to

show the robbery of the axe from him; however, it doesn't account for Jim and Ben Allison's knowledge of the crime. Smith claimed they were witnesses. Henry Frisbee died April 19, 1912, and is buried in the Keenerville Christian Church Cemetery in Madison County. Columbus Frisbee is also buried in Madison County having lived from January 27, 1882 to March 13, 1910.

[160] Applications for Pardons, Reprieves and Commutations, N. C. Archives.

[161] A similar modern event occurred in Florida in 1989, when the State of Florida prepared to execute Ted Bundy. Bundy began confessing new murders which he claimed to have committed. For a time, it looked as if his date of execution would be postponed, so that states could verify the new confessions. Finally on January 24, 1989, Florida carried out the execution. Many thought Bundy was simply inventing new data to prolong his life. What weight can be give accusations so strong as those made by Peter Smith?

Chapter 6: We Shall Meet on That Beautiful Shore

The Superior Court term of February 1905 in Madison County lasted two weeks and is unique in its history. Two men were convicted of rape in separate instances, and each was sentenced to death. Charlie Stines was convicted of raping Sarah Collins in her home near Hot Springs, and Peter Smith was convicted of raping Eva Suttles. Both Stines and Smith, while awaiting the decisions on their appeals, had reasons to hope for the best. At that time, five men had been sentenced to death in Madison County, but only one was actually executed.

In 1883, the office of the North Carolina Attorney General began collecting statistics on crime. From 1883 to 1902, 1,261 persons, almost all men, were tried for a capital felony. Only twelve were hanged. In the early years of the twentieth century, North Carolina was averaging about one hanging a year. During those years, eighteen lynchings were recorded. The death penalty was no more a surety then than it is now.

Evincing no doubt of Peter Smith's guilt, the North Carolina Supreme Court affirmed his conviction on May 23, 1905:

A minute examination of the record shows that the prisoner has been fairly tried by an able and unusually painstaking judge and has been convicted upon evidence that leaves no reasonable doubt of his guilt. He fully deserves the penalty. He must pay for the shocking crime he has committed.

In 1905, North Carolina law assigned the duty of setting execution dates to the Governor, who then issued a death warrant. Some states still use this procedure, but North Carolina Governors became tired of this burden and a procedure was used later where the convicted person was brought back before a Superior Court Judge to set the date. On June 5, 1905, Governor Robert B. Glenn issued a death warrant to the Sheriff of Madison County:

Whereas Peter Smith charged with rape in a bill of indictment found by the Grand Jury of Madison County in the Superior Court was at the February 1905 term thereof duly tried and convicted of said crime and the penalty of death adjudged.

And whereas, upon his appeal to the Supreme Court it has been decided that there is no error in the record of proceedings and said judgment has been affirmed at February 1905 term thereof, which with the opinion has been duly certified and made known to me.

Now therefore, by virtue of the authority vested in me by law, I, R. B. Glenn, Governor of North Carolina do command you that on the 1st day of August, A.D., 1905 at the usual place prescribed by law in said county, you proceed to carry said judgment into execution by hanging the said Peter Smith by the neck until he is dead.

Some people believed that Eva Suttles failed to make enough of an outcry when she claimed rape, but the citizens of Madison County did not fail to raise an outcry when Peter Smith's execution date was set. On July 10, 1905, the Governor commuted his death sentence until September 1905. Later, the Governor gave Smith an execution date of September 14, 1905. Governor Glenn changed the execution date to September 29, 1905. Finally, Governor Glenn set the execution date for October 2, 1905.

Obviously, Governor Glenn was having trouble dealing with this case, as well he should; there was growing pressure on him. An aforementioned letter to Glenn from Thomas N. James was written on the letterhead of the Madison County Bank and prominently featured the fact that the bank was the "largest capitalized bank in the county." J. M. Gudger, Jr. was listed as President. Gudger earlier served as Solicitor-District Attorney for Western North Carolina and was later elected to the United States Congress. His name would have been recognized immediately in the Governor's office. J. H. White and J. F. Redmon were listed as vice presidents, and the author of the letter, Thomas N. James, who was shown on the letterhead to be cashier of the bank, signed his name beside the words "State Executive

Committee." In 1905, Madison County was one of North Carolina's few reliably Republican counties. Democratic Governor Glenn would obviously have been aware that granting a reprieve or commutation would please the prominent members of his own political party.

Glenn also would feel the squeeze from what would now be called the Religious Right. Two missionaries began making Peter Smith, an illiterate and impoverished man from one of North Carolina's most rural areas, their mission. Suddenly this simple man, thought to be a common, if particularly vicious, criminal, was a featured persona in big-city newspapers down in Asheville. Visited by missionaries and attorneys, he could have been easily forgiven for relishing all the attention. Peter Smith reportedly took to religion, and missionaries and newspapers alike showed an interest in the progress of his salvation. On September 12, 1905, the *Asheville Citizen* reported:

> Smith declares his innocence; a thing which, however, is quite usual with those of whose guilt there is no doubt and declares that he is a Christian and ready to die. He held a regular reception at the jail Sunday. A number of people coming to hold religious services with him and many more out of curiosity.

It is easy to find examples of condemned persons who, during the time of intense publicity before execution, seem to enjoy their newfound fame. Religious conversions may well be sincere, but as Peter Smith's religious fervor strengthened, so did the belief that his life would be spared. He was reportedly weakening. Once able to roam the rugged mountains of Madison County, bolstered by new friends and notoriety, Smith claimed illness.

When execution remained set for September 14, 1905, the Sheriff of Madison County took him from the Buncombe County Jail where he was held as a safe keeper, to Madison County. The Sheriff also brought Sol Hensley, another prisoner who was a witness in a different case. Smith and Hensley were handcuffed together. Smith begged not to be so handcuffed, stating that he was too weak to escape.

Before his execution on October 2, the *Asheville Citizen* reported on October 1, 1905,

With his last hope of a commutation of sentence taken away by Governor Glenn's refusal to stay execution, watched day and night by prison guards, and counting the time he has to live by the hours and minutes, Peter Smith, convicted of criminal assault, and sentenced to hang tomorrow, lies prostrate in a cell in the Madison County jail at Marshall. The nerve that he displayed during his confinement here and the courage he showed upon leaving for the scene of his execution seem to have deserted him and it is reported that it may be necessary to carry him to the gallows tomorrow morning when the time for executing the sentence of the court arrives.

On the morning of October 2, 1905, after Smith accused the Frisbee men, he was brought at 12:30 p.m. to an elevated platform where he faced a throng of citizens who came to observe his hanging. The Sheriff asked a local doctor to apologize to the crowd that only a few persons could observe the hanging. The sheriff retired to his office where he received a telegram at 12:55 p.m. from Governor Glenn that denied any further reprieve.

The *Madison County Record* of October 6, 1905 gave a succinct account of the hanging:

At 1 o'clock Sheriff Cole told Smith that it was time to go and he was assisted from his chair and walked with the Sheriff to the gallows. Rev. C.O. Gray, who has been very attentive to the doomed man, advising and praying with him since he was brought to this jail, and Rev. L. B. Compton and P. L. Maness, and two lady missionaries, who were his spiritual advisers while in the Asheville jail, accompanied the prisoner to the scaffold where by his request they sang a hymn, "Sin can never enter there."[162] After the hymn Rev. Compton read a chapter and then offered a fervent prayer that brought tears to the eyes of strong men. This was the only time that the prisoner showed any sign of emotion, breaking down and weeping bitterly. The prisoner then asked for one more hymn, "Is Thy Heart Right With

God?"[163] Smith was then carried onto the trap where Sheriff Cole, assisted by deputy sheriff Nick White and Sheriff Reed of Buncombe, arranged his clothing, opening his collar to properly adjust the cap and rope. Smith gave a last hearty embrace to deputy sheriff Nick White saying: "You have been good to me." Smith then smiled and said "goodbye" to those around him.

Peter Smith's final words according to the *Madison County Record* were addressed to those witnessing the ceremony before the private hanging:

> Friends, I meet you now for my last time, but I am going to a better place. All take warning. I have been charged with many things. God knows how they are and not the people. I have been kicked about a good deal, but they are done kicking me around now, for I will soon go away. I am ready to go home. I will not say but a few words as I am too weak to talk, but don't think that I am scared. I have made peace with my God and am going home to him. I can't come to you any more, but you can come to me if you serve God. I love my friends and my enemies alike. I am going home. Serving God is the best work of man. I have had some time to serve with Him and am going home to Him in a few minutes. I am not guilty of the crime as charged against me. I am sick and can't talk any more. Good-bye friends.

Jesse James Bailey, who was at the hanging, recalled his impressions. Smith was hanged behind a black screen. "I can't remember what material we had back then but it was a material that you could see through if the sun hit it right." Eldridge Leake remembered that his father attended the hanging. His father, then active in Republican Party politics, was allowed to be one of the few witnesses.[164] The Sheriff reluctantly walked to the wooden lever, placed his hand on it, and walked away, demonstrating that he was having a difficult time. He again walked to the lever, and without great conviction, pulled the lever that sprang the trap door. Leake said the hanging of Peter Smith had had a profound impact on his father, who referred to it often. The *Asheville Citizen* hailed this hanging to be the "most successful ever held in this state. It being evident to all that the deceased suffered no agony."

Governor Glenn, who took strong measures to prevent lynching, was bombarded with requests to commute Smith's death sentence, and obviously agonized over the outcome. He wrote the following letter to the *Asheville Citizen*:

> The State contends that the prosecutrix' character was good; the defendant denies this, so I said she might not be all she ought to be. Still a bad woman, even if she were one, cannot be assaulted and this woman is so corroborated that I have no doubt of the prisoner's guilt. The judge and solicitor refuse to recommend commutation, and being convinced by the evidence, I decline to interfere. R. B. Glenn, Governor.

When Governor Glenn granted a reprieve for the execution set for September 14, 1904, he was visiting Boston, Massachusetts, and acted through an assistant. While in Boston, he took steps to set up an extraordinary interview. Rumors reached him that Eva Suttles had recanted her testimony, and the Governor requested by letter that Solicitor Mark Brown, in the presence of the presiding judge and the defense attorney, interview Eva Suttles to confirm her version of events. I. N. Ebbs was away from his residence when the letter from the Governor arrived. In his absence, Solicitor Brown arranged that Eva Suttles be brought to Asheville, where he and Presiding Judge Moore interviewed her. Solicitor Brown reported to the Governor that Eva Suttles continued to maintain that she was raped by Peter Smith. On September 19, 1905, after the Eva Suttles interview, I. N. Ebbs received his letter from the Governor. Ebbs wrote the Governor that day and made a not too subtle objection of the procedure:

> I have been informed that the Solicitor has caused Eva Suttles to be carried before him at Asheville. I have had no notice of such course being taken except what

others have told me. Inasmuch the Solicitor has given
me no notice to that effect.

Considering the historic consternation that the word *carried* has
caused in this case, one wonders if I.N. Ebbs deliberately chose
this word to express his indignation with the procedure.

Jasper Ebbs' testimony continues as an enigma. He is only
a year younger than his brother, I.N. Ebbs. The brothers must
once have been close. Jasper Ebbs held positions of authority. As
a Justice of the Peace, he performed the marriage ceremony for
Eva Suttles' mother, Martha Smith and her father on December
15, 1888. Jasper Ebbs, though not a formally educated man, was
a well-respected one, with many folks on Spring Creek accepting
his position of leadership.

In the Smith trial, Jasper Ebbs was called as a witness by
his brother I. N. Ebbs. Attorneys call witnesses whom they believe
will be helpful to their client's cause and indeed Jasper Ebbs was
able to testify that the mood of the crowd at Friezland School was
violent and that he allayed mob action. This was in keeping with
Peter Smith's contention that he did not flee arrest but was fearful
for his life. On cross-examination, Jasper Ebbs was the lone witness
who testified that Smith earlier said he went to Eva Suttles' house.
Without doubt Solicitor Brown appreciated what Jasper Ebbs
would say on cross-examination, but Lawyer Ebbs appears to have
been surprised by this testimony. The defendant made vigorous
objection in his appeal to Jasper Ebbs' testimony. Part of the
strained relationship between Jasper and I.N may have been
political. Jasper was an influential Democrat (Justice of the Peace
appointments were political plums given only to those who were
truly helpful in party politics), and I. N. Ebbs was a prominent
Republican.

After the trial, Jasper Ebbs served for an astounding fifty
years on the Madison County Board of Education.

I. N. Ebbs, when admitted to the practice of law in North
Carolina, failed to inform the North Carolina Bar Association that
he was convicted in the United States Court for the Eastern District
of Louisiana of forgery on December 4, 1903. In 1908, the
Committee of Grievances of the North Carolina Bar Association

gave Solicitor Mark W. Brown a report of this and Solicitor Brown filed a disbarment proceeding with the Superior Court. The judge in Asheville gave Esquire Ebbs opportunity to respond and Ebbs declined. The Superior Court judge then determined that Ebbs was convicted of five counts of forgery and altering receipts and accounts with intent to defraud the United States of America. The judge ordered that Ebbs be disbarred. Ebbs, represented by former Solicitor, James M. Gudger, appealed to the North Carolina Supreme Court, and in a divided court, the majority ruled that to have defrauded the United States in that manner did not represent, under the statutes, a justification for disbarment in North Carolina. I. N. Ebbs died September 16, 1950.

Republican Mark W. Brown was re-elected Solicitor in November 1906. Madison County always voted Republican, but Brown's district, which included Buncombe and several other western North Carolina counties, usually voted for Democratic candidates. In winning election, Brown's majority in Madison County was reduced considerably from his margin of four years earlier because he was opposed by Guy V. Roberts, a popular Democratic lawyer who lived in Madison County. The people of Spring Creek always voted Democratic. Brown later became President of the North Carolina Bar Association. When he died on July 25, 1929, he was eulogized as one of the most respected members of the Buncombe County Bar.

Alexander Suttles traveled all day to attend the hanging of Peter Smith,[165] and was satisfied that justice was done. After the hanging, Alexander Suttles, Eva, his son James, and his daughter Ida, walked to Sevier County, Tennessee where they caught a surrey to Coal City. Alexander became a coal miner, then worked for a while in Knoxville, Tennessee, but tired of the flatlands. He and his son James returned to Sandy Mush in Buncombe County near the Madison County line, where he bought a small farm. In 1909, he married a second wife, Marinda Keener, and later married a third time. When he died on November 1, 1951, he was survived by his third wife, Rachael Stines Suttles. Alexander Suttles lived a long time and was well respected, but he accumulated little wealth and was buried at a church cemetery without a headstone.

A reporter for the *Asheville Gazette News* on October 3, 1905, wrote that Peter Smith gave him two letters prior to his execution. One letter was from Smith's young son and the other was from his wife. Neither attended the execution.

> The letters from his wife and child were simple farewells and explained that the reason that they did not come to see him was because they had no shoes. The little fellow's letter ended with a pitiful appeal: "Oh, papa, I want you to see if you can't get some of them to get me a pair of shoes."

As for Smith himself, his performance on the day he was hanged, waiting until then to name persons who allegedly murdered Hannah Plemmons, insured the continued debate over his guilt. His continued denial of guilt, at first, resulted in the Governor extending the dates of his execution, and in the end, created a mystery that continues to this day in Madison County. Peter Smith's last minutes on earth generated a newspaper editorial that noted his seeming fixation on a life in Heaven as he spoke his last words and wondered whether he could go to eternity with a lie on his lips. Many pondered whether he was, in fact, guilty of the crime charged. For better or worse, Peter Smith is likely to be remembered in this part of this world for generations to come.

The Smith execution highlighted many concerns about the execution process itself, and whether the Sheriff's and public's interests were being well-served. The role of the news media, as always, was put under the spotlight, as was the circus atmosphere surrounding what should have been a most solemn event. Making executions private rather than public did not prevent a ghoulish aspect to the proceedings. More hangings followed that of Peter Smith, but North Carolina leaders were clearly positioning themselves for a new way of doing things.

Eva Suttles went with her father to Tennessee and migrated eastward with him back to Knoxville, Tennessee. She married Nude Leeper in 1909, and lived the rest of her life in Knoxville. She returned to Western North Carolina when her father died, and on rare occasions, to visit her brother James' children. She spent her last years in a nursing home. Her son, Pat, recalls that she had a recurring dream where a man tried to put a wire around her neck. Eva Suttles Leeper died August 6, 1981, the last survivor of the Spring Creek incident.

After New York instituted electricity as the means of executing criminals, other states followed suit. North Carolina Governor Robert B. Glenn, in his final address to the General Assembly at a special session in 1908, said:

> All executions for capital offenses should be held in the State's Prison at Raleigh, and not in the county where the offense was committed, and should be by electrocution, and not by the old and *barbarous* (emphasis added) mode of hanging. I believe this change can be made without any amendment to the Constitution, and it will, in my judgment, prove very satisfactory.

The North Carolina Governor was repeating the words of the New York Governor.

Robert D. Gilmer was Attorney General of North Carolina in 1909. In his report to Governor Glenn on January 1, 1909, he also recommended change in executions:

> I recommend that all criminal executions or hangings take place at the State Penitentiary, under the control of the State Prison authorities. Cost should not be considered when public morals are at stake, but I maintain that it is far cheaper to bring a prisoner to the State's Prison as soon as he has been convicted of a capital felony and there hold him until his execution than it would be to erect a scaffold or gallows and enclosure and pay a death-watch in the several counties of this State.
>
> It will also have the effect of checking the mock heroism which attends so many executions, and of assuring the prisoners of a speedy death at the hands of persons familiar with the work, rather than a bungling execution at the hands of sheriffs who are totally unfamiliar with hangings.

North Carolina grew tired of public hangings and provided for private hangings which permitted limited numbers of persons to observe. In 1909, North Carolina eliminated executions in the county seat. The General Assembly that year made statutory provision for executions to be conducted with electricity at Central Prison in Raleigh.

Governor Glenn continued in office until January 1909. After Peter Smith's hanging, he issued more warrants for hanging to be performed by the local sheriffs. Preston Daniels was hanged by the neck until dead in Martin County on December 16, 1905. Two men were ordered by the Governor to be hanged in 1906, four in 1907, three in 1908, and two in 1909. Glenn commuted some sentences. The last North Carolina hanging took place in Elizabethtown, the Bladen County seat. Henry E. Spivey was hanged by Sheriff J. M. Clarke, on Friday March 11, 1910. One week later, Sheriff Clarke was an invited guest to watch the first execution by electricity to occur in North Carolina.

Walter Morrison, "crying bitterly, but not loudly"[166] was led from his cell to an electric chair invented by E. F. Davis of New York at Central Prison in Raleigh, North Carolina. "Having lost his nerve as he faced the mysterious electric chair so different from the familiar gallows, Walter Morrison piteously called for mercy, until the head-gear had been adjusted," wrote the *Raleigh News and Observer* the next day. His body absorbed three shocks of 1,800 volts. Between the second and third shocks, Doctors McGeachy and Riddick found the pulse faint and the heart still throbbing. "Going mighty hard'" was Dr. McGeachy's assessment. Electrician Davis later explained that this was natural but that death had already taken place. Extinguishing life took six-and-one-half minutes. The *News and Observer* reported that there was none of the sensational shouting or hysterical screaming that have so often attended hangings. North Carolina's new humane method of executions was deemed successful. Sheriff Clarke, whose every appearance "indicates cool nerve" stated that, "I hung one last Friday, and I would rather see one hung any time than to see one electrocuted."

Footnotes

[162] C. L. Brittain's photograph shows no women on the platform where Peter Smith made his statements to the crowd. Moreover, the *Madison County Record* account says the religious group accompanied Smith to the scaffold. This would be consistent with the fact that no women appeared on the platform since the scaffold was concealed from the public view. It appears that the newspaper account may have published items not totally in sequence. The *Record* spoke of the prayer that brought tears to the eyes of strong men, giving the indication that this prayer was made in public and therefore on the platform. If women were allowed to witness the private hanging that would be a deviation from the norm of that era.

[163] "Is Thy Heart Right with God" still has some current use.

> Have thy affections been nailed to the cross?
> Is thy heart right with God?
> Dost thou count all things for Jesus but loss?
> Is thy heart right with God?
> Is thy heart right with God,
> Wash'd in the crimson flood,
> Cleansed and made holy, humble and lowly,
> Right in the sight of God.

"Sin Can Never Enter There" was written by C.W. Naylor and copyrighted in 1902. Its music was written in shape notes which were popular music in rural mountain churches. For the most part, this song does not now appear in church hymnals. It is based on an interpretation of Revelation 21:27 and puts forth the idea that a person while still alive on earth must seek forgiveness of particular sins otherwise that person cannot enter Heaven:

> Heav-en is a ho-ly place, Filled with glo-ry and with grace,
> Sin can nev-er en-ter there; All with-in its gates are pure,
> From de-file-ment kept se-cure, Sin can nev-er en-ter there.
> If you hope to dwell at last, When your life on earth is past
> In that home so bright and fair, You must here be cleansed from sin,
> Have the life of Christ with-in, Sin can nev-er en-ter there,
> You may live in sin be-low, Heav-en's grace re-fuse to know,
> But you can-not en-ter there; It will stop you at the door,
> Bar you out for-ev-er-more, Sin can nev-er en-ter there.
> If you cling to sin till death, When you draw your lat-est breath,
> You will sink in dark de-spair, To the re-gions of the lost,
> Thus to prove at aw-ful cost, Sin can nev-er en-ter there

[164] Mountain Republicans contend that good roads exist where Democrats live. Actually, there are few good roads anywhere in Madison County, but politics has been a factor in North Carolina road building history. Madison had a Republican history and there had been little historic incentive for the predominantly Democratic Legislatures and Governors to improve roads in this county. Eldridge Leake was a prominent lawyer from Madison

County. He began his adulthood as a Republican, but later switched to the Democrats and attained statewide stature. His son, Larry, has been a state senator and currently is chairman of the State Board of Elections. Larry told this writer that his father was able to get an important road for Madison County. Governor William B. Umstead once summoned Eldridge Leake to the Executive Mansion without revealing his purpose. The Governor wanted Leake to serve as Madison County election chairman for Alton Lennon, the candidate for United States Senator in the Democratic primary of 1954. Eldridge Leake demanded that first the road from Walnut to Spring Creek be paved. The deal was made and the road was paved. Madison County under Leake's leadership went for Lennon, although Kerr Scott was actually elected United States Senator in 1954. W. Kerr Scott was elected North Carolina Governor in 1948. Madison County voted Republican and the Republican candidate for Governor, George M. Pritchard, received more votes in Madison County than did Scott. Kerr Scott never fully bonded with Democratic Party leaders in the county and infuriated them by hiring stalwart Republican and private attorney Clyde M. Roberts to represent the State of North Carolina in some highway comdemnation proceedings.

[165] F. N. Suttles of Hendersonville, North Carolina was the source of much of the personal and family data about Alexander Suttles and others of the Suttles family.

[166] *Raleigh News and Observer*, March 19, 1910.

CASE IV

LAW'S ALTERNATIVE

Chapter 1: First Degree Murder

In 1893, North Carolina, following the examples of other states, divided murder into two categories. In so doing, North Carolina exempted more murders from the death penalty. In an early case decided by the North Carolina Supreme Court after the passage of the 1893 law, the North Carolina Justices wrote that North Carolina was the last state to make this division:

> The passage of the act of 1893 marks an era in the judicial history of the State. As far as we can ascertain, every other State had previously divided the common-law kind of murder into two classes. The theory upon which this change has been made is that the law will always be executed more faithfully when it is in accord with an enlightened idea of justice. Public sentiment has revolted at the thought of placing on a level in the courts one who is provoked by insulting words to kill another with a deadly weapon, with one who waylays and shoots another in order to rob him of his money, or poisons him to gratify an old grudge.[167]

When President George Washington took his celebrated tour of the southern United States, he went south near the eastern coast but returned along the western borders of the states. He stopped in Charlotte, Salisbury, and Salem. These places represented North Carolina's westernmost towns of consequence, even though Washington referred to Charlotte as a "trifling place." Rowan County, with Salisbury as the county seat, then extended to the extreme western part of the state that itself stretched all the way to the Mississippi River. Daniel Boone began his western excursions from Salisbury and in the minutes and documents of the Court of Quarter Sessions and Pleas for Rowan County is maintained Boone's original signature. Waightstill Avery, North Carolina's first Attorney General, was admitted to the practice of law in that court since the western counties of North Carolina were created from land that once was Rowan County.

As Daniel Boone traveled west, he pioneered a trail leading through Deep Gap into what is now the Town of Boone in Watauga

County. The early pioneers into eastern Tennessee were at first called the Watauga Settlers. It was this area, together with all its other western land, that North Carolina ceded to Congress soon after the Revolutionary War. Yet Watauga County was not formed until 1849, and most of its territory was taken from Ashe County. Like Avery County, Watauga County never had a major railroad, although the two counties shared the narrow gauge Eastern Tennessee and Western North Carolina (ET & WNC) Railroad. A railroad went through the Todd community, a landmark on the Ashe and Watauga County line. Until modern times, like other areas not served by the railroad, Watauga County was isolated from the outside world and its commerce and trade.

D.C. McCanless served as one of the first sheriffs of Watauga County. As Sheriff he also was tax collector. His claim to fame was to flee with his girlfriend and the county's tax monies, west where he was, reportedly, killed by Wild Bill Hickok.

On February 27, 1865, General U.S. Grant ordered Major General George Stoneman to conduct a raid against the Virginia and Tennessee Railroad to destroy the rails all the way into Lynchburg, Virginia if he could. Stoneman set out from Knoxville moving through Morristown's Bull's Gap across Iron Mountain to Boone. On March 28, 1865, Stoneman's forces were resisted by the Watauga Home Guard. Stoneman was only slightly delayed and then moved on into Wilkesboro and north into Virginia.

For long-time residents of Watauga County, two events stand out over the past sixty years: the flood of 1940 and the winter of 1960. After torrential rains had already fallen across the county for several days, two additional inches of rain fell between five and six o'clock on August 13, 1940. Sixteen people died and at least 30 homes were destroyed. Fed by erosion on clear-cut slopes, mudslides ravaged many areas, including one that was estimated to have carved a swath 500 feet wide and 75 feet deep in the Stony Fork Community.

The winter of 1960 began with mild weather but as the season progressed toward spring, snow and temperatures fell for weeks on end. Food, medicines and animal feed were airlifted to Watauga and Ashe Counties. Eighty-four inches of snow fell during that winter, a record that would stand until the winter of 1995-96, when the higher elevations of Watauga County received 125 inches.

Watauga County has never been plagued with serious crime. Murders are rare, and multiple murders are rarer; only four multiple murders have taken place in the county's history.[168] Prior to murder being divided into first and second degrees, no one was ever convicted of murder or of any other capital offense in Watauga County. Few persons were ever convicted of first-degree murder since then.[169]

Yet one section of Watauga County gained notoriety for its violent history. Pottertown sits on the slope of Snake Mountain, one of the most beautiful and remote areas of the county. Yet anyone researching court records for the names of murder victims or of those accused of crime in early Watauga County history finds the name Potter more than any other.

James Marvin Potter is a gentle person. He has been a sawmiller, a millwright, a machinist, and a meat cutter. As a boy, he attended Pottertown School. His father owned one of the first motor vehicles in his poor community. The school teacher at Pottertown boarded with this family. To get to high school, James Marvin Potter had to walk in mountain terrain for one-and-a-half miles to ride the school bus. Now elderly, Potter continues to work. He remembers the past:

> Within a span of about 500 yards there have been nine killings. This is the place where Sam Ellison killed Howard Hockaday, and over here Glen Brown killed Burchie Potter, at this place Boone Potter killed his father, and over there the Snyder brothers killed their father, Will. This is where Campbell was killed and Broom was killed there. Boone and Clarence Potter killed the deputy, Howell, at this spot and shortly up the road is where the posse killed Boone. I think the reason for all these killings is because the people here were suspicious of outsiders.

Marvin Potter saw one of the killings; his brother's. Pottertown had once been called Tamarack, lying on the Trade, Tennessee, mail route and part of the Watauga County Township known as North Fork; on the headwaters of the north fork of the New River.

Pottertown was once so isolated and considered so dangerous that for many years sheriffs did not venture there. Attorney Wade Brown, once Mayor of Boone, also served as Chairman of the North Carolina Parole Commission and in the North Carolina General Assembly. Brown was able to use his influence to get the first road cut through Meat Camp into Pottertown. Even this difficult dirt track vastly improved the circumstances for Pottertown residents. It was paved by the North Carolina Department of Transportation in 1999.

One of the founders of Pottertown, John Potter, is reputed to have discovered a vein of pure silver on one of the nearby mountain knobs. John would supposedly collect silver until he filled his saddlebags, then take the ore to Kentucky where it was minted. No one else, not even his wife, who helped him transport the ore, ever knew the location of the mine. John Potter would blindfold her en route. The secret of the mine's location died with him.

Mr. Austin South was a long-serving Clerk of Court in Watauga County. He had family ties to the Potters. Before his death he wrote an unpublished manuscript about the Potters. According to Austin South, the Potters left Pennsylvania after President Washington put down the "Whiskey Rebellion." Abraham Potter was an early settler, with ties to Kentucky and Virginia.[170]

If North Carolina could ever boast a wild western frontier, Watauga County would fit the bill. Among its early characters was Joseph T. Wilson, who gave himself the name Lucky Joe Wilson.[171] Lucky Joe Wilson was a deserter from the Union Army during the Civil War. He was later pardoned by Tennessee Provisional Governor, Andrew Johnson. His background included a stint as a Deputy U. S. Marshall in Johnson County, Tennessee, when he was alleged to have forged several hundred dollars in witness tickets. He escaped from jail in Knoxville, Tennessee, and then became a Postmaster in Piketon, Kentucky. He left there amid questions of stolen postage and registered money. When he returned to North Carolina, he was arrested in Ashe County by a United States Marshal and returned to Piketon, Kentucky. While in jail there, he convinced authorities that he was dead by lying perfectly still. By using this ruse, he escaped from Pike County Jail, and then returned to Watauga County.

On June 3, 1883, together with two accomplices, he stole horses belonging to Henry Main. When Lucky Joe came under suspicion, he assisted those seeking the thieves. Later, one of his compatriots confessed to the crime and named Lucky Joe as well. Wilson fled to Kentucky. Eventually, he was convicted of this crime in Ashe County Superior Court, and spent eight years in prison.

On May 7, 1883, the Watauga County Grand Jury indicted Wilson for an offense that occurred on March 1, 1883, the larceny of one horse from Henry Main. Joseph S. Adams was Solicitor for Watauga County and his district included Ashe County as well. The case was tried in Ashe County in the fall of that year. After Wilson was convicted, the Supreme Court upheld his conviction. Lucky Joe used his young son as an alibi, but the private attorney who was assisting Solicitor Adams argued to the jury that for Wilson to call a son whom he could control but fail to call his own wife was not credible. This attorney said in the presence of the jury that Lucky Joe's wife was present in the courtroom and that he saw her. In so doing, the lawyer deliberately put facts before the jury that were not in evidence. The judge instructed the jury not to consider this. The judge said that he was reading during the prosecutor's argument at the time and since he was not in the courtroom, no objection was made. Further, the judge said that he would not have permitted this argument if he were present in the courtroom. The Supreme Court ruled that this jury argument was inappropriate and expressed its opinion that juries would "recoil" whenever tactics of this type were used. Even so, they declined to reverse the conviction.

After the jury convicted and the judge sentenced Lucky Joe, he was granted bond until the next term of court until the Supreme Court ruled on his appeal. After the Supreme Court ruling, he was confined in the Watauga County Jail. On March 6, 1884, he escaped. The *Lenoir Topic* of March 19, 1884, reported, "One of the most adroit escapes known in criminal history was effected today (March 6) by Lucky Joe Wilson, a famous chief of a gang of desperados infesting this state." According to that article, Lucky Joe caught a chicken, killed it, and placed the blood on his clothing and body. The night was cold. Wilson scraped in snow and ice from outside and kept his hands and feet nearly frozen. As he lay motionless, the jailer discovered him and called for help. It was determined that Lucky Joe was dead, and his "body" was placed in a coffin. Later, when he was alone, Lucky Joe Wilson got out of the coffin and fled.

The publicity given to this incident created such an uproar that the Watauga County Jailer felt obliged to report his version. H. L. Huggins, the Watauga County jailer, wrote The *Lenoir Topic* on April 2, 1884, and blamed others for the escape. Huggins maintained that he sent for the chairman of the Watauga County Commissioners, D. B. Dougherty, who in turn, summoned two doctors, W.B. and M. B. Councill, who thought the prisoner was critically ill and ordered his removal to the Coffey Hotel. Huggins maintained that he dissented and expressed his judgment that Wilson was faking.

Lucky Joe was captured and began service of his 10-year sentence on May 12, 1884. He was 37 years old. He served until February, 1893, when he was discharged from prison.

In a nice twist of fate, Lucky Joe Wilson joined in the posse who went seeking Boone and Clarence Potter, bringing unkind commentary from a Justice of the North Carolina Supreme Court. Later, Lucky Joe would die in prison in Statesville, North Carolina.

In October 1902, Isaac Hodge complained to Justice of the Peace Burnett Smith that Boone Potter broke into his residence. The Justice of the Peace issued a warrant for forcible trespass. Earlier, Isaac Hodge testified before the Grand Jury where Boone Potter was charged with murdering James M. Broome. Throughout this narrative many of the same names will recur, in this instance a fact used by Boone and Clarence Potter to claim that certain people were out to get them.

Issuing a warrant was easy: the problems developed in getting it served. To serve a warrant means that the person charged must be physically arrested. Burnett Smith later testified at the trial of Clarence Potter, "the people of our country were afraid of the Potter men."[172]

Connor of the North Carolina Supreme Court later dealt with legal issues in the Clarence Potter case. He had this to say about this posse:

> I make no comment on the unfortunate man who lost his life (Amos Wellington Howell). Whether he was a 'brave officer' or not I do not know, and I forebear saying more, upon the record before us, than that it is fortunate for the administration of our criminal law that it is not the custom to proceed as these men did in the arrest of persons charged with violating the law.[177]

The Supreme Court rarely makes such a condemnation.

North Carolina permitted persons to resist an unlawful arrest, and such a rule always had the potential for disaster. Many folks in criminal justice think that the law should compel citizens to submit to arrest and then challenge the legality of the arrest later if they are so inclined. Such a rule would alleviate some of the dangers inherent to law enforcement officers as they attempt arrests. A significant change was made to this rule in modern times, but in 1902, the law permitted Boone and Clarence Potter to resist unlawful arrests.

November 5, 1902 was headed toward a confrontation as two violent young men were confronted by a posse whose de facto leader spent eight years in prison for horse stealing and whose membership was made up of enemies of the young men.

As could have been predicted, gunfire broke out. Wellie Howell was shot by Boone Potter, and Clarence Potter struck Wellie in the head with a large rock. Clarence was arrested, but Boone Potter, although wounded by a bullet, fled.

Wellie Howell died November 21, 1902. The Watauga County Grand Jury indicted both Boone and Clarence Potter for the first-degree murder of Amos Wellington Howell in March 1903. Clarence Potter, who was held in custody since his arrest in November 1902, was put on trial for first degree murder, convicted, and became the only person in Watauga County ever to be sentenced to be hanged.

Lucky Joe Wilson spent part of the night of November 4, 1902 with a woman before he joined the other posse members at

Isaac Hodges' house. During Clarence Potter's trial, which began March 28, 1903, Lucky Joe testified for the State. Defense attorney Will Lovill inquired about this woman, and forced Lucky Joe to testify that she was considered less than respectable: the time-honored strategy of attacking witnesses' character.

All of the Town of Boone's legal community became involved in the trial. E. F. and Will Lovill, together with W. H. Bower, represented the defendant, Clarence Potter. District Attorney Moses N. Harshaw was assisted by private attorneys Romulus Z. and Frank A. Linney and E. S. Coffey. Romulus Z. Linney was from Alexander County but bought land on Rich Mountain in Watauga County. Linney and his son had a considerable law practice in Watauga County.

The defense lawyers disputed the facts surrounding Wellie Howell's death.[178] Calvin Turnmire was not asked to join the posse at first: Howell, Lucky Joe Wilson, Hamby and Snyder spent most of the night together at Isaac Hodges' home. Howell, on the early morning of the shooting, November 5, 1902, went to Calvin Turnmire's residence to ask him to join the posse. Turnmire was initially asked to read the warrant to Clarence Potter, but Turnmire declined this opportunity since "I can't read to do any good." It was the practice to read warrants verbatim whenever a person was arrested.

On the night of November 4, 1902, the men of the posse formed a plan because they anticipated trouble. Under the plan, two men were to concentrate on Clarence Potter and the others on Boone Potter. Lucky Joe testified that he advised Wellie Howell not to get involved in this matter because Boone Potter would never be arrested, but Howell said that he had warrants and was confident that he could handle the situation.

A rainy November 5, 1902 dawned. Boone Potter worked at Frank Miller's saw mill. Early in the morning, Boone Potter drove a wagon with a team of mules into an area where the group of armed men waited in hiding. Clarence Potter sat on the wagon on the right side, next to Elbert Heck. As the three men jumped off the wagon, Calvin Turnmire suddenly confronted them and called Clarence Potter out. Clarence Potter moved toward

Turnmire for four or five steps and Turnmire advised Clarence that he was under arrest and that Turnmire had a warrant for him. Hamby read the warrant to Clarence. All three of these men testified at Clarence Potter's trial but Clarence Potter's testimony differed from theirs; Hamby and Turnmire said that Clarence told them that the day of arrest was not convenient, since he had to help Boone haul logs and that his father would sign his bond. Clarence testified that Turnmire gave Clarence Potter permission to change clothes since it was raining and his clothes were wet. Boone Potter stood some 15 steps away. Everyone agreed that Clarence got back on the wagon and that Boone got the mules moving in a trot. Turnmire and Hamby said that, as Clarence got onto the wagon, Boone had bounced on it as well and said, "Come on Clarence." Both Potters then got on the wagon and Boone was whipping the mules ("pouring cash on"). Clarence said at the trial that he was simply going to change clothes as he was given permission to do. Clarence maintained that Boone always made the mules trot when there was no log on the wagon. The posse, however, thought that the two men were attempting to escape and began running after the wagon.

When the wagon came to the creek, it slowed and Amos Wellington Howell crossed a footlog to the other side first. Clarence said that he and Boone Potter got off the wagon on the right side, and that their companion got off on the left side. Clarence Potter testified that he heard Howell make some statement to Boone Potter and that Boone asked Howell to show his authority, implying recognition of an impending arrest. Clarence said that at this point Howell drew his pistol on Boone and fired first, without provocation.

Boone Potter, contrary to his practice, was not armed, but Clarence carried a handgun under his bib overalls. According to Clarence, Boone grabbed the weapon from Clarence and fired once or twice on Howell. Clarence testified that Howell then threw the gun on Clarence and that:

> I (Clarence) picked up a little rock and threw it to keep
> him from shooting any more. About this time Boone
> and me started off to get away from these fellows. We
> ran a little piece together then I turned to the right and

he kept to the road. Joe Wilson, Snyder and Howell, I think, were after Boone and they shot a few shots. Hamby and Turnmire was after me. Hamby shot a few shots at me. I gave up and came back.

Turnmire and Hamby contradicted Clarence, saying that Clarence Potter gave the pistol to Boone instead of Boone grabbing it, and that Boone Potter was first to fire a weapon at Wellie Howell. Lucky Joe Wilson recalled that Boone Potter told Clarence Potter, "shoot 'em or give me the pistol." According to Wilson, Clarence Potter gave the weapon to Boone Potter, who fired the first shot. The state's witnesses agreed that Clarence Potter hit Wellie Howell in the head with a large rock after Howell was shot by Boone Potter. Clarence Potter was convicted of first degree murder, sentenced to be hanged, and appealed to the North Carolina Supreme Court.

Several difficult issues had to be resolved by this trial, namely, the legality of the posse and the right of defendant to resist an unlawful arrest. The defendants could have been found to have acted in self-defense, or convicted of a lesser charge than murder. Strangely, the defense team ignored these avenues, concentrating instead on whether the evidence showed premeditation. In making this strategic decision, the defense attorneys seem to have reconciled themselves to the likelihood that the jury would believe that Boone Potter fired the first shots and that he did so before either he or Clarence were put in danger. This strategy was designed to insure a conviction of a lesser offense than first degree murder, the best verdict they thought they could get for their client. During both the trial and the appeal before the Supreme Court, the defense argued that no evidence existed of premeditation on Clarence Potter's part, and no evidence existed of a conspiracy between Boone and Clarence to kill. Such a theory left open the possibility that Boone Potter acted with premeditation when he fired first at Wellie Howell, but that Clarence Potter's actions warranted only a charge of second degree murder.

Boone Potter did not testify since he remained at large as a fugitive, living in Wyoming. After Clarence Potter's conviction,

Boone Potter was arrested there and was interviewed by a reporter for *The Sheridan Post*:

> He talked readily about all of the charges against him, saying that when he killed the officer, five persons were after him and that one of them shot him after he had thrown up his hands. He says that he then got his gun and began shooting. He declared his willingness to go back to North Carolina; said he had employed good attorneys and would undoubtedly be cleared when his case comes to trial.[179]

Boone Potter's statement to the newspaper conflicts with the accounts of the witnesses at the trial, including Clarence's testimony. Boone's absence worked to Clarence Potter's advantage, and allowed Clarence to contend that whatever Boone Potter had in mind could not be imputed to Clarence Potter.

David M. Furches, later Chief Justice of the North Carolina Supreme Court, wrote in 1895 in another case:

> The facts in this case present a very bad tragedy, to use no stronger word. But we have nothing to do with that. This is a Court of appeals upon errors of law appearing in the transcript of record. We do not try the prisoner, but simply pass upon the correctness of the trial below. And, if we shall find error in the trial below, this does not acquit the prisoner, but only sends the case back for another trial.[180]

Furches' statement helps in understanding the role of the appellate courts. One appealing a conviction in criminal court is not entitled to have the appellate judges pass judgment upon the facts or to second-guess the jury's decision. The party appealing must assemble the trial transcript together with the appropriate court documents and have them delivered to the District Attorney who must agree that the record on appeal is correct. If the parties do not agree, the judge settles the record of the case on appeal. In Clarence Potter's appeal, the Supreme Court Justices were critical of the transcript and thought that they did not have a concisely stated record of the testimony before them.

The trial judge said the defendant would be guilty of first degree murder if the jury found facts showing one of three scenarios. First, if Clarence Potter premeditated the act and intentionally struck Wellie Howell on the head with a rock, bringing about the death of Wellie Howell, then he would be guilty. The appellate court took no issue with the judge's charge in this respect.

Second, the judge charged the jury that Clarence Potter would be guilty of first degree murder if Boone Potter premeditated murder and intentionally fired a gun into the body of Wellie Howell, killing him, and Clarence Potter had aided and abetted Boone Potter in some manner. There was some evidence showing that Clarence Potter had aided Boone. For instance, one version of the facts was that Clarence passed the gun to Boone Potter after Boone had said, "Shoot them or give me the gun." The Supreme Court found no error here.

Third, the trial judge charged the jury that it should find Clarence Potter guilty of first degree murder if it finds that Boone Potter and Clarence Potter conspired to resist arrest by taking the life of any one of the officers who was authorized to execute a warrant for arrest and that the two cousins acted in concert to accomplish this conspiracy. The judge recited that the jury could consider the events at the sawmill in making this finding. The sawmill stood some three hundred yards from the creek where Amos Wellington Howell was felled. Justice Walter A. Montgomery of the Supreme Court, who wrote the majority opinion for the court, opined that the jury should not have been permitted to find a conspiracy to resist arrest and to kill a posse member if necessary to resist arrest, based on facts which may have occurred at the sawmill. Boone Potter stood fifteen steps from Clarence at the sawmill and there was nothing that suggested that he knew there was a warrant for him. Montgomery thought that the events at the sawmill might demonstrate a conspiracy to resist the arrest of Clarence Potter, but could not be construed to show a conspiracy to kill. Since the judge had authorized the jury to infer facts that were not proved, there would have to be a new trial.

Justice Henry G. Connor of the court agreed with Montgomery, but additionally, wrote of Boone Potter:

> His conduct (at the saw mill) appears to me to be entirely consistent with that of a man in his station of life making his daily bread by his labor; he had unloaded his wagon and I can see nothing in his conduct inconsistent with what might have been expected of a man of his occupation.

Justice Connor, clearly, was not convinced that Boone Potter was able to overhear the conversation between Turnmire and Clarence Potter and that he was simply directing Clarence to leave with him, not thinking that he was impeding any effort to arrest. Connor did express his opinion that premeditation was later formed at the creek where the violence occurred.

The Supreme Court granted Clarence Potter a new trial, but the opinion was narrowly drawn, rejecting the defendant's argument that no evidence existed of premeditation. The justices likewise rejected counsel's contention that no evidence pointed to a conspiracy. They ruled that the trial judge overreached, and permitted the jury to give an interpretation to facts that the court felt could not be justified. This victory did not bode well for Clarence Potter's future and Justice Connor wrote:

> Upon his own showing, this uneducated young mountaineer, before reaching his majority, is guilty of murder in the second degree. It is more than probable that, at the best, he will forfeit to the State more than a score of years of his freedom.

Walter Clark was elected Chief Justice in November, 1902. He had been an Associate Justice and served so long on the court as an associate justice that he was involved in the formulation of the law relating to first and second degree murder. Originally, any malicious killing of a human was murder and punishable by death. Following enactment of the 1893 statute, the North Carolina courts began critical interpretations of this new law. Several murder cases—those involving Wade Patrick and G.W. Locklear from Robeson County, Edward J.

Fuller from Cumberland County, Gabriel Thomas from Pamlico County, and William Gadberry from Yadkin County— were reversed by the North Carolina Supreme Court because the majority of the justices found that the trial judges misinterpreted the new law.[181]   A conspicuous pattern developed in that Justice (later to be Chief Justice) Walter Clark regularly dissented whenever the Supreme Court granted a new trial in a murder case. Clark's interpretation of the new law made it easier for the State to obtain convictions of first degree murder. North Carolina's Supreme Court at the time consisted of five justices and some of the court's opinions show the judges often strenuously disagreed.

The statute's language addressed the meaning of premeditation and deliberation. As early as 1896, the North Carolina Supreme Court settled on this definition:

> What does the law mean by the word 'premeditation'? The word 'premeditate' means to think beforehand, as where a man thinks about the commission of an act and concludes or determines in his mind to commit the act; he has thus premeditated the commission of the act. The law does not lay down any rule as to the time which must elapse between the moment when a person premeditates or comes to the determination in his own mind to kill another person and the moment when he does the killing, as a test. It is not a question of time. It is merely a question of whether the accused formed in his own mind the determination to kill the deceased, and then at some subsequent period, either immediate or remote, does carry his previously formed determination into effect by killing the deceased. If there be an intent to kill, and a simultaneous killing, then there is no premeditation.[182]

One long-standing rule provided that when the State's evidence showed a killing with a deadly weapon then malice was presumed and the burden actually shifted to defendant to show that the killing was other than malicious.[183] Failure by defendant to meet this burden meant he was guilty of murder. Justice Clark wanted to extend this principle to proof of premeditation as well, so that a killing with a deadly weapon would have raised a presumption that the killing was done with malice and with premeditation. During the formative years of the first degree murder laws, the majority of justices rejected Justice Clark's position and this arena continued to cause dissention on the court. The court said that ruling on premeditation should fall to the jury, not to the judge. North Carolina courts ruled that premeditation did not have to be prolonged, but could be instantaneous so long as it preceded the killing. In the Potter case, Justice Connor noted, "I cannot but regret that it so frequently occurs that such widely divergent views exist in this Court in regard to the plainest principles of the criminal law." Clarence Potter's case set precedent on some important points, with plenty of disagreement from the opposing side. Chief Justice Clark voted to affirm the conviction.

Justice Clark thought that the judge had conducted the trial in all respects fairly and according to law:

> There was sufficient aiding and abetting, combining and conspiring, to make the prisoner guilty, whether (as is doubtful) the prisoner or Boone killed the deceased. Though the judge recited the evidence, as it was his duty to do, he did not, as the opinion assumes, tell the jury that the action in putting the horses into a lope was a conspiracy or combination, nor could the court tell them it was, nor that it was not. The remark 'Shoot, or give me the pistol,' is certainly some evidence, taken with the other circumstances, of a combination or conspiracy—the pursuit of a common design. . . .The motion for the pistol, the accompanying remark, and the handling it over under the circumstances, the immediate use of it by Boone, and the prisoner joining in the attack with a rock, certainly constituted some evidence (and very strong evidence) of aiding, abetting, combining and conspiring; and, if there was any evidence, it was properly left to the jury. The court told the jury that they should examine the evidence, and if, upon all the evidence and circumstances, the jury was satisfied of premeditation and deliberation, etc. Upon all the authorities, unless they are to be overruled, a moment of premeditation, no matter how

brief, is sufficient, if the jury find that there was premeditation and deliberation.

Chief Justice Clark expressed his concern that reversing this conviction would promote lawlessness:

> If there is no liability to capital punishment for taking the life of an officer under the circumstances of this case, then the only safe method of serving process on those defying the state's authority will be service by mail or with a shotgun; and the Legislature should so provide, authorizing the officer to fire first. The life of the officer is worth at least as much to the state and to his family and friends as that of the defiant lawbreaker, and the life of the latter is not the only one that should be regarded with tenderness in the administration of the law. No case could be presented more strongly demanding the capital sentence of the law than this, where two men who had been defying the law and the service of its precepts are halted by an officer with the state's process in his hand, and one of them motions to the prisoner for his pistol, which is passed over to him by the prisoner, and both united with pistol and rock in taking the officer's life, for no other cause than he was there honestly, faithfully endeavoring to obey the trust the state had confided in him. Is the state not strong enough, is it not just enough, to vindicate its majesty, and execute the law against the willful murderer of its own officer when its process is thus defied, and its officer slain, without provocation or excuse, for no fault save that he was endeavoring to do his sworn duty? Shall the condition of him who defies the law be so far better than that of him who shall attempt to execute it that the officer may lose his life, but the lawbreaker cannot? The state certainly cannot have faithful service which is more tender of the life of him who resists and slays an officer in the discharge of duty than careful to throw the terror of its power as a shield around the officer who would execute its orders.

Despite Justice Clark's fervor, the other justices voted Clarence Potter a new trial. A term was set for June, 1904, but Judge Neal continued the case because Clarence Potter maintained that one of his witnesses could not attend that session of court. On August 11, 1904, Clarence Potter stood trial the second time for his life for the murder of Amos Wellington Howell. Justice Connor of the Supreme Court predicted that Potter would be found guilty of at least second-degree murder, but the jury found Potter not guilty.

Community sentiment favored Clarence Potter. The *Watauga Democrat* on April 9, 1903 wrote:

> Some of the state witnesses who, it appears, were determined to hang a Potter, and in the absence of Boone Potter, the prime actor in this drama, Clarence must pay the death penalty at all hazards. And then to know that some of these witnesses who had hounded this boy to the gallows are men of the most damnable character themselves makes this death sentence more horrible. No one claims that this boy is not guilty of a crime, and a very serious one, and richly deserves punishment, but it seems to us that, everything considered, for him to die on the gallows as an accessory, while the principal in the crime is at large and no effort made to capture him, would be indeed a dark spot on the escutcheons of Watauga County and the Old North State.

These sentiments, widely circulated throughout Watauga County, both reflected and affected public opinion.

Likewise, the opinion written by the Chief Justice of the Supreme Court, also expressed skepticism that the head injury inflicted by Clarence Potter caused the death of Wellie Howell or that the evidence showed either premeditation or a conspiracy. The court did not accept either phase of the argument but rather said that the judge should not have allowed the jury to consider the activities at the sawmill as evidence of a conspiracy. Even so, the attorneys must have been encouraged that the evidence was not convincing to the Chief Justice or to the editor of the *Watauga Democrat* that Clarence's actions actually resulted in death of Wellie Howell.

At the second trial, Clarence changed his tune. He initially testified that Boone Potter grabbed the pistol from Clarence after the two men and their companion got onto the wagon and the posse stopped the wagon at the creek. For Clarence to give the weapon to Boone after trouble had started could be construed as Clarence assisting Boone Potter. At the second trial, the attorneys wanted to remove any evidence allowing this taint. Clarence Potter's testimony[185] at the second trial was that he handed the pistol to Boone Potter so that Clarence Potter would not have on his person a concealed weapon. The officer already told Clarence that he was being arrested for carrying a concealed weapon. We don't know if the jury believed Clarence Potter's second story, but the latter testimony would give credence for intent beyond just helping Boone Potter.[186]

The American Bar Association's rule of professional conduct prohibits a lawyer from counseling or assisting a witness to give false testimony. This rule is accepted by many state bar associations including that of North Carolina, but prosecutors generally view it as unenforceable since no meaningful forum exists to enforce the rule. It is violated often and usually without consequence. For Clarence Potter to have changed his testimony in regard to the passing of the weapon from him to Boone seems substantial; his attorneys would know better than anyone that he lied somewhere along the line. The bar rule regulating lawyers' conduct had not yet been instituted, and it is possible that this tactic strengthened the belief that Boone Potter alone killed Amos Wellington Howell.

Joseph T. Wilson did not appear as a witness in the second trial. The state's attorneys may have made a decision not to call him in any event, but he was in the County Prison in Iredell County. On June 9, 1904, the *Watauga Democrat* wrote:

> On Monday evening "Lucky Joe" Wilson was bound to court, tried and convicted for an assault on his daughter with a deadly weapon to wit: a heavy horse halter. There was also a case pending against him at this term of Court for beating his wife. He was drunk

on Monday evening when he left town and had with
him his wife.

During the term of court beginning June 6, 1904, Lucky
Joe was given a sentence of five years on the Iredell County roads.
Wilson died during this confinement.

The defense legal team in the second trial abandoned its
earlier arguments that there was no evidence of premeditation
and conspiracy because the Supreme Court had rejected that
argument. During the second trial, the lawyers relied upon another
strategy that the deputation of Howell was void. The deputation
that was signed by Justice of Peace Burnett Smith, missing in the
first trial, appeared at the second trial. Lucky Joe's wife testified
that after the first trial she found the deputation stuck between the
lining and fabric of Lucky Joe's coat. The coat was ripped, she
said, and the deputation was caught in the rip.

The state's evidence took another strange twist: the
warrants issued against Boone Potter and Clarence Potter were
missing. The Supreme Court noted that the clerk was unable to
produce the warrants during the appeal even though they were
introduced into evidence during the first trial. Now the warrants
simply vanished. Moreover, there was evidence that the warrant
against Boone Potter was materially altered after the shooting
incident. The original date of the alleged event was changed and
the allegations of conduct were changed as well. To prove this,
the defendant called one of his own attorneys, who confirmed the
alterations of the warrant.

To cast further doubt into the legitimacy of both the posse
and the warrant process, the defendant showed that Calvin
Turnmire did not post a bond as constable with the Register of
Deeds. Defendant's strategy was to show that the warrant was
void and that the posse's efforts to serve the void warrant were
themselves illegal, and thus the defendant was entitled to offer
resistance.

The defense team contended that the warrant against
Clarence Potter for carrying a concealed weapon was issued in
bad faith since Hamby and others were seeking to use the criminal
law solely in a vindictive manner against Clarence Potter. Carrying

this argument further, the defense lawyers contended that the entire effort lacked legitimacy—the warrant was void, the deputation was nonexistent, the posse was bogus and Citizen Potter would then be in a legal position to defend himself against such an unwarranted attack. Alternatively, Clarence's team advocated that the jury should find that Clarence cooperated with the posse and was given leave to go to his residence and change clothes. Furthermore, the warrant was not formally read to Clarence and the arrest was not legally perfected. Clarence also sought to show that Wellie Howell fired the first shot, and that this would justify Clarence defending himself and coming to the defense of his cousin, Boone.

Judge Thomas McNeill instructed the jury that it could find Clarence Potter guilty of first degree murder, guilty of second degree murder, guilty of voluntary manslaughter, or not guilty. The judge told the jury that there was no fixed time required in law for premeditation to occur. He spoke of the law of excusable self-defense. He told the jury:

> In passing upon the powers and authority of the officers, you are instructed that the mode by which the legality of process for the purpose of justifying an arrest is tested is this: process absolutely void does not protect the officer, but for mere error or irregularity of process making it voidable only, if the Sheriff or other officer be killed, whilst attempting in good faith, to execute it, such killing if done by the accused with deliberation and premeditation is murder in the first degree; if done without premeditation or deliberation but with malice, express or implied is guilty of murder in the second degree, but if done under legal provocation and in the heat of blood and upon sudden impulse, but without malice, and without deliberation and premeditation, is guilty of manslaughter.
>
> In the case of a warrant issued by a justice of the peace, in a matter in which he has jurisdiction to issue it, the person executing the warrant, when acting in good faith, is under the special protection of the law, and a killing

of an officer, or other person authorized to execute it is a felony, if done willfully to avoid arrest and the grade of the felony is determined by the ingredients entering into the offense and which I have just distinguished. An officer or other person authorized to make an arrest, and attempting to make an arrest under process, informally or defectively setting out the charge, if the process issued from a court having jurisdiction to issue it, has the full protection of the law interwoven around him in the performance of his duties in good faith.

A justice of the peace in extraordinary cases, may appoint anyone not a party to execute a warrant, and his decision is conclusive as to when such extraordinary cases arise for the exercise of such power. If you find from the evidence that Justice Smith appointed Mr. Howell to execute the warrants and administered an oath to him as such deputy at the time, you are instructed that he had the power to appoint him for that purpose. You are further instructed, if you believe the evidence, that he had the jurisdiction to issue the warrants against Boone Potter and Clarence Potter, you are further instructed that if Esquire Smith did appoint Howell to execute the warrants, that Howell had the power to summon other persons to aid him in making the arrest, and any person summoned by him for this purpose who willfully refused or neglected to obey the command is himself guilty of a misdemeanor.[187]

The jury found Clarence Potter not guilty. Juries are not required to explain their verdicts, and there is no known document that recorded the reasoning of the Potter jury. The judge's charge clearly authorized the jury to consider the lawfulness of the warrant and the legality of the deputation. Based on this charge, it is certainly possible that the jury found that Amos Wellington Howell was not lawfully authorized to make the arrests of Clarence and Boone Potter. Perhaps the first law enforcement officer to have been killed in Watauga County had not been an officer at all.

The second trial focused entirely on the gunshot wound as being the singular cause of death. A full reading of the judge's charge to the jury in the second trial reveals that the judge never used the word "rock." In the first trial, the judge charged that a pistol is a deadly weapon and similarly gave an instruction that a rock under the circumstances described by the evidence also becomes a deadly weapon. The second trial had no similar charge involving the rock. Finally, in the first trial, the judge told the jurors that Clarence Potter could be found guilty in effect under two theories: that he struck Amos Wellington Howell with a rock and this injury caused Howell's death, or alternatively, Potter could be guilty if Boone Potter shot Howell causing his death under circumstances showing that Clarence was a participant by aiding and abetting or by conspiring to carry out a common plan. In the second trial, the judge did not give the jury the option of finding Clarence guilty based on his slaying Howell with a rock.

When Boone Potter shot Wellie Howell on November 5, 1902, the .38 caliber bullet passed through the flesh of Howell's bicep, into and under the breastbone. Howell dropped his weapon but did not stagger. Howell was able to stoop to retrieve his weapon, but at that time Clarence Potter threw a rock and struck Howell on his right temple. Some witnesses said the rock weighed from eight to ten pounds, but others described the rock being around two pounds. Howell fell to his knees and then onto his left side, bleeding freely from his arm, breast, and head. When both Boone and Clarence Potter fled on foot, Wellie Howell joined in the chase, running some fifteen feet. He made a statement that he did not feel so bad.

After Clarence Potter was apprehended, all of those in the posse, together with Clarence, went first to the residence of John O. Potter who forbade them from coming to his house. The party, consisting of Wellie Howell, Stilley Snyder, Calvin Turnmire, Joseph T. Wilson, Will Hamby, and Clarence Potter walked to the residence of David M. Wilson that stood 1/4 mile from the shooting site. Howell lay down on a bed. Howell made statements and was able to talk coherently. Wilson said to Howell, "Wellie, I warned you against this, but you are killed, aren't you?" Howell answered, "No, I'm not hurt very bad." Wilson, continuing the interrogation, asked, "How come you to get shot, Wellie, and who shot you?" Wellie Howell answered, "Boone Potter did, but I shot him first." Explaining why he did not shoot Boone Potter again, Howell said, "When he shot me, it took the use of my arm and I dropped my pistol. But the shot I gave him will kill him. I went to reach down with my left hand for my pistol and Clarence Potter hit me with a rock and kindly addled me till I couldn't get hold of my pistol again. Then when I came kindly to myself these parties were gone."

Dr. Reece Graham attended Wellie Howell on the Wednesday night he was injured. He did not examine the head wound because it was bandaged. He determined that the projectile had passed through the muscle of the arm into the breast. The following day Dr. Graham removed the lead ball from the front part of Wellie's breast. Wellie was able to attend a church service on Saturday, and Dr. Graham saw him there. The church was located three-fourths of a mile from David Wilson's residence. On the same day, Wellie rode a horse to his parents' home in what is now the Fleetwood section of Ashe County, accompanied by Dr. Graham for the first part of the trip. The doctor thought that Wellie's wound was healing nicely.

Dr. Reece Graham was one of the first medically trained persons in the part of Ashe County that adjoins the Pottertown area of Watauga County. The Graham family has a long tradition of education in the medical and dental fields.[188]

There is no direct route from Pottertown to the Fleetwood section of Ashe County. The current road running through Meat Camp into Pottertown was not constructed in 1902. The existing road was primitive. Wellie Howell's grandfather, William Howell, lived in a house in Todd, North Carolina, which is currently owned by the Ben Blackburn family.. Although one cannot know what route Wellie Howell traveled, the most direct route that existed then would have taken him toward Todd, approximately midway between David Wilson's home and the Howell residence in Fleetwood. The Howells, large landowners and slave owners, built their stately home before the Civil War, but the large house was burned by General Stoneman.

Wellie would have traveled over a mountain to Todd, and then from Todd on a primitive trail that generally followed the New River, to Fleetwood.[189] In 1902, one traveling by horseback would have confronted a meandering trail that followed the hills and on occasion forded and re-forded the river. The fifteen-mile trek from Pottertown to Fleetwood might have meant an overnight stay at Grandfather William's.

Mrs. Lizzie Howell Fairchild[190] had a carefully preserved tin photograph of her uncle Wellie Howell. Amos Wellington Howell was buried on a hill behind his father's house, side by side with two little brothers who died in infancy. The Howells sold this property long ago. Following Mrs. Fairchild's directions, the grave of Amos Wellington Howell was located in March 1991. The grave lies in a pasture off the Water Tank Road in the Fleetwood section of Ashe County, on a hill. A fine stone once marked the grave. This little family cemetery lies, somewhat neglected, on privately-owned land. The headstone was discovered under a layer of soil and covered by grass, with its wording still legible.

Wellie's mother Rachel testified at both trials. Mrs. Howell testified that when Wellie came to her house, and for the remainder of his life, he complained of a throbbing in his head. He had a wound through to the bone where the band of his hat rested. She testified that her son lost a great deal of blood from his arm. He was able to walk around during this time. On Thursday, November 20, 1902, Wellie swooned away. He could hear talk and felt a dull throbbing in his head until his death. Dr. John C. Testerman gave his mother instructions, and she did what she could for her son. Wellie Howell died November 21, 1902, at about 3:00 p.m.

Dr. Testerman testified that he practiced medicine for 20 years, and that he was principally educated in the area where he lived—that is Ashe County. This could only mean that he had little formal education in medicine since there was no medical school in the area. He learned medicine as an apprentice. Testerman saw Amos Wellington Howell two or three days before his death. Howell was very weak. Testerman could tell that the pistol ball had passed under the arm into the front of Wellie's breast. This doctor attributed the cause of death to be weakness and loss of blood. In Dr. Testerman's opinion, a small amount of blood on the brain could have precipitated death, but was secondary to the bullet wound itself.

Dr. William Roby Blackburn had been practicing medicine for 14 years. He was educated at the College of Physicians and Surgeons. In the early 1900s, several medical schools were known as colleges of physicians and surgeons, but the one attended by Dr. Blackburn is currently a part of the University of Maryland Medical School. Dr. Blackburn testified that he saw Wellie Howell on November 6, 1902. The pistol ball had passed under the bone of the arm and into the chest for about four or five inches to a point within an inch of the median line. Howell complained of a headache. In Dr. Blackburn's opinion, both injuries, one caused by a rock striking the head and the other caused by the pistol ball, caused Wellie Howell's death.

Dr. Graham believed that death occurred as a result of secondary hemorrhaging from the gunshot wound. The pistol ball was in an area where it likely struck an artery. Dr. Graham stated that all gunshot wounds are liable to secondary hemorrhaging, and that a skull fracture might cause pressure on the brain and produce a clot. A Dr. Crowson testified that he saw Howell on the evening he was shot. Howell's clothing was wet with blood from his arm. This doctor did not observe a fracture of the head. The Justices of the Supreme Court made it clear that they thought the gunshot wound was the fatal wound, but the medical evidence was open to interpretation.

Dr. Page Hudson was North Carolina's first Chief Medical Examiner.[191] Dr. Hudson was given summaries of the doctors' testimonies and those of the other witnesses who described the deteriorating condition of Wellie Howell, along with other testimony and evidence. Doctor Hudson emphasized that he could give no conclusive opinion without an autopsy, but ventured his comment:

> In my opinion the head injury was the lethal one. I suspect that the impact of the stone to the head caused the somewhat slow accumulation of blood under the dura, the lining on the outside of the brain, that we call a subdural hematoma. For the arm wound (presumably from the same bullet) to cause the death in 11 days, the

mechanism should have been bleeding or infection. The material presented does not indicate that he had any significant amount of either after the initial hemorrhage.

Hudson stated that the characteristics of a subdural hematoma are "sneaky." In the first hours or even a couple of days, there would be few appreciable signs, but as the slow bleeding begins to increase toward the end, he would expect increasing problems. At the end, unconsciousness for a period of time would be expected. Howell, in the early days, after the shooting, could have done the physical things described.

The bullet wound, Hudson said, could cause secondary hemorrhaging by injuring, not severing, an artery or major vein. In such a case the injured vessel would remain weakened as the body appeared to grow stronger. After a week or so there could be a "traumatic aneurysm" where the weakened vessel finally erupted. Dr. Hudson likened this to an injured inner tube. Such a condition is rare, but would provide the most likely explanation for death if there was a sudden burst of bleeding after the initial injury. Certainly the two injuries could have interacted and each contributed to Wellie's death.

According to Lizzie Fairchild, Uncle Wellie was the oldest of seven children. Sometime after his death, his parents moved to Pennsylvania. Wellie Howell's last surviving sibling died in 1977. No relative survives who was alive in 1902.

After returning to his mother's home, he had grown visibly stronger, and on the date of his death, he walked a mile to the post office in Oval. Oval no longer exists as a community but the grand old building which once housed the post office still stands. "Uncle Wellie got hot and reopened the wound and bled to death before they could ever get it stopped."[192]   Preserved for a while by the family, the bloody blanket was eventually discarded. Mrs. Fairchild knew nothing about injuries from any rock. "I did not know anything about the rock. I have never heard of that." Other family members repeated this version. The version of Wellie Howell walking to the post office was not told during the trials, but this version makes it clear the bullet wound was fatal.

After his second trial, Clarence Potter left the Watauga County Courthouse a free man. Potter historians contend that Clarence Potter killed several other persons.[193] He is reputed to have shot his mother, not fatally, in the hip. On another occasion, Clarence Potter was disarmed during a trial in Watauga County. Clarence Potter spent his last days hospitalized in Tennessee, died at 82 years old at Eastern State Hospital in Knoxville, Tennessee, on September 21, 1965. Cause of death was said to be exhaustion due to cerebral vascular accident; other contributing conditions were chronic brain syndrome associated with cerebral arteriosclerosis with psychotic reaction.

Clarence Potter was buried in Dyson Grove Cemetery near Butler, Tennessee. He remains the only man ever to have been sentenced to be hanged in Watauga County. His sentence provided for hanging at the "usual place of executions in Watauga County," and since this judgment was never carried out, there was never established a usual place for hanging. He lived in the Trade, Tennessee, area. Clarence Potter lived many of his remaining years outside North Carolina. People still remember him walking the streets of Boone, always carrying a gun in an unconcealed shoulder holster. He often was provoked to draw the gun and all too frequently used it. Clarence Potter seemed to have thoroughly enjoyed his notoriety.

Footnotes

[167] *State vs. Fuller*, 114 N. C. 885 (1894)

[168] Doctor Franklin Main murdered his wife, Vennie Mae Main, daughter, Iona Main Potter, wife, and neighbor, E.A. Ellison on July 31, 1960 in the Meat Camp section of Watauga County. Mrs. Main actually lived until August 16, 1960. Doctor (Dock) Franklin Main then killed himself. On February 3, 1972, unknown killers strangled and simultaneously drowned Bryce and Virginia Durham and their son Bobby in the bathtub of their residence near Boone. No one was ever put on trial for these murders. Hubert S. Wagner killed Ronnie Earl Moody and Dexter Sebastian Byrd on Christmas Day, 1926. He was indicted in Watauga County for first degree murder but the case was moved to trial to Wilkes County, where Wagner was found guilty of second degree murder. Albert Anderson burned John and Bessie Jones to death in their residence on July 17, 1952. He was allowed to plead guilty to being an accessory before the fact to arson and two murders and was sentenced to three terms of life imprisonment.

[169] Clarence Potter, who is a subject of this book, was the first one to be convicted of first degree murder in Watauga County. William Baldwin was convicted of first degree murder of Blowing Rock Town Marshall J. W. Miller on July 6, 1909, and was sentenced to death. But Baldwin got a new trial and was convincted of manslaughter. He got another new trial, and on September 7, 1911, he was found not guilty.

Execution by electricity began in North Carolina for crimes that happened after March 6, 1909, and Baldwin's death sentence was one of North Carolina's first under this new law. Baldwin is the only person sentenced to death by electricity in Watauga County.

Leonard W. La Fond and Jo Ann Severson pleaded guilty to the first degree murder of their traveling companion, Lewis A. Finn, on April 27, 1956 and were both sentenced to life imprisonment.

John Denver Potter was convicted in 1977 of the first degree murder of Ferd Snyder. At the time of the offense, the United States Supreme Court ruled the death penalty unconstitutional, and Potter was sentenced to life imprisonment.

Phillip Lee Young and Dwight David Presnell were convicted of the first degree murder of J. O. Cook in 1983. Young became the third person sentenced to death in Watauga County, but the Supreme Court changed his sentence to life imprisonment.

Daniel Brian Lee was sentenced to death on April 26, 1990, for the first degree murder of Jennifer Gray, but sentencing occurred in Avery County even though it was a Watauga County case.

Kenneth Coffey on November 27, 1995, and Bobby Bragg on February 26, 1996, were convicted of first degree murder of Marvin "Coy" Hartley and both were sentenced to life imprisonment.

Lamont Claxton Underwood was convicted on July 21, 1997 for the first degree murder of Victor Gunnarsson on December 3, 1993. Underwood was sentenced to life imprisonment. This case had an international angle because Gunnarsson was a suspect in the assassination of Swedish Prime Minister Olaf Palme.

Shelby Jean White was convicted in Watauga County on July 1, 1998, of first degree murder in Avery County, and sentenced to life imprisonment.

Arthur Ashley Burton pled guilty to first degree murder of Kimberly Kameter on May 29, 2001, and he was sentenced to life imprisonment.

Tony Carlton Barker pleaded guilty to first degree murder of Justin Knight on February 11, 2002, and was sentenced to life imprisonment without parole.

[170] Elizabeth South Storie wrote *My Killing Kin*, (The Reprint Company, Spartanburg, South Carolina, 1991), which devotes considerable space to the Potter ancestry.

[171] Arville Perry, late of Boone, was a collateral descendant of Lucky Joe. Perry was, for many years, a deputy sheriff whenever the Democrats held the Office of Sheriff. In the mid 1970s, a cache of tear gas canisters

exploded and Arville Perry was disabled and he then retired. Perry talked at great length about Lucky Joe Wilson and produced a newspaper clipping written by Nancy Alexander which appeared in the *Lenoir News Topic* on May 25, 1957. Lucky Joe has numerous descendants living in Watauga County and some discuss their ancestor with amusement while others remain mum.

Ralph Wilson and Forrest B. Wilson were sources for the Wilson narrative together with the Alexander article.

[172] Narrative transcript of Clarence Potter Trial, Original Records of the Supreme Court North Carolina Archives.

[173] Narrative transcript of the testimony, original cases files of the Supreme Court, North Carolina Archives.

[174] Revised Code chapter 24, section 11.

[175] Composite from the narrative transcript, original case files of the Supreme Court, North Carolina Archives.

[176] The Snyder family did not fare well in its relations with the Potters. At the Spring term of Watauga County Superior Court in 1903, Clarence Potter was indicted for assault of C.S. Snyder with a deadly weapon, a pistol, and serious injury was alleged. There was an accumulation of assault charges against Clarence Potter that were still pending in 1911, and an entry in the Watauga County Clerk of Superior Court office shows these charges: "Ordered retained on docket until the expiration of two years sentence which defendant (Clarence Potter) is serving on Gaston County roads. To be dismissed at that time if defendant leaves the state." Banishment from a state was a tool used by the courts of the past. In addition, criminal cases were dismissed if the defendant might join the military. Such remedies did not serve criminal justice well, although they may have been useful to particular jurisdictions.

[177] *State vs. Potter*, 134 N. C. 719 (1904)

[178] Summarization of the testimony is from the narrative transcript Supreme Court Original case files North Carolina Archives.

[179] *Sheridan Post*, Sheridan, Wyoming, August 27, 1903. This is the only recorded incident where Boone Potter talked about the death of Amos Wellington Howell.

[180] *State vs. Gadberry*, 117 N. C. 811 (1895)

[181] Opponents of the death penalty often say that numerous death penalty convictions are overturned by the appellate courts and this shows an uncertainty or lack of skill on the part of lawyers and judges in dealing with death penalty issues. Periods of repetitive reversals by the appellate courts usually occur when there is a significant change in the law, and in such cases, it takes time to develop an understanding of the new law.

[182] *State vs. Dowden*, 118 N. C. 1146 (1896)

[183] Shifting the burden of proof to the defendant would now be unconstitutional. Current law allows the jury to infer malice but the jury is not compelled to do so and the defendant has no burden of proof.

[184] Leonard Greer has lived all his life in Watauga County. He is interested in history. His explanation, based on things he had been told, for the not guilty verdict in the second trial was, "There were many guns in the town of Boone," implying an atmosphere of intimidation.

[185] Handwritten judge's notes, North Carolina Archives.

[186] Since there was no conviction, a transcript of the testimony was never made. Not even a narrative form of transcript exists. The judge's handwritten notes are in the North Carolina Archives and his charge to the jury is in the Watauga County Clerk of Court office. Both were used as a source for determining the testimony at the trial.

[187] Judge's handwritten notes, Loose file, Watauga County Clerk of Court.

[188] Dr. James Graham of Boone is a dentist of note. Dr. Reece Graham was a brother of one of his ancestors. Dr. Reece Graham was well educated and attended medical school at one of the precedents of the University of Maryland School of Medicine. He had an extensive practice.

[189] It is said that the New River is among the oldest of all rivers in the world. In 1917, a railroad was built into Todd following the course of the river. When this railroad was abandoned, a paved road was built there. Popular now with bicyclists, this narrow road is a stretch of level pavement for several miles. It parallels the river and provides both a spectacular view and a glimpse into history since its surrounding lands are not greatly developed. It is bordered by rolling farmlands and is a place without too many passing motor vehicles.

[190] Ohh—Ben Blackburn. He enjoys libraries, and old records are a source of joy for him. His interest and help were profound. He is a lineal descendant of Amos Wellington Howell's ancestors, and considers himself to be a distant cousin of Wellie Howell. Among his family archives is a photograph of Cousin Wellie. Ben's family could not identify the photograph until Ben helped with this book. Wellie was identified by Mrs. Lizzie Howell Fairchild. In 1990, when Ben Blackburn first learned of the author's research, he was merely interested until he learned that Amos Amos Wellington Howell was related to him. Then he became enthusiastic. In March 1991, Blackburn introduced Mrs. Fairchild to the author.

[191] Superbly educated in medical science and possessing a deep, resonant voice, Dr. Hudson became a favored witness in criminal cases all over North Carolina. The medical examiner system began in North Carolina in the 1960s. Dr. Hudson put together a staff which was often raided to fill similar positions in other states. He is now a consultant after a stint on the faculty at East Carolina Medical School. After testifying several times in Madison County, he became a part time resident there.

[192] Conversation with Mrs. Lizzie Howell Fairchild in March 1991.

[193] James Marvin Potter remembers that Clarence Potter would say when asked why he killed so many people, "Yah God, Honey, they needed it." Prosecutors know well that violent people tend to be recidivists. Proponents of capital punishment can point to specific deterrence. One who is put to

death will not kill again. Much of Clarence Potter's mayhem was not committed in North Carolina.

Chapter 2: Bluster, Myth, and an Attempt at Reality

The two trials of Clarence Potter add to the understanding of the historic evolution of the death penalty. However, Clarence Potter's story is not complete without his more infamous cousin, Daniel Boone Potter. Boone Potter, aka "Boonie," "Booner," or "Little Dan," was Clarence's double first cousin. Boone's mother was Clarence's blood aunt and Boone's father was Clarence's blood uncle. Every old-timer in Watauga and Ashe Counties can tell a story about this young man.[194] Some stories, that equated Boone Potter with the notorious killer, Billy the Kid, are obviously legends.[195] In Boone, as in many pioneer towns of the early twentieth century, young men openly carried guns when they were venturing out not only into the woods but also into the community.[196]

Boone Potter's exploits impressed young Potter children and they all learned the stories of whom he killed and how he killed them.[197] Historically, we know that he did kill several men. Only a few of the Potters in Pottertown were responsible for the notoriety of the family for fighting and killing.

The Ashe County Public Library has old records from Pennsylvania on microfilm, and the records depict the Potters as respected and even esteemed in that state. J.O.J. Potter served as a Justice of the Peace, and James Marvin Potter's father was a respected merchant. The bluster and myth surrounding Boone Potter makes serious research difficult and necessary.

Pottertown, remote and isolated, was unruly—the law did not often venture there. Travel up to Snake Mountain was long and arduous, and folks did have some reason to fear for their safety. James Marvin Potter remembered one occasion when Boone Potter was arrested by the Watauga County sheriff; but he escaped en route to Boone and jail.

Lurid newspaper accounts contributed to his legend, and to the difficulty in separating fact from fiction. Some relatives say Boone died at the age of 21, and during the trial of Clarence Potter, Clarence estimated the age of his cousin Boone to be 23. The headstone on Boone Potter's grave (which has an erroneous date of death) shows that he was 25 and was born on September 30, 1879. The United States Census for 1900 shows that Boone Potter was born in December of 1879. If this is accurate, then Potter, who died on April 23, 1904, would have been 24. Robert C. Rivers, the former editor and proprietor of the *Watauga Democrat,* concluded that Boone was about 26 when he died.

When the posse killed Daniel Boone Potter, it made headlines throughout the state. As will be shown later, Will Hamby fired the weapon that killed Boone. The *Asheville Citizen* said on April 24, 1904, that Potter had cut his "third notch" in killing John Hamby in the mountains of Johnson County, Tennessee. The story was wrong. The event occurred in Pottertown in Watauga County and it was Will Hamby who killed Boone Potter, not the other way around.

The *Greensboro Patriot* (dated April 27, 1904) continued the charade: "Desperado on the Warpath." In a dateline from Roanoke, Virginia, the *Patriot* reported that Boone Potter killed a man named *Hamberry in Johnson County, Tennessee* and that he escaped and was heavily armed. In fact, Boone Potter lay dead. The *Charlotte Daily Observer* also got it wrong.

The word *desperado* was used to describe Boone Potter in the *Statesville Landmark*, the *Watauga Democrat*, the *Greensboro Patriot*, the *Asheville Citizen*, the *Charlotte Daily Observer*, and the *Sheridan Post* of Sheridan, Wyoming. Governor Charles B. Aycock referred to Boone's alleged killing of Amos Wellington Howell as a *"foul"* murder. North Carolina extradited Boone Potter back to his home state from Wyoming, an expensive venture involving the payment of a reward.

During the Clarence Potter first degree murder trials, Dr. Crowson testified that he examined both Amos Wellington Howell and Boone Potter. Potter was shot one-half inch from the left nipple. Boone Potter was in a hurry and did not have time for the doctor to probe. The bullet, which exited his body, could not have been fired by someone standing in front of him, Crowson said.

Boone Potter fled North Carolina after shooting Wellie Howell. Governor Aycock offered a reward of $200.00 for his capture. The Watauga County Commissioners offered a reward of $50.00. Lucky Joe Wilson boasted that he would chip in another $50.00.

On Sunday morning, August 2, 1903, a young man who called himself Donnelly walked into the Post Office in Sheridan, Wyoming. Awaiting his arrival was Sheridan Town Marshal C. H. Grinnell. The Marshal arrested Donnelly, claiming that he was really Daniel Boone Potter, a fugitive wanted for murder in North Carolina. Donnelly denied the allegation. For the first and only time in his life, Boone Potter was photographed, and the mug shot sent to the Sheriff of Watauga County for identification. Word returned to Marshal Grinnell that he had indeed captured the fugitive. Obviously, Grinnell had information from a source in Watauga County or he would not have been lying in wait for Boone Potter in Wyoming. The clannish nature of the Potter family suggests that only someone who was intimately connected with the family could have provided this information.

On August 5, 1903, Watauga County Solicitor Moses N. Harshaw requested that Governor Aycock requisition Boone Potter from the State of Wyoming. Three days later, Aycock sent a telegram to Wyoming Governor Fenimore Chatterton: "Please have authorities in Sheridan hold Boon Potter for requisition wanted here for foul murder." Aycock then made a formal request for extradition and named James S. Squires from Caldwell County as agent to take custody of the fugitive. Arrangements were made to house Boone Potter in the Caldwell County Jail rather than the Watauga County Jail. On August 13, 1903, Boone Potter escaped from the Sheridan County Jail. At the time of escape, he continued to maintain that his name was Donnelly.

The *Sheridan Post* wrote that Potter used a broomstick and a chair spindle to reach under the steel door and force the bolt holding the lever upward. Potter then walked outside the steel enclosure and took a stove poker and picked a hole through the brick wall. The county jail was used to confine Potter because the town jail was deemed insecure and Sheridan officials were told "Potter was a very bad man." It seems as though newspapers could not get the facts right—the *Post* reported that Potter was wanted for the murder of "two deputy sheriffs in North Carolina."

On the day of Potter's escape, Sheriff Neilson did not follow his habit of padlocking the cell because he did not feel well and thought that escape was impossible. Potter was soon caught. Once news reached Watauga County, Boone's past caught up with him, and for the first time, Potter admitted his identity to newspapers and the public in Wyoming.

North Carolina agents J. S. Squires and J.N. Harshaw arrived in Sheridan, Wyoming, on August 24, 1903, but they found the town marshal unwilling to relinquish Boone Potter until he was paid the reward. Squires telegraphed Governor Aycock, who was staying at the Battery Park Hotel in Asheville. At 11:07 a.m. on August 25, 1903, Governor Aycock sent Governor Chatterton a telegram: "Town marshal Sheridan refuses to surrender Ben (sic) Potter wanted here for murder. He will be paid reward on receipt of account. Please have him deliver Potter to my agent." The officers left with Boone Potter on a train headed for North Carolina that very day. In September, 1903, the State of North Carolina paid J.S. Squires $490.40 for expenses in delivering Potter from Wyoming to Lenoir, North Carolina. C. H. Grinnell was paid $203.10 for reward and expenses by the citizens of North Carolina. On December 7, 1903, the Watauga County Commissioners paid C. H. Grinnell the reward of $50.00 that county had proffered. No record exists of Lucky Joe Wilson ever paying out his reward.

On December 18, 1903, Boone Potter and a cell mate, Archie Wilkes, escaped from the Caldwell County Jail in Lenoir. The *Lenoir Topic* of December 23, 1903, described the act and, according to that article, Potter removed a steel bar from the cell sink. Using that bar, Boonie broke the combination lock to the iron case where the draw bars were locked and the keys were kept. Boone then took the keys, reached through the door and unlocked the cell. He took the steel bar that he had used earlier and knocked a hole in the wall to the jail and left in a manner similar to that of his escape in Sheridan, Wyoming. Archie Wilkes surrendered shortly thereafter. Boone made good his escape, and returned to Pottertown where he lived openly. During this time, Potter was always heavily armed, carrying two handguns and a rifle. Sheriff McCall of Caldwell County offered a two-hundred dollar reward for the capture of Boone Potter.

On April 2, 1904, the dead body of Charles Campbell was found near the Potter residence. Campbell had a gun shot wound to the side of his head and a serious injury to his hand. Charles Campbell was charged with murder in Burke County, and was placed in confinement in Catawba County at Newton awaiting his trial. Campbell escaped from jail on March 24, 1904. Before his escape, he came to know Clarence Potter, who was also confined in the Catawba County Jail while his appeal for the first degree murder of Amos Wellington Howell was being heard in the Supreme Court. A few days after his escape, Campbell showed up in Pottertown. Clarence Potter told Campbell that Boone would give him refuge. Campbell arrived in Pottertown in bitter cold and in poor shape after his escape. Boone Potter was suspicious of Campbell and on April 1, 1904, asked his mother, Clarence Potter's aunt, to visit her nephew in the Catawba County Jail. Mrs. Potter talked with Clarence Potter, and on the following day, Campbell was found dead.

H. L. Weaver was the Watauga County Coroner in 1904. He organized a coroner's jury and conducted an inquest over the body of Charles Campbell. Dee Etta Potter, Boone's sister, purported to be the only eyewitness to the death of Charles Campbell. She testified that Campbell shot himself with a .38 caliber handgun, and as he fell to the ground, his hand struck a rock inflicting the serious injury to the hand.[198] The coroner's jury heard from Dr. F. M. Greer who testified as a physician.[199] The coroner's inquest concluded that Charles Campbell killed himself.[200] Locally, the death of Campbell was not reported in the newspaper, and the matter, strangely, generated little interest. Outsiders already took their cue that they were not welcome in Pottertown. Yet there were some who were skeptical about Campbell's death, especially in Caldwell, Burke, and Catawba counties, where Campbell was well known.

Dr. J. R. Campbell of Newton, North Carolina, who was not related to Charles Campbell, studied the Watauga County inquest, working on information that a .38 caliber bullet entered Campbell's head near his ear. There were no powder burns on the deceased's head. Dr. Campbell thought there would have been powder burns to the head had the deceased fired the shot, even if the handgun were held at extreme arm's length. If it were murder, Boone Potter was the obvious suspect. Moreover, in Dr.

Campbell's opinion, the injury to Campbell's hand was more consistent with a bullet wound than an injury caused by striking a rock as Campbell fell. Dr. Campbell thought the deceased had thrown up his hand as the gun was fired, and the bullet passed through the hand.[201]

On Saturday, April 23, 1904, a posse consisting of Deputy Sheriff J. W. Miller (Willet Miller), Jonas Winebarger, Will Hamby and Dave Regan armed themselves with shotguns filled with buck shot load and hid near the residence of Boone's mother, Mrs. Enoch Potter, close to the Ashe County line. Boone Potter and a driver were on a wagon trip to Elk Park, North Carolina. As the two men approached the residence, the men of the waiting posse sprang up, pointing shotguns at the two men. Hamby demanded that Potter surrender and Potter initially said "all right," but then wheeled around and jumped off the back of the wagon. In a single motion Potter fired his handgun at Jonas Winebarger and hit him in the shoulder. The three other men of the posse fired and Potter was struck in the shoulders and arms with buckshot, but was able to flee into the woods. The men of the posse took wounded Jonas Winebarger to Will Hamby's home while Potter returned to his mother's home.

Potter then dispatched a small boy to tell the posse that Potter intended to kill them. While Will Hamby waited on the porch of his house, he saw Boone Potter stealthily approach the house. Hamby and Potter exchanged several shots and Boone Potter fell mortally wounded. Potter was taken to his mother's house and died within a few hours. He was buried that Saturday afternoon beside his father, Enoch. His grave was marked with a rock. Sometime later, engraved headstones were placed on Enoch's and Boone's graves. Boone Potter's stone states that he died April 30, 1905 (rather than April 23, 1904). In reporting on the duel between Potter and Hamby, the *Watauga Democrat*, in worthy style, proclaimed the duel was "An exhibition of bravery and recklessness rarely seem among men."

Shortly after Boone Potter's death the Statesville *Landmark* reported that Potter confessed to the killing of Charles Campbell on his deathbed. This rumor was then repeated in the *Charlotte Observer*, *The News Herald* of Morganton, *The Weekly News* of Lenoir and other papers. According to this reported confession, Potter continued to have strong suspicions about Campbell and finally aimed his revolver at Campbell's head. Campbell reflexively raised his hand, the bullet glanced off the hand and struck him in the head. Boone Potter was also reported to have said that he bribed the jailer who permitted his escape from the Caldwell County Jail, but papers soon began to challenge this reported confession. *The News Herald* of Morganton asked Deputy Sheriff J. W. Miller about Boone's deathbed confession. Miller, who stayed with Boone Potter and his family after Potter was shot, said:

> If he said anything about having killed Campbell or that he bribed the jailer at Lenoir to let him out of jail I have yet to hear of it. I was at the home of Potter some two hours after he was shot and he seemed unable to speak above a whisper. I think the reports to which you allude are all probably unfounded.[202]

John Church lived in Pottertown and was one of the jurors on the Coroner's Jury that held an inquest over the body of Charlie Campbell. He said:

> There is no doubt at all about how Campbell met his death. It was a clear case of suicide. Potter's sister, the only eye witness, told how it was done, and her testimony, and the condition of the corpse, and all the surroundings, were so conclusive that no question was raised as to it being a case of suicide.

For many, it remains hard to believe that Boone Potter made a confession while dying, and it did not end the matter of whether Campbell's death was a suicide.[203] The Potter family knew what happened.

In a crime ritual of the era, questions arose as to the payment of the reward. The Caldwell County sheriff offered a reward after Boone Potter escaped. The Watauga County posse claimed the reward, but the Caldwell Sheriff refused to pay it. He contended that he offered a reward for the arrest and delivery to him of Potter, and that those terms were not met. The Sheriff's personal reward was not paid.

Boone Potter's short, violent life and his death, created both fact and fiction in the accounts of his life and misdeeds.

The April 29, 1904, Statesville *Landmark* published:

> Boone Potter, Desperado Brief History of the Career
> of the Watauga County Murderer—Began His Career
> of Crime at the Age of Ten—Four or Five Killings
> Accredited to Him—His Father one of his Victims.

The author of this article is not identified and one hopes that the writer made efforts to verify his work. The article itself shows the work is based on the report of one unnamed source: "in conversation with one who has had more or less association with the Potter family for a few years, the following is learned." Later the *Watauga Democrat* published the same article. Whatever its deficiencies in verifying information, the *Landmark* article appears to be the only piece written at the time attempting to report history rather than create a legend. But can it be authenticated?

The *Landmark* stated:

> Boone's first desperate deed was when he was about
> ten years old, when he defied a band of revenue officers.
> Boone and his father were traveling with a load of
> blockade liquor when the revenue officers attacked them,
> shooting at them. The father ran but Boone remained
> and returned the fire.

Using the date shown as date of birth on Daniel Boone Potter's tombstone (September 30, 1879) this event should have happened about 1889. There is no record of this incident. Revenue officers were officers of the United States government and under the statutes of the times, ten-year-old boys could be prosecuted as adults. The law then provided that infants under seven years of age were conclusively presumed to lack capacity to commit crimes, and accordingly could not be indicted or punished. A child over fourteen was, by contrast, considered to be fully responsible for his actions. And for the younger children, an aggravated battery using a deadly weapon could be sufficient to rebut the presumption of incapacity based on age.[204] Returning fire, as the newspaper article described, does not constitute a battery, but would tend to show a "mischievous mind" which the courts ruled would also rebut the presumption. A narration that federal officers and a ten year-old boy engaged in a shootout with no charges being brought seems unlikely. Of course, it could have taken place somewhere outside North Carolina.

The *Landmark* article continues:

> Although he was never arrested for it, a murder was credited to Boone about four years ago. A man named Bloom came to the Potter neighborhood and settled. While it is not known that Bloom was a dangerous character he was suspected of evil intentions. He carried pistols and was always heavily armed. Bloom was leaving his house one day when he was shot in the back and killed. It is generally believed that Boone shot him.

The dead man's name was James M. Broome and his body was found on the morning of December 2, 1900,[205] outside the residence of Enoch Potter. He was shot in the back and it appeared obvious that he was murdered.

A Coroner's inquest was held and the jury questioned members of the Enoch Potter family. Potter family members asserted that Broome killed himself. The coroner's jury ended inconclusively. Coroners' juries were composed of local people, who could easily be subjected to intimidation or could have shared in the prevailing distrust of outsiders coming into the area.

Boone Potter actually granted a newspaper interview some years later to the *Sheridan Post*. This interview took place after Boone escaped and was recaptured in Sheridan, Wyoming, after exaggerated reports that Potter had made it "out west" from Watauga County. Potter's statements in the August 27, 1903, edition of the paper were about a tramp who was in the neighborhood for several days and whose body was found in front of the Potter house. Potter said "the tramp committed suicide with a revolver and my entire family was tried for his murder and acquitted." (An apparent reference to the Coroner's Inquest.) Broome's death contributed to the notion that strangers were not safe in the Pottertown section of Watauga County.

At the spring 1903 term of Watauga County Superior Court Isaac Hodge and W. R. Hamby appeared before the Grand Jury and persuaded the grand jurors to issue a presentment charging Daniel Boone Potter with the murder of James Broome on December 1, 1900. That presentment does not constitute a formal accusation. Solicitor Moses N. Harshaw never followed the presentment with a bill of indictment. Will Hamby already exhibited animosity toward Potter, ultimately killing him. Hodge was the person who swore out a warrant against Potter, setting in motion the events that led to the shooting of Amos Wellington Howell.

The *Landmark* next claimed "five or six years ago Boone killed a negro in West Virginia." This accusation follows the Potter legends that Clarence Potter killed a Negro in Virginia. Only the Potters themselves could have revealed these matters outside the state. Considering their propensity to brag about their exploits, those murders could have happened but were never verified. The *Landmark* article continued:

> The deed that brought him before the public was when he killed his father about two years ago. In regard to the cause of this act it is understood that Boone's father, Enoch Potter, supported a woman who lived with him but who was not his wife. Enoch owned considerable land which he was selling off, taking notes payable to this woman. Boone Potter resented this illegal discrimination against his mother and championed her cause. The two men, Boone and Enoch, were in different rooms of the Potter home. Enoch heard Boone denouncing him for his action in regard to the land. He went to the door of the room where Boone was and shot him twice with a Smith & Wesson pistol, one ball taking effect in the breast and the other in the abdomen. Boone returned the fire with a Winchester rifle, the ball taking effect in Enoch's bowels. He died from the

injuries two weeks later. Boone was acquitted in the court on the ground of self defense.

This incident was well documented. Sworn testimony was given and is preserved in the North Carolina Department of Archives. The story is worth repeating.

J.O.J. Potter was one of Boone Potter's kinsmen, and a Justice of the Peace in North Fork Township serving Watauga County in 1902. On May 16, 1902, Justice Potter issued a warrant charging D.B. Potter with the murder of his father, Enoch. The warrant was issued based on an affidavit of T. J. Ray. On the same day, Justice Potter conducted a preliminary hearing to determine whether Boone Potter should be bound over for Superior Court. At the conclusion of the hearing, Justice Potter determined that "D.B. Potter, Jr.,[206] the defendant, be discharged upon the grounds that the act and homicide of which he stands charged was committed wholly and absolutely in self defense." The effusive language used by Justice Potter was not unusual in court papers, and considering his family connection, suggests that the Justice of the Peace was making a strong point.

Several people witnessed both the shooting and events afterwards, including Justice Potter. Enoch Potter lived in a two-story house, upstairs with his wife Evelina. Sarah Ellison lived downstairs. At the time of the shootings, on April 11, 1902, Abraham Potter, Enoch's brother, and Abraham's wife, Selena Potter, went to Enoch's residence seeking to purchase the Potter home. The company also included both female residents of the home, Evelina Potter and Sarah Ellison, and their children, including Boone. Justice of the Peace Potter arrived late but in time to witness the shooting. T. J. Ray came at the request of Enoch Potter to write a deed and notes for the payment of money. These witnesses gave written statements that fully account for what happened.

Enoch Potter decided to move to Oregon. His brother, Abraham, agreed to buy Enoch's real estate. Boone Potter cautioned his mother not to sign the deed without receiving a share in the proceeds. T. J. Ray was a neighbor whom Enoch asked to come over to write for him. Following is T. J. Ray's statement:

I received word from Enoch Potter to come to his house on the night prior to the shooting. He wanted me to do some writing for him, but did not go till next morning. I saw Booney and the balance of the family first and saw no signs of any trouble. I asked Booney where his father was. He informed me he was upstairs. I then went up and found Enoch and shook hands with him and he soon introduced his business after which we drank some whiskey.

He told me that he and Booney had had a falling out the evening before and that he came dam ny[207] shooting him and he went on to say that he would shoot his own boy as quick as any body else if he fooled with him. A little child was standing by about 2 yrs old, which he said he would shoot as quick as any body if it agrevated him enough.

Then he said he wanted me to write a deed; as he had sold his land to his brother Abe, and intended to go to Organ at once. He then sent his daughter after paper, pen and ink and Abe Potter & wife said to tell Abe & his wife to come down at once to fix up that trade, for he wanted to have the deed registered before the sun went down. I wrote the deed then the deceased sent for a justice of the peace[208] & he came to take the acknowledgment. When the J.P. arrived the deceased ordered the J.P. to go downstairs & take the acknowledgment of his wife Evelina. Just after the writing of the deed I wrote three notes of one thousand dollars each. Said notes were made payable to Enoch Potter. In a few minutes the J.P. and Evelina called Enoch to come in the adjoining room; as they wanted to speak to him. When the deceased was absent Booney Potter came in the room. I was called for in a short time to bring my pin and ink in the room where Enoch was at. I went in the room where Evelina Enoch and the J.P. were at. Just as I went into the room Enoch handed me the deed and said: Write Evelin's name. She is willing to sign her name but she cannot write her name.

I ask Evelina if she was willing for me to sign her name to the deed. She said: speaking to Enoch I am willing to do what is right and I know you are so I think you ought to sign one of the notes over to me. At this remark, the deceased seemed to fly in a passion & began cursing her, and said: God Damn you if you don't want to sign this deed don't you do it, you can go to Hell and all your damn proceeds. Just then I heard Booney speak in the adjoining room, but failed to understand what he said. Just then Enoch reached for his pistol in his belt, and raised to his feet with his pistol in his hand and started into the room where Booney was and said as he went:

God damn him I will settle it with him. As soon as he turned the door out of my sight through the door I herd three shots fired in rapid succession. There was screams and cries that Booney was killed. I past by Enoch who had set down on the head of the stairs I went on in the room and found Booney lying on the bed on his back. I found a bullet hole in the upper part & one in the lower part of his chest. From the nature of the wounds I thought Booney Potter would be dead in a few minutes. I hurd some one inform Enoch that Booney was thought to be dying and asked him if he wanted to see him and speak to him before he dyed, and he said: God damn him let him dye and go to hell. I don't want to see him. Afterwards, the deceased showed sorrow that the trouble had arisen. I told the defendant that his father was shot in the leg.

Those who were present at the scene thought that Daniel Boone Potter was mortally wounded, while the wound to Enoch Potter was less serious. Both wounded men were cared for, but Boone began to recover while Enoch Potter's condition worsened. Enoch Potter died on April 15, 1902, as a result of complications from his injuries. His tombstone erroneously reads, "Enoch Potter 1855-1903." Boone Potter convalesced, and no official action was taken against him. On May 16, 1902, T. J. Ray appeared before J.O.J. Potter (both of whom were present at the time of the shootings) and Ray swore as follows:

> T. J. Ray being duly sworn complains and says: on or about the 11th day of April 1902 D. B. Potter, Jr. did engage in an affray with and assault Enoch Potter with a deadly weapon to wit: a gun and that the said Enoch Potter died from the efforts of said assault on or about the 15th day of April, 1902.

Justice of the Peace J.O. J. Potter issued an arrest warrant. Deputy Sheriff J. C. Miller filled out a return on the warrant showing that he took Boone Potter into custody on May 16, 1902. Boone undoubtedly was present at the preliminary hearing but there is no record of his statement. Selena Potter's statement is enlightening:

> I was in the room with my husband Abraham Potter, Boonie Potter and others when Enoch Potter came to the door with pistol in his hand. I being near the door I put my hands on his breast and told him not to shoot Boonie. As he entered the room he said 'Dan God dam you what is up'; and just at that time he fired his pistol in the direction of Boonie. I did not see Boonie shoot Enoch as my back was toward him. The first word I heard after the shooting was Boonie said 'Lord have Mercy on me Pa has killed me.' We then got Boonie on the bed and washed him in camphor. I thought he would be dead in a few minutes. Then I went down stairs to where Enoch was. He said 'Salenia I am shot.' I told him I hated it awfully bad, and Enoch said: 'I shot to kill and I ment to kill, and all I hate is that I did not get another shot or two.' While I stood there Enoch said to me: 'Salenia do you think little Dan will die?' I told him I thought he would and he looked at me and asked me if I would ever see old Enoch hung. I told him I would not if I could help it. Just before Enoch come to the door, little Boonie said: 'Uncle Abe all I want is for mother to have what is right.' Boonie said this while

he was listening to Enoch curse his mother. That is all
I heard Boonie say."

If Boone Potter had died, the witnesses' statements could easily
have implicated Enoch Potter. Enoch Potter manufactured and
sold illegal liquor, and his son grew up in an environment of heavy
drinking, violence, and suspicion of outsiders. Evelina Potter's
statement follows:

> I was called up stairs to sign deed. When asked to sign
> said I was willing to do what is right & I know you are
> but I think I should have one of the notes made payable
> to me, then he said 'God dam you & your proceeds'
> and other curse words at the same time reached for his
> pistol & started for the adjoining room saying 'God
> dam him I will settle him' Just as he turned the door out
> of my sight I heard two or three shots fired very fast.

> The night before shooting after Boone had gone to bed,
> I heard Enoch curs him very violently and say 'if you
> say ary word I will go in there & shoot you' at this
> Boone said 'Pa I don't want any trouble or quarrel with
> you but lets just wait till morn. I will leave immediately
> after the shaving' I entered the room to Boone & he
> said he thought his pa had killed him & said if he had
> not been compelled to that he would not have shot his
> pa for the world. Boone soon went down stairs to his
> father's bed side & told him that he would not have
> shot him for the world if he Enoch had not shot him
> first. At this Enoch seemed to become enraged &
> reached for this pistol & cursed Boonie. At this I asked
> Boonie to go out of his fathers room, which he and
> Enoch hollowed for me to come to him. I told Sarah
> Ellison that Enoch had shot B, and that I didn't want to
> be killed I didn't go because I feared I would be that by
> him upon entering the room.

Statements were taken from Dee Etta Potter and Abraham
Potter consistent with those of other witnesses. Alex Ellison
reported that he had spent the night before the shooting with Boonie
Potter and that Enoch Potter had cursed Boone. Sarah Ellison gave a

statement that she did not know what had happened upstairs in the house, because she was downstairs at the time. A person whose name was Victory Wilson was interviewed but stated that she knew nothing. T. J. Ray appears to have conducted the investigation, and witnessed all statements.

Family matters aside, Potter's ruling that the killing was justified, legally speaking, barely holds water. First, no relative is going to be impartial in such a case and should never be the one to rule on it. Second, J.O. J. Potter also witnessed the events, making it doubly impossible for him to render a fair and neutral judgment. The ruling did not follow the law of the time which stated that whenever a person used a firearm to intentionally inflict a wound on another and the victim died from that wound then two things were presumed. First that the killing was unlawful; second, that the killing was committed with malice. The defendant then had the burden of proving self-defense.[209] Whether the proof was sufficient to show self-defense would be a question for the jury. The usual practice in the event of such a death would be for the Solicitor to submit a bill of indictment. In instances when such bills were returned as true bills, Solicitors showed no hesitation in trying cases of this type before a jury.

Watauga County Solicitor Moses N. Harshaw lived in Caldwell County. Then, Solicitors worked part time, often maintaining a private law practice at the same time. Harshaw probably came to Watauga County only three or four times a year. There is nothing that indicates Harshaw even knew of this case. Justice Potter's conclusion would not have prevented Harshaw from submitting a bill of indictment to the grand jury, yet it seems that Justice Potter's decision was fully accepted. None of the witnesses was ever subjected to cross-examination. From the statements they gave, a ruling of self-defense may have been the appropriate conclusion, although such a ruling was tainted by legal impropriety. The *Landmark* article of April 29, 1904, reported:

> The crime for which Boone was last wanted and for which he went to Montana to escape arrest was the killing of Deputy Sheriff Howell about a year ago. Boone and a cousin, Clarence Potter, rocked a man's

house. A man for whom the Potters bore no love was instrumental in issuing a warrant for them and in having Howell deputized to serve the papers. The officers found the Potters in a wagon going along the road. The warrant was read to Clarence and he agreed to surrender but in a jiffy the Potters jumped from the wagon, one on each side. Clarence had a pistol which he passed across the wagon to Boone, the latter using it with deadly aim on Howell. Clarence was arrested but Boone escaped and went West. He was arrested three months ago in Montana, brought to Lenoir and put in jail."

The incorrect reference to Boone Potter's arrest in Montana instead of Wyoming is part of a host of erroneous reporting in the case, up to and including the ultimate irony of his tombstone carved with the wrong dates for his birth and death. His inscription reads:

Daniel Boone Potter
September 30, 1879
April 30, 1905

Boone Potter died April 23, 1904. Like his father's tombstone, the date of death is incorrect.

Boone Potter was the first person to be killed in Watauga County by a law enforcement officer in performance of his duties. He also is the first person to have killed a law enforcement officer in the performance of his duties.[210] For these and other misdeeds, he remains both a legendary figure and one who is important to the legal history of the county.[211]

Footnotes

[194] Alfred Adams was venerable, witty, and told stories with great exuberance. A respected banker, he knew the history of most of the longstanding families in Watauga County. Alfred loved to tell stories about Boone Potter. One story was related to the fact that Boone always carried a gun. As a young boy attending school, Boonie once rolled a .45 caliber bullet down the floor, an act that created consternation in the teacher. Adams relished telling about Boone's father, Enoch, who owned a house with two stories. On one floor lived his wife and the children of the married couple

and on the other floor lived a woman, who was not married to Enoch, and their child. Enoch would go from floor to floor as he chose. When Enoch and Boone shot each other, and while it appeared that Boone would die, Enoch said that Boone would be the fifth person killed by him. Hearing those stories was an inspiration for me to develop a hobby of studying old trial transcripts and court records.

[195] Billy the Kid and Boone Potter both died young men. The numbers of people that each killed may have been exaggerated. Those who wanted to magnify The Kid claimed that he killed a person for each year of his life. Similarly, some Potters make the same claim for Boone Potter. Neither assertion is probably true. There certainly is one similarity. Pat Garrett who killed The Kid was buried beside him, and Boone Potter is buried beside his father, Enoch, whom he killed.

[196] Alfred Adams said that as a young man, he occasionally armed himself when he was dating someone from a different community in Watauga County.

[197] See Storie, Elizabeth South, *My Killing Kin*, (The Reprint Company, Spartanburg, S. C. 1991.)

[198] *The News Herald*, Morganton, N. C., May 12, 1904.

[199] Minutes of the Watauga County Commissioners.

[200] *The News Herald, Ibid.*

[201] *The News Herald*, Morganton, North Carolina, May 5, 1904.

[202] *The News Herald*, Morganton, North Carolina, May 12, 1904.

[203] At one time committing suicide resulted in a forfeiture of the deceased's estate to the crown. North Carolina, for a long time, made it a criminal offense to attempt suicide. Those cases that are suicide do not implicate the criminal law and the prosecuting attorney has no involvement. Even so there are numbers of cases ruled to be suicide, where the family does not accept the conclusion, and district attorneys are often confronted with the most contentious situations. One powerful politician told the author that whenever law enforcement could not solve a murder, it labels it suicide. The number of suspicious suicides in the vicinity of the Enoch Potter house is certainly troubling. The coroner's inquest appears to have too easily accepted the version of Boone Potter's sister, who had an obvious interest in protecting her brother.

[204] Juvenile law came almost full circle. Years after 1889, juvenile laws were passed which protected children by setting up a system where their offenses were tried in juvenile court. In some states the juvenile age was eighteen but in North Carolina it was sixteen. As juvenile violent crime becomes so appalling, many states now try juveniles in adult court.

[205] Potter legend among current generations (see Storie, *My Killing Kin, Ibid.*) is that the killing occurred on Christmas Eve in 1900, but this cannot be true. The minutes of the meetings of the Watauga County Commissioners show that one of the Coroner's jurors was J. H. Canter and that on December 4, 1900, Canter presented an account to the commission-

ers for services as coroner's juror in the inquest over J. M. Broome and he was paid $2.00 for his services. E. F. Potter, a relative of Enoch, was commissioned to summon witnesses. Based on the date alleged in the presentment of the grand jury, the author determined the date of Broome's killing to be December 2, 1900.

[206] Boone Potter had an uncle named Daniel Boone Potter. The use of the nomenclature Daniel Boone Potter, Jr. is not technically correct. The documents recording the preliminary hearing is the only place where this author has encountered the use of the word "Jr."

[207] Nigh is a colloquialism used for the word "near." The spelling "ny" was the witness Ray's spelling.

[208] J.O.J. Potter was never specifically mentioned by name in the written statements of T. J. Ray or any other witness. Elizabeth South Storie in her book mentions that J.O.J. Potter was the Justice of the Peace who was requested to come to the Potter residence, and that he was a witness to the events. James Marvin Potter told this writer that his relative, J.O.J. was present in the house. J.O.J. Potter lived in the neighborhood. Although there may have been other justices of the peace in the area, the Potters would have preferred that their kinsman assist them rather than an outsider.

[209] Until 1975, the defendant had the burden of proving that he acted in self defense. In that year, the North Carolina Supreme Court decided *State vs. Hankerson*, 288 N. C. 632 (1975). That decision was prompted by the United States Supreme Court decision in *Mullaney vs. Wilbur,* 421 U.S. 684 (1975), which held that it violates the due process clause of the U. S. Constitution to place the burden of proof on the defendant in a criminal case. The decision may not have required the interpretation that the North Carolina Supreme Court gave it, but the law is now clear. The State must prove beyond reasonable doubt that the defendant did not act in self-defense. Relieving the defendant of the burden of proof has undoubtedly resulted in some acquittals where there might have been a conviction earlier.

[210] The reader should recall the earlier discussion about the contentions that Amos Wellington Howell was not properly deputized and that he was acting without lawful authority.

[211] Some time ago the author published in several newspapers, the story of Mary Jane Crowson's drowning of her infant son. One prominent citizen commented that he found the story important because he grew up believing that our values had "gone to Hell" in recent times, and the story taught him that many decades ago there was a similar form of decadence.

Bibliography

Books

Biennial Report of the Adjutant General of North Carolina for the year 1923

Biennial Reports of the Attorney General of North Carolina 1894-1896

Capps, Francis E., ed. *Gradwohl's Legal Medicine*, 2nd edition, Bristol: John Wright & Sons, 1968

Code of North Carolina, Revisal of 1905, Sec. 3285

Corbitt, David Lee, ed. *Addresses and Papers of Governor Clyde Roark Hoey 1937-1941*. Charlotte, NC: Presses of Observer House, Inc., 1944

Encyclopaedia Britannica: A Dictionary of Arts, Sciences, Literature, and General Information, Benefit of Clergy & Negro. Cambridge University Press, 1911

Gilmer, Robert D. (Attorney General). *Biennial Report of the Attorney General of North Carolina. 1907-1908*

Glenn, Robert B. The Governor's Message to The General Assembly of North Carolina of 1907, *Public Documents*, Session 1907 Vol. 1, E. M. Uzzell & Co.State Printers and Binders, 1907

Glenn, Robert B. The Governor's Message to The General Assembly of North Carolina Special Session 1908, *Public Documents*, Special Session 1908, Vol. 1, E. M. Uzzell & Co. State Printers and Binders, 1907

Hayes, Kyle and Johnson J. Hayes. *Autobiography and Additional Hayes Family Data*. Wilkesboro, NC: 1980

Laws of the State of North Carolina Enacted in the Year 1816. Thomas Henderson State Printers, 1817, Ch. XX

Moenssens, Andre A. *Fingerprints and the Law*, Philadelphia, PA: Chilton Book Company, 1969

North Carolina Code of 1935, Article 17

North Carolina State Prison Descriptive Register Of Convicts, Vols. 9 and 10, North Carolina Archives, Prison Department

Perkins, Rollin M., *Perkins on Criminal Law*, 2nd edition, Mineola NY: Foundation Press, 1969

Proclamation offering Reward for Apprehension of Criminals 1874-1890, North Carolina Archives, pages 55 & 56

Public and Private Laws of North Carolina, Special Session 1868, Chapter 21

Public and Private Laws of North Carolina, 1879, Chapter 221

Register of Convicts, Volume II, North Carolina Archives

Reprieves from 1880. North Carolina Archives, Governor's Office

Reprieves 1904-1919. North Carolina Archives, Governor's Office

Requisitions for Return of Criminals, 1871-1883, North Carolina Archives, Governor's Office

Requisitions for Return of Criminals, 1883-1892, North Carolina Archives, Governor's Office

Revised Statutes of the State of North Carolina, Raleigh, 1837, "Crimes and Punishment Chapter XXXIV

Saunders, William L. (Secretary. of State). *The Colonial Records of North Carolina*, Vol. 2. Raleigh, NC: P. M. Hale State Printer, 1886

Schenck, David._David Schenck Diaries_, (Typed Copy) Vol. 8. Chapel Hill, NC: Southern Historical Collection, University of North Carolina. October 12, 1879

Sheppard, Muriel Early. *Cabins in the Laurel*. Chapel Hill, NC: UNC Press, c1935, 7th printing 1978

Sobel, Robert, and John Raimo, eds. *Biographical Directory of the Governors of the United States, 1789-1978*. Westport, CT: Meckler Books, 1978

Young, Perry Deane. *The Untold Story of Frankie Silver: Was She Unjustly Hanged?*: Asheboro, N.C: Down Home Press, 1998

Governors' Papers

Governor Robert B. Glenn Papers, loose papers, North Carolina Archives.

Governor Graham papers, loose papers, North Carolina Archives.

Governor Clyde R. Hoey Papers, loose papers, North Carolina Archives.

Governor Cameron Morrison Papers, loose papers, North Carolina Archives.

Commutations and Reprieves, Thomas J. Jarvis to Robert B. Glenn, 1880-1907, North Carolina Archives.

North Carolina Reports

Freeman vs. Ponder, 234 N.C. 294 (1951)
In Re Ebbs, 150 N.C. 44 (1908)
Ponder vs. Davis and Crowder, 233 N. C. 699 (1951)
Ponder vs. North Carolina State Board of Elections, 233 N. C. 707 (1951)
State vs. Angel, 29 N.C. 27 (1846)
State vs. Bell, 103 N.C. 438 (1889)
State vs. Thomas Boon(e), 80 N. C. 461(1879)
State vs. Thomas Boon(e), 82 N. C. 637 (1880)
State vs. Carroll, 27 N.C. 139(1844)
State vs. Coffey, 210 N. C. 561 (1936)
State vs. Crowson, 98 N. C. 595 (1887)
State vs. Cunningham, 72 N.C.469 (1875)
State vs. Gosnell, Gunter, and Thomas, 208 N.C. 401 (1935)
State vs. Gragg, 122 N. C. 1082 (1898)
State vs. Gray, 5 N.C. 147 (1806)
State vs. Hall, 142 N. C. 710 (1906)
State vs. Haney, 67 N.C. 467 (1872)
State vs. Henderson, 180 N. C. 735 (1920)
State vs. Kearney, 8 N.C. 53 (1820)
State vs. Murphy, 157 N. C. 485 (1911)
State vs. Pate, 121 N. C. 659 (1897)
State vs. Potter, 134 N. C. 719 (1904)
State vs. Rinehart, 75 N. C. 58 (1876)
State vs. Rucker, 68 N. C. 211 (1873)
State vs. Seaborn, 15 N.C. (1833)
State vs. Silver, 14 N. C. 332 (1832)
State vs. Smith, 138 N.C. 700 (1905)
State vs. Stines, 138 N.C. 686 (1905)
State vs. Whitson, 111 N. C. 695 (1892)
State vs. Wilson, 104 N.C. 868 (1889)
State vs. Wilson (Joseph T.), 90 N.C.736 (1884)
State vs. Yeates, 11 N.C.187 (1825)

North Carolina Court of Appeals

State vs. Moore, 39 N.C. App. 643(1979)

United States Supreme Court Reports

In Re Kemmler, 136 U. S. 436 (1890)
Powell et al. vs.Alabama et al., 287 U. S. 45 (1932)
Witherspoon vs. Illinois, 391 U.S. 510 (1968)

Avery County Clerk Office

Book of Oaths
Minute Docket vol. 8 page 230
Minute Docket vol. 8 page 283
Minute Docket vol. 8 page 294

Avery County Register of Deeds Office

Board of Commissioners Minutes April –July 1936

East Tennessee State University Library, Johnson City, Tennessee

Carolina Clinchfield and Ohio Railroad Archives

Journal Articles

Franklin, H. Bruce. "Billy Budd and Capital Punishment: A Tale of Three Centuries," *American Literature 69* (June 1977): 337-359.

Hughes, Thomas P. "Harold P. Brown and the Executioner's Current: An Incident in the AC-DC Controversy," *Business History Review* 32 (Spring 1958): 143-165.

Mitchell County Clerk of Court

Minute Docket 1923
Loose files concerning John Goss and Grand Jury Reports

Mitchell County Register of Deeds Office

Board of Commissioners Minutes 1927

North Carolina Archives

Madison County Criminal Minute Docket
Mitchell County Board of Commissioners Minutes, 1923
Peter Smith File
Records of Justice of the Peace, Madison County

Yancey County Court Minute Book, 1934-1848
Yancey County Minute Book, Spring Term 1875

North Carolina Dept. of Correction

Management Information and Research
Reed Coffey file

North Carolina Supreme Court Records

State vs. Reed Coffey, July Term 1936, No. 218 Record on Appeal, Old
Records Building, North Carolina State Government, Raleigh

Personal Family Archives

May Irene Coffey Pyatte
Letters of Mrs. Lilly Coffey

Spruce Pine, Town of

Minutes of Town Aldermen during 1923
Loose papers

Watauga County Clerk of Clerk

Criminal Docket A
Criminal Judgment Docket C
Minute Docket J
Minute Docket O
Loose papers 1903
Loose papers 1904
Judge's Instructions 1905

Watauga County Register of Deeds

Watauga County Commissioners' Minutes Book 4

Wake County Vital Records

Death Certificate Vol. 69, page 378

Web Resources

"Chicago Race Riot of 1919," Encyclopedia Britannica, 2003,
http://www.britannica.com/eb/article?eu_24357&tocid=0

Florida Corrections Commission. "Execution Methods Used by States," June 1997, http://www.fcc.state.fl.us/fcc/reports/methods/emstates.html

North Carolina Department of Correction. "Execution Methods - Lethal Injection." (Statutory amendment signed into law October 29, 1998.) http://www.doc.state.nc.us/dop/deathpenalty/executio.htm

Newspapers

Asheville Citizen
November 13, 1901, "One Hanging In A Year"
February 26, 1902, "Johnson And Foster Forfeited Their Lives On The Scaffold," page 1
August 25, 1903, "Buncombe Sheriff Reed Invited To Attend Hanging In Iredell"
April 24, 1904, "North Carolina Desperado Cuts Third Notch," page 1
April 27, 1904, "Potter on Deathbed Confesses To Murder Of Charles Campbell"
September 12, 1905, "Smith Goes To Marshall On No. 11," page 1
September 14, 1905, "Peter Smith Gets Respite," page 1
October 1, 1905, "Peter Smith Prostrated," page 6
October 3, 1905, "Standing On The Shores Of Eternity Peter Smith, Hanged Yesterday At Marshall, Declares His Innocence," page 1
September 28, 1923, "Spruce Pine Mob Drives Negroes Out Of The Town," page 1
September 30, 1923, "Alleged Negro Assailant Now In Custody," page 1
October 3, 1923, "Shot, Signal Flashes And Scurring Figure Call Troops to Arms,"page 1
October 4, 1923, "People And Places in Spruce Pine," page 3
December 9, 1923, "A Triumph Of Law," page 4
October 5, 1935, "Electric Chair Takes Lives Of 3 Madison Men"
April 6, 1936, "Avery County Officer Is Slain At His Home," page 1
April 7, 1936, "Youth Charged With Murder Of Avery Officer," page 1
July 9, 1936, "Coffey Is Being Tried In Death Case In Avery," page 1
July 10, 1936, "Find Avery Man Guilty Of Murder," page 1
August 5, 1937 "Hoey Commutes Death Sentence of Reed Coffey," page 8
August 7, 1937, "Exum Died Gas Chamber"
October 15, 1936, "State Supreme Court Dismisses Death Pleas," page 1

Asheville Daily Citizen
April 2, 1894, "Tragedy In Mitchell," page 1

Asheville Gazette News
October 3, 1905, "Smith Has Named The Frisbee Boys," page 1

Atlanta Constitution
September 29, 1923, "Troops To Keep Order As Blacks Return To Work,"
      page 1
October 2, 1923, "More Guardsmen To Spruce Pine," page 1

Avery Advocate
April 9, 1936, "H. Coffey Murdered," page 1
July 9, 1936, "Coffey Faces Gas Chamber," page 1
October 15, 1936, "Reed Coffey Loses Appeal," page 1
August 5, 1937, "Coffey Gets Life Term," page 1

Bakersville Enterprise
April 4, 1894, "Lynched! By One Hundred Men," page 1

Charlotte Daily Observer
April 26, 1904, "Boone Potter Shot To Death," page 1

Charlotte Observer
October 2, 1923, "Concord Troops At Spruce Pine Take Up Duties At
      Once," page 1

Christian Science Monitor
October 1, 1923, "Governor Demands Mob Violence Ban"

Comet, Johnson City, Tennessee
April 5, 1894, " Lynched At Bakersville"

Greensboro Patriot, Greensboro, North Carolina
April 27, 1904, "Desperado On The Warpath"

Hickory Daily Record, Hickory, North Carolina
October 1, 1923, 'Goff Is Captured Taken To Raleigh"
October 2, 1923 "Squad Of State Troops Guard 9 Negro Laborers"

Johnson City Chronicle
September 29, 1923, "Military Guard At Spruce Pine To Keep Peace In
      Community," page 1
September 30, 1923, "National Guardsmen On Duty In Spruce Pine, N.C.,
      Community," page 1
October 2, 1923, "Soldiers Protect Negroes At Spruce Pine, N.C.," page 1
October 3, 1923, "Signal Lights And Some Shooting Stir Spruce Pine Up
      A Bit," page 1
October 7, 1923, "Green and Peter Brick Were Arrested"
October 9, 1923, "Troops Which Have Been On Duty. . ."
October 4, 1923, "Workers Returning To Labor On Roads About Spruce

Pine," page 1
October 23, 1923, "John Goff Guilty," page 1
October 24, 1923, "Seventy-Seven Men Indicted By Mitchell County
        Grand Jury,"page1
November 14, 1923, "Bakersville Boys Accused Of Crimes In Court," p.1

The Lenoir Topic
March 19,1884, "An Adroit Escape," page 1
December 23, 1903, "Boone Breaks Jail"
May 25, 1957, "Lucky Joe Rouses People Of Western North Carolina,"
        page 1
Madison County Record
October 6, 1905, "Execution of Peter Smith," page 1
October 13, 1905, "Peter Smith Who Was Hanged Here October 2," page 5

Marion Progress
October 4, 1923, "Old North State Ranks High In Highway Work"
October 11, 1923, "Nearly 200 Negroes Deported," page 4
October 18, 1923, "11 Mitchell County Men Bound Over For Rioting"
October 25, 1923, "Goss Negro Is Sentence To Electric Chair"

Marion Record, Marion North Carolina
April 6, 1894, "Judge Lynch In Mitchell County"
April 13, 1894, "A North Carolina Lynching"

Marshall News Record
May 14, 1970, "Peter Smith Hanged In Marshall Oct. 5, 1905," page 6

Messenger, Marion, North Carolina
June 25, 1897, "The Linville River Railroad"

New York Herald
August 7, 1890, "Kemmler's Death By Torture"

New York Times
December 9, 1923, "Will Use Powers As Governor To Prevent Lynchings,"
        section II; page 1

New York Tribune
August 6, 1890, "Kemmler Will Have Another Night Of Misery and
        Suspense"
August 7, 1890, "Errors And Misunderstanding Made The Execution
        Painful To The Witnesses"

News Herald, Morganton, North Carolina
April 28, 1904, "Boone Potter Killed," page 2
May 5, 1904, "Campbell Killed By Potter," page 2
May 12, 1904, "Denial That Potter Killed Campbell," page 1
The North Carolina Citizen, Asheville, North Carolina
June 3, 1875, "Execution of Cunningham," page 3

Raleigh News and Observer
March 10, 1910, "The First Electrocution Ends Walter Morrison's Life"
October 6, 1923, "Get Nowhere In Move For Truce At Spruce Pine"
October 23, 1923, "Death Penalty Is Imposed On Goss"
October 24, 1923, "Jury Brings In Many True Bills," page 2
December 1, 1923, "Goss Gets Stay Of One Week More," page 12
December 8, 1923, "John Goss Dies Admitting Crime, " page 9
May 3, 1937, "Governor Tells Prisoners About Faith And Rewards," page 1

Sheridan Post, Sheridan Wyoming
August 13, 1903, "Potter Is Out," page 10
August 27, 1903, "Officers Arrive," page 1

Spartanburg Herald
October 2, 1923, "Of Interest in Spartanburg. . ."

Spartanburg Journal
September 28, 1923, "Negro Laborers Forced To Leave Spruce Pine,
        N.C.," page 1
September 29, 1923, "Think Trouble At Spruce Pine Over, " page 1

Statesville Landmark, Statesville, North Carolina
April 7, 1903, "2 Murder Cases at Watauga Court"
April 29, 1904, " Boone Potter, Desperado," page 1
October 4, 1923, "Negroes Back In Spruce Pine," page 1

Tri-County News Journal
March 30, 1989, "The Old Story Of Hol English Lynched For Murder,"
        page 4

Washington Post
October 1, 1923, "Ask More Troops At Spruce Pine"

Watauga Democrat
May 14, 1896, "The Grand Jury At Mitchell. . ."
November 13, 1902, "Deputy Sheriff Houck"
November 27, 1902, "Mr. Howell, Son Of Mr. Phelix Howell. . ."
April 2, 1903, "Superior Court Convened & B. F. Long, Judge"
April 9, 1903, "At 2:p.m. On Wednesday Of Last Week. . ."

December 31, 1903, ""Sheriff Of Caldwell Co Offered $200 Reward"
April 14, 1904, "Clarence Potter Who Was Found Guilty. . ."
May 5, 1904, "A Short History Of Boone Potter," page 2
June 9, 1904, " 'Lucky Joe' Again In The Tolls," page 1
June 16, 1904, "The Clarence Potter Case. . ," page 1
August 11, 1904, "Venire For The Trial Of The Potter Homicide Case Was
        Drawn On Monday," page 1
August 18, 1904, "Clarence Potter Acquitted," page 1

The Weekly News (Lenoir, North Carolina)
December 25, 1903, "Boone Potter Free"
April 29, 1904, "Boone Potter Dead," page 2

INDEX

Town, county and location names which are not otherwise identified are understood to be located in North Carolina.

Symbols

About the Author

James Thomas Rusher is a native of Salisbury, North Carolina. He graduated from the University of North Carolina School of Law in 1967 and has since that time been licensed to practice law in North Carolina. Since 1971, he has been a prosecuting attorney in a mountain district in Western North Carolina. He was elected District Attorney in the Twenty-fourth Prosecutorial District of North Carolina in 1982, and has been re-elected to that position four times. The Twenty-Fourth District includes five small rural counties: Watauga, Avery, Mitchell, Yancey, and Madison.

He retired from public office at the end of December 2002.